Psychology Education and Training

Much of the psychological research in the last century has been conducted in the global North West; hence, many prevailing theories and methodologies reflect the philosophical framework and shared cultural knowledge of this region. Other world views and cultural contexts have, as yet, not had the same opportunity to develop scientific insights that come to the attention of global audiences. *Psychology Education and Training* is the first truly international effort to generate a framework for common standards in psychological education and training across the globe.

Psychologists have long studied human beings in their sociocultural context, but new challenges, such as globalization, and new insights, such as into the relationship of the brain and behavior, need that education and training keep pace with such rapidly evolving developments. The chapters in this book were generated by an international conference which resulted in the Dornburg Accord. While anchored in higher education, the focus is on the generative and translational psychological science needed to fulfill psychology's responsibility to society. *Psychology Education and Training* is the first book of its kind to cover both historic strengths and the requirements of emerging fields. It also deals with balancing the universalities and cultural specificities of psychological processes, the adjustments to academic curricula required to support national needs, as well as with the credentials and regulations required to assure the quality of psychological services.

Psychology Education and Training is unique in providing initial data and concurrent assessment of various components of education and training in psychology across the globe. The book is a must for faculty members, advanced students of psychology and policy-makers who are interested in the issues that shape their societies.

Rainer K. Silbereisen is Research Professor of Developmental Psychology and Director of the Center for Applied Developmental Science at the University of Jena, Germany. He is Past-President of the International Union of Psychological Science (2012–2016). His main research interests are in human lifespan development from a biopsychosocial perspective and in the role of social and cultural change in positive and maladaptive human development.

Pierre L.-J. Ritchie is Full Professor at the School of Psychology, University of Ottawa, Canada, where he is also Director of the Centre for Psychological Services and Research. He is the former Secretary-General of the International Union of Psychological Science (1996–2012). His scholarly interests address health policy, education and training, as well as ethics in health practice and in research involving human participants.

Janak Pandey is currently Vice-Chancellor of the Central University of Bihar, Patna, India, having served as Professor of Psychology at the University of Allahabad for three decades. His research interests focus on social and cultural psychology, with a special interest in the study of contemporary issues.

Psychology Education and Training

A global perspective

**Edited by Rainer K. Silbereisen,
Pierre L.-J. Ritchie
and Janak Pandey**

Routledge
Taylor & Francis Group

LONDON AND NEW YORK

First published 2014 by Psychology Press

Published 2023 by Routledge
4 Park Square, Milton Park, Abingdon, Oxon OX14 4RN
605 Third Avenue, New York, NY 10017

Routledge is an imprint of the Taylor & Francis Group, an informa business

British Library Cataloguing in Publication Data
A catalogue record for this book is available from the British Library

Library of Congress Cataloging in Publication Data
Psychology education and training : a global perspective / edited by Rainer K. Silbereisen, Pierre L.-J. Ritchie, and Janak Pandey.
      pages cm
   Includes bibliographical references and index.
   1. Psychology—Study and teaching (Higher)   2. Psychologists.
   I. Silbereisen, R. K. (Rainer K.), 1944–
   BF77.P759 2014
   150.71'1—dc23

                                                              2013027263

ISBN: 978-1-84872-151-7 (hbk)
ISBN: 978-1-84872-427-3 (pbk)
ISBN: 978-1-315-85153-2 (ebk)

Typeset in Times New Roman
by RefineCatch Limited, Bungay, Suffolk

Contents

**Commentary on 'Roles and responsibilities of international
psychology organizations for PET'**   253
TÉA GOGOTISHVILI

Contributors

Lawrence Aber is Albert and Blanche Willner Family Professor in Psychology and Public Policy at the Steinhardt School of Culture, Education, and Human Development, and University Professor, New York University. His basic research examines the influence of poverty and violence at the family and community levels on the social, emotional, behavioral, cognitive and academic development of children and youth. He is an internationally recognised expert in child development and social policy. See steinhardt.nyu.edu/faculty_bios/view/J._Lawrence_Aber

Oscar Barbarin has a PhD in clinical psychology and is the Lila and Douglas Hertz Endowed Chair and Professor in the Department of Psychology at Tulane University in New Orleans. His research has focused on universal mental health screening for children and the family impact of life-threatening childhood illness. His current research focuses on the early development of math skills, executive function and self-regulation in vulnerable children. See tulane.edu/sse/psyc/faculty-and-staff/faculty/barbarin.cfm

Andreas Beelmann is Professor of Psychology and Chair of the Department of Research Synthesis, Intervention and Evaluation at the University of Jena, Germany. His main research interests are meta-analysis of social interventions and development and prevention of problem behaviors in children and adolescents. See www.uni-jena.de/svw/devpsy/staff.html

Allan B. I. Bernardo is Professor of Psychology at the University of Macau, Macau SAR China. His main research interests are lay beliefs and intergroup relations in hierarchical societies, learning motivation, and hope theory. See www.umac.mo/psychology/staff_BERNARDO.html

Merry Bullock is Senior Director of the Office of International Affairs at the American Psychological Association in Washington, DC. Her current research and scholarly interests are international development, policy, history of psychology and developmental science. See www.merrybullock.net

Cheryl de la Rey is Vice-Chancellor and Principal and Professor of Psychology at the University of Pretoria, South Africa. Her main research interests are intergroup relations, leadership and gender. See www.up.ac.za.

Rocío Fernández-Ballesteros is Emeritus Professor at the Autonomous University of Madrid and Director of the Research Unit on Assessment and Aging. Her main research interests lie within the field of geropsychology, in particular aging in changing societies, as well as in psychological assessment and evaluation. See www.uam.es/personal_pdi/psicologia/rfb/CVINGLES.pdf

Téa Gogotishvili has a PhD in psychology and is an EAGT Accredited Psychotherapist, Supervisor and Professor at the St. Andrew Georgian University, Tbilisi, Georgia. She is also Head of the D. Uznadze Center for Psychology Education and Counseling in Tbilisi. Her main research interests are clinical psychology, psychotherapy, antisocial behavior prevention and psychosocial rehabilitation. See www.sangu.edu.ge

Judy E. Hall is Executive Officer of the National Register of Health Service Psychologists in Washington, DC. Her interests relate to credentialing and professional education and training standards of psychologists across the world. See www.nationalregister.org

Buxin Han is Professor of Psychology and Deputy Director of the Key Lab of Mental Health at the Institute of Psychology, Chinese Academy of Sciences, Beijing. His main research interests are healthy life-span development and psychology of religion. See sourcedb.cas.cn/sourcedb_psych_cas/en/epsychexpert/200907/t20090714_2073858.html

Pascal Huguet has a PhD in social psychology and is Director of Research at the National Centre for Scientific Research (CNRS), Aix-Marseille University, France and is Head of the Brain, Behaviour and Cognition Institute also in Marseille. His research focuses on the social regulation of cognitive functioning: he has a special interest in the effects of social presence on human and non-human primates, social comparison processes, autobiographical memory, and gender stereotyping. See www.federation3c.com/

Kwang-Kuo Hwang is currently National Chair Professor at the Department of Psychology, National Taiwan University, Taipei, Taiwan and National Policy Advisor to the President of Taiwan. His main research interests are related to the indigenization of psychology and social science in Chinese society and the foundation of Chinese psychology. See www.victoria.ac.nz/cacr/aaspsite/aasp/AASPExecutive/Kwang-KuoHwang.aspx

Victor N. Karandashev is Professor of Psychology at Leningrad State University, St. Petersburg, Russia and Aquinas College, Michigan, USA. His main research interests are the internationalization of psychology education and training and the psychology of romantic love. See http://victor.karandashevs.ru/

Ingrid Lunt is Professor of Educational Studies and Director of the Doctoral Training Centre for the Social Sciences at the University of Oxford where she is also Vice Principal of Green Templeton College. Her main research interests are higher education, particularly in a European context, and systems of professional qualification and regulation. See www.education.ox.ac.uk/about-us/directory/professor-ingrid-lunt/

Maria Regina Maluf is Professor of Psychology at the University of São Paulo, Brazil. Her research focuses primarily on educational and developmental issues: literacy teaching; instruction that facilitates learning mainly for children endangered by poverty; and theory of mind development. See www.mrmaluf.com.br

Wolfgang H. R. Miltner is Professor of Psychology and Chair of the Department of Biological and Clinical Psychology, University of Jena, Germany. His research focuses on the biological-bases of attention, learning, error monitoring, emotion and altered states of consciousness and its applications for the diagnosis and treatment of mental and physical disorders – anxiety, pain, paresis, facial palsy. See www.biopsy.uni-jena.de/en/people/administration.html

A. Bame Nsamenang is Professor of Psychology and Learning Science and Head of the University Cooperation Division at the University of Bamenda, Cameroon. He is also Director of the Human Development Resource Centre (HDRC) www.thehdrc.org. His research interests are in African childhoods, youth development and teacher preparation. See www.unige.ch/fapse/SSE/teachers/dasen/Nsamenang.htm

Janak Pandey is currently Vice-Chancellor of the Central University of Bihar, Patna, India, having served as Professor of Psychology at the University of Allahabad for three decades. His research interests focus on social and cultural psychology with special interest in the study of contemporary issues. See www.iupsys.net/index.php/profiles/166--janak-pandey-profile

José M. Peiró is Professor of Work and Organizational Psychology at the University of Valencia, Director of the Research Institute of Human Resources Psychology (IDOCAL), and Senior Researcher at the Research Institute of Economics (IVIE) Valencia. Spain. He is President of the International Association of Applied Psychology. His main research interests are occupational stress and well-being, youth labor market entry, and climate and leadership in organizations. See www.uv.es/~jmpeiro/cv_affiliation.html

Martin Pinquart is Professor of Developmental Psychology at Philipps University at Marburg, Germany. His main research interests focus on influences of individual and social conditions on human development. See www.uni-marburg.de/fb04/ag-pp-ep/pinquart/index_html.

Pierre L.-J. Ritchie is Full Professor at the School of Psychology, University of Ottawa, Canada, where he is also Director of the Centre for Psychological Services and Research. He is the former Secretary-General of the International Union of Psychological Science (1996–2012). His scholarly interests address health policy, education and training as well as ethics in health practice and in research involving human participants. See www.socialsciences.uottawa.ca/psy/professor-profile?id=245&pageID=1

Rainer K. Silbereisen is Research Professor of Developmental Psychology and Director of the Center for Applied Developmental Science at the University of Jena, Germany. He is Past-President of the International Union of Psychological Science (2012–2016). His main research interests are in human lifespan development from a biopsychosocial perspective and in the role of social and cultural change in positive and maladaptive human development. See www.rainersilbereisen.de

Ava D. Thompson is Associate Professor of Psychology at the College of The Bahamas and Executive Director of The Bahamas Institute for Child and Adolescent Mental Health (BICAMH) in Nassau, Bahamas. Her main research areas are culturally relevant pedagogy, indigenous and international psychologies and child and adolescent mental health. See www.iupsys.net/index.php/profiles/31004-ava-thompson-profile

Foreword

The International Union of Psychological Science (IUPsyS) is honored to present this current contribution on *Psychology Education and Training: A global perspective*, edited by my IUPsyS colleagues Rainer K. Silbereisen, Pierre Ritchie and Janak Pandey, which takes this vast and often conflicting area to new heights.

As the overarching global voice of psychology, representing over 100 national and international psychology organizations, and in response to national member needs, IUPsyS has actively considered over the last four years the systems and structures of education and training for psychologists internationally. To this end, IUPsyS is also considering whether it makes sense to develop guidelines and standards for education and training in psychology globally and the feasibility of a more international curriculum for both researchers and practitioners in the various fields of psychology. If this were to happen, a transparent and accountable global psychology dispensation could be created where there would be greater portability and mutual recognition of training and qualifications with the resultant ability to work competently internationally to ensure the best possible psychological interactions and outcomes for the greater public good. *Psychology Education and Training: A global perspective* is the culmination of the first phase of this massive undertaking, and it relies on evidence gleaned from a variety of sources representative of psychology globally, not least of which were the responses from over 40 countries to the IUPsyS questionnaire on education and training.

IUPsyS recognizes that, while the role and status of psychologists and their regular contributions to society are taken for granted in certain developed psychology dispensations, the position is often tenuous at best in large parts of the rest of the world. It behoves us to ensure that there is greater common understanding of what constitutes a psychologist and what can be expected when one consults with a psychologist in a variety of different settings, especially psychologists' core competencies. This will engender greater trust in the immense work that psychologists individually and severally engage in daily in numerous public and private contexts all over the world.

Psychology Education and Training: A global perspective is required reading for those involved in any facet of education and training in our multicultural world.

Saths Cooper, PhD
President: IUPsyS

Acknowledgements

The editors of this book would like to thank the following individuals and organizations who have helped in the making of this book. First, we would like to thank all contributors who gave their time not only to attend the Dornburg Conference, which formed the basis of the book, but for their willingness and patience in dealing so well with all the subsequent editorial machinations. Without their efforts, there would be no book. The entire endeavour was supported by the International Union of Psychological Science (IUPsyS) as part of its activities to serve the discipline and society. Improving the education and training of psychologists, the core of this book, has high priority in the strategic plan governing IUPsyS. We are very thankful for the engagement of its leadership.

As with all projects, the principal actors have been supported by the endeavours of others behind the scenes. Here we would especially like to mention the work of Stefanie Gläser and Katrin Müller, both of the Department of Developmental Psychology and the Center for Applied Developmental Science, University of Jena, Germany, and of Philip Grandia of the School of Psychology at the University of Ottawa. Stefanie was the main organizer of the Dornburg Conference, thereby playing a large role in its undoubted success; Katrin liaised with contributors and the publishers throughout the project and generally kept all involved in the project on track and on time; and Philip assisted with the review and synthesis of the thematic chapters and commentaries.

Verona Christmas-Best served as a valued colleague in helping plan the Dornburg Conference and by acting as Managing Editor for the book. She has been tireless and effective in making major contributions to the book's organization and in editing many of the chapters, especially those whose authors' first language is other than English. The Editors are very grateful for her sustained intellectual and practical engagement with all parts of what became the Dornburg Accord and this book.

Finally, thanks must also go to the Center for Applied Developmental Science (CADS) and the University of Jena, which supported the Dornburg Conference by allowing use of its conference center, situated in the beautiful and ancient Dornburg Castle, close to Jena. The University, which appropriately has a significant link to the history of psychology through Professor William Thierry Preyer – commonly held to be the founder of developmental psychology and to have published the first textbook of developmental psychology in 1882 – also supported work on this book by the provision of office space, secretarial support and other means.

Part I
Introduction

Introduction to psychology education and training

A global perspective

Rainer K. Silbereisen and Pierre L.-J. Ritchie

Why concern ourselves with psychology education and training (PET)? The simple answer is that we have a responsibility to enable the education and training of the next generations of psychologists for careers in academia and practice. Educators have a proactive obligation to ensure that future psychologists are prepared to deal with the sustained changes in societies and cultures which present new challenges for psychology's composition and outreach. The 'we' in the second sentence refers initially to the editors and authors of this book, who have a shared commitment to the many issues of psychology education and training addressed here. All are scientists and/or representatives of organizations concerned about what defines psychology, whom it serves, and how the next generation of psychologists should be prepared for the opportunities that await them.

Changes affecting psychology

Current global challenges certainly have an impact on psychology. Globalization itself encompasses unprecedented international exchange affecting virtually all aspects of local, national and regional economies, communication and cultural diffusion. Many people are not prepared for this and have difficulties in dealing with the risks and opportunities in new market economies (Silbereisen and Chen, 2010). The pace and magnitude of extensive worldwide migration, for instance, confronts belief systems and cultural traditions. We have sadly observed how more proximate contact has increased the risk of deeply rooted conflicts being activated in some areas of the world. Similarly, globalization can reduce or increase disparities. In either case, there are consequences for social structure and concomitant psychological factors affecting, for example, mental health and family systems. Countries in sub-Saharan Africa, for instance, are mostly ill-positioned to take advantage of globalization for several reasons, but particularly due to low educational provision and lack of foreign investment. This consequently divides society and inequalities within societies widen (Perrons, 2004).

Most of the world has recently experienced wide-reaching economic recession. One of the contributing factors has been irresponsible risk-taking by some of the main decision-makers involved. To date, this is poorly understood; psychological expertise is required to understand such behavior and achieve better decisions in the future (Wuermli *et al.*, 2012). The shake-up of repressive political regimes at the end of the twentieth century often resulted in the old elite regaining power. The new voice people had begun to express is becoming muted again. The large-scale disturbance of ecological balances by old and new industrial superpowers increases the threat of natural and man-made disasters. In all these examples, the related human activities confirm why psychology is asked to recommend solutions. As leaders of the discipline, we must acknowledge that we have not yet always achieved the scientific or applied competence to offer well-founded information and insights, or practical solutions.

To illustrate the claim that social and cultural change present new demands and opportunities for psychology, let us briefly consider one of the most profound changes affecting primarily (but no longer limited to) the North-West of the globe – population aging. In many countries, the proportion of people over 65 years has been growing steadily over recent decades and with it the burden of age-related chronic illnesses and related disabilities. According to data reported by Karel et al. (2012), the prevalence of neurocognitive disorders (e.g., dementia) among those 65 and older is 10 percent. This figure prompts the need for new research. There has been a scarcity of longitudinal studies that distinguish between the later consequences of disorders already evident earlier in life, and mental health problems that develop in old age. Moreover, the aging population in many countries is not only diverse in terms of ethnicity due to worldwide migration, but also in terms of unique generational experiences (e.g., baby boomers in the global north and those affected by economic crises earlier in life in various parts of the world).

Against this background, it is alarming to realize that in the USA for instance, psychological health service providers currently spend less than 10% of their time, on average, with adults older than 65 years (Michalski and Kohout, 2011). To close the gap between projected needs and current offerings requires a doubling of service time; this presents opportunities for the next generation of psychological practitioners. However, the psychology education and training to which we are accustomed seems to be particularly underdeveloped with regard to such challenges (Pinquart, 2007). In Chapter 4 of this book Fernandez-Ballesteros both articulates the problems and proposes a model of expertise that can serve as a basis for psychologist educators.

The examples cited may appear exaggerated to some and less relevant to others. Nonetheless, we observe that their effects are already being overshadowed by new challenges concerning the development, socialization, and education of children, youth and young adults. For example, the sweeping technological changes that resulted in the characterization 'knowledge societies' require large-scale investment in early education to overcome the societal divides related to opportunities for a successful life (Heckman, 2011). Educational systems must also be tailored to the needs of populations with diverse backgrounds. Beyond the traditional fundamental areas that define a 'good education', decision-makers are increasingly aware of the importance to social cohesion of promoting the knowledge and skills necessary for appropriate behavior in complex social groups.

All this, of course, has implications for the work of psychologists as scientists and practitioners. To create the opportunity for such contributions to society and human well-being, the discipline must build on both its historic strengths and the emerging areas. While taking full advantage of technological innovation, in both instances new educational frameworks and approaches are required.

What is psychology?

There are indeed new societal challenges – both in nature and scope – that require adjustment of the traditional canons of psychology. Before proceeding with further consideration of how to get there, it is pertinent to offer a few thoughts on what we understand to be the core of the discipline. First, as Magnusson (2012) put it, psychology deals with 'the human being and society'. It is also understood that animals can contribute to an understanding of psychological processes. Psychology deals with the unique role of individuals as the core players in societal and cultural processes. Thus, psychology and its realization through research and practice addresses the individual as an active 'biopsychosocial' being involved in dynamic interaction with a context, be it proximal or distal.

Psychology as a science is part of a family of related sciences that also investigate dynamic interactions between individuals and their environment, but which focus on different aspects. Although psychology is often identified as a social science, a recent study by Witte and Strohmeier (2013) of what is actually accomplished in (basic) psychological research (the 'disciplinary matrix') revealed a much broader overlap with biology. Both disciplines are strong in confronting empirical data with hypotheses, thereby using a statistical inference rationale, but psychology is somewhat more oriented toward testing existing theories rather than the development of new concepts and models. That said, some sub-fields of psychology, like cognitive, social, and biological psychology, have particularly well developed research paradigms. This has had important implications for psychology's value as a neuroscience and potential in the emerging area of epigenetics. Based on the analysis of research projects funded by a national science foundation, Witte and Strohmeier (2013) conclude that to be better aligned to the approach of biology, psychology should complement its emphasis on theory testing by greater emphasis on theory development. Moreover, in contrast to other disciplines, psychology appears to be over-homogenous in its methodological approach. Thus, it could profit from greater intellectual engagement prompted by enhanced utilization of other approaches, such as model development and qualitative field studies.

Psychologists study (mainly) human beings in their larger societal and cultural context. From this platform, it is evident that cross-disciplinary research is required to explain how individuals develop and manifest their capacities for dynamic interaction with multiple contexts across the lifespan. This is a highly complex process; consequently, no one scientific discipline can shoulder the demands of formulating all explanatory concepts, providing methodologies, and planning interventions. Instead, psychology has to join in concerted action with other sciences toward understanding the dynamic interaction between individual and society.

As the remarks on prototypical research methodologies of psychology already show, this collaboration has to go beyond the usual partners, such as sociology or economics, and encompass biology and other life sciences. More specifically, the many facets of neuroscience and research on the gene–environment interaction, which are increasingly becoming coherent disciplines in their own right, offer especially fruitful prospects for strengthening the interface between psychology and biology. In Chapter 5 Wolfgang Miltner makes a contribution to our thinking about this in the context of psychology education and training.

A prominent recent example is the enriched understanding of psycho-biological aspects of stress as a mediating link between environmental pressures and lasting effects on the neurocognitive and behavioral system of humans. Stressors, such as the disruption of family processes following large-scale disasters, result in epigenetic modifications of DNA-coded cellular effects on physiological processes related to the stress system. These often relatively long-lasting changes in sensitivity to stressors have an impact on the development of brain functions and behavioral repertoires (Silbereisen *et al.*, 2013). Without exaggeration, for the first time one can state that we, as psychologists, have a clear understanding of the cascading microprocesses at the cellular level that link environment and individual behavior.

While psychology is the science of individual behavior, behavior itself is influenced in its ontogenesis and microgenesis by the various layers of ecology around us, ranging from families to societies and cultures. However, it is also correct that it is the categorization, classification and diagnostic tools of psychology which enable us to distinguish among various patterns of behavior. Without psychology's scientific expertise, our new scientific allies (sometimes our adversaries and competitors too) would not know which human behavior results from the conditions and processes within their own realm. This is a good example of the importance of being theory-driven, albeit informed by emerging empirically derived knowledge achieved through methodological rigour.

This example also validates Magnusson's (2012) affirmation that 'scientific progress is the change in the content and boundaries of disciplines over time, as a result of scientific breakthroughs and successive progress' (p. 25). This process reveals times of rapid change as well as longer periods of stability and even stagnation. As a consequence, established sciences such as psychology become better suited to new challenges, and new disciplines also may emerge. This is a permanent process, well-known from natural sciences. We would be wise not to regard it as a matter of losing one's territory. Of course, the new questions and new boundaries require an adjustment among all the players, whether they be established scientists (and practitioners) or novices in the field who can contribute to psychology education and training.

Science is not about single cases but about careful generalizations. In the case of the science of psychology, it aims at insights into the dynamic interaction between individuals and environments. Societies and cultures as particular expressions of environment are not only diverse; they also change over time. Any generalization has its limits. We as psychologists need to gain knowledge about the specificities of the societies and cultures that influence how individuals function and develop in their world. We want to understand the principles characterizing human functioning in various contexts as well as the mechanisms by which these principles work. These aims have two implications.

First, there may be principles and mechanisms that apply similarly in almost all environments over time, and there may be other principles and mechanisms that apply only to certain environments. Finding an answer to which of the alternatives is true is an empirical question. Second, scientific questions are typically framed and focused by paradigmatic views. One well-established practice is to take psychological approaches and research traditions originating in the Western world as the absolute reference, even implying that its results are 'free' of any cultural bias or limitation. Given the understanding of psychology proposed here, this belief is not only inadequate, but underscores that psychology education and training must address the diversity of the human existence and its possible manifestation in different principles and mechanisms across societal and cultural borders. The chapters by Barbarin, Hwang and Nsamenang (Chapters 6, 7 and 8 respectively) are particularly pertinent to the consideration of this dimension.

The state of the discipline of psychology varies considerably across countries, cultures and societies. Psychology's future evolution must take account of these variances and the importance of setting priorities for the respective content and pace of development among them. This has noteworthy intellectual and ethical implications for PET. Nonetheless, it also speaks to the importance of generating and adopting common principles to guide the education and training of the next generations of psychologists.

Beyond all the recent changes in the focal issues and methodologies of science in general, and of psychology in particular, according to one source (see www.nature.com/nature/journal/v484/n7395/full/484442a.html) still only 2 percent of the scientific papers published within the social sciences deal with the new world challenges, such as globalization, economic shock and ecological degradation. Correcting this imbalance is not only an issue of innovative research programs and funding opportunities. It also goes to the heart of the creative power of any discipline – its young scientists and their education and training.

A new deal for psychology education and training

In summary, the recent changes in the discipline of psychology resulting from new concepts and methods linked (among others) to new biological and ecological approaches call for adjustments of psychology education and training. This adjustment is also required to meet new challenges to societies and cultures around the world, such as globalization, that sensitized psychology to the distal conditions beyond the individual, which were traditionally underrated in their complexity and change over time. The chapters by Lunt and Bullock (Chapter 2 and 3 of this book) capture this dimension from regional and from global perspectives.

This scenario was the background for various activities within the International Union of Psychological Science (IUPsyS) that led to the Dornburg Conference,[1] and this book. IUPsyS activities are guided by a strategic plan, which articulates the Union's service to the discipline and society for each quadrennial period of governance and substantive activities. In its current version, four components characterize the strategic priority designated as Development of the Discipline's Common Core: education and training, ethics, responsible conduct of research, and the recognition of psychologists. All four are interrelated in many ways. Sadly, recent examples of scientific fraud and other ethical lapses remind us that nurturing and supporting integrity is a fundamental element of education and training as well as collegial exchange.

The intense competition for new ideas and funding led some researchers to confabulate data for experiments that never took place, thereby not only betraying the scientific community, but also exploiting the trust of young investigators in compromising their own qualifications by utilizing such data (see https://www.commissielevelt.nl/wp-content/uploads_per_blog/commissielevelt/2013/01/final reportLevelt1.pdf). These widely publicized affairs are not unique to psychology. They represent only a tiny fraction of research conducted, but nevertheless they have done great damage. Greater public recognition of psychology and psychologists was harmed; the existing regulation of research was found wanting; basic rules of ethics in psychology obviously were not internalized well enough; and above all, these cases made clear that psychology education and training should be improved to go beyond systems of knowledge and include issues such as transparency and replicability (e.g. research designs, apparatus and data acquisition and retention). These topics are not new but, as evidenced by the recent high level of activity supported by national science foundations in response to the problems, the leaders of our discipline believe that new efforts and better articulated standards are vital to the discipline's well-being and as a service to society (see www.councilscienceeditors.org/i4a/pages/index.cfm?pageid=3361).

Before the Dornburg Conference, which comprised a 22-strong international faculty and a select group of young scholars from four countries, an IUPsyS workgroup had carried out a survey among the Union's national member organizations on how psychology education training is handled in their respective countries. The survey addressed the organization of studies, the nature of qualifications gained at various levels, the core elements of the curriculum offered, basic facts about technical equipment, and the institutional structure of academic units devoted to psychology. The survey is addressed comprehensively in Chapter 1 of this book by Pinquart and Bernardo. Based on some 40+ responses, we gained first insights into an interesting pattern that showed many commonalities and relatively little country specificity. This rather homogeneous pattern should not be misunderstood as evidence for similar needs concerning psychology across countries, and consequently for providing entirely similar education and training of desired competencies. Rather, the high share of commonalities probably reveals the normative power of psychology models from the established and best-resourced players in the discipline, especially as conducted by psychology in North America and Western Europe. We determined to look beyond the status quo, important though it was as a point of departure. This decision guided the planning of the conference and the conception of this book.

The structure and message of the book

In selecting the international faculty for the Dornburg Conference, who are also the authors of the chapters to follow in this book, we sought colleagues from multiple perspectives. Following exchanges among the co-editors and chapter authors, we reaffirmed that it was desirable to have diverse views rather than compel adherence to a narrow and likely artificial homogeneity. Hence, there is no single dominant cultural, ideological or philosophically based orientation. Concurrence with the Dornburg Accord by all participants, therefore, gives rise to optimism that there will be a common way forward. Across the diversity represented in this book is a commitment to psychological science that adheres to rigorous methods of observation and data-collection, notwithstanding different cultural contexts and theoretical orientations.

The general topic of psychology education and training needs to be organized in smaller units, covering pertinent issues, such as what it means to study psychology. It also needs to examine what is required to work as a researcher or a practitioner within a society that demands more than a reflection of the science construed by psychologists. Decision-makers increasingly push for greater accountability, comparability of qualifications, and the protection of the recipients of psychological services.

With this in mind, we have organized the book in a particular way. It begins with a review and analysis of the survey as a description of the current context in which psychology operates in the realm of education and training (see Chapter 1). There are other sources available that report research, practice and training on psychology in various regions of the world, but the IUPsyS survey was the first to bring information on a vast range of issues in a comparable format, and based on intensive pre-testing. Respondents were in most cases actively involved in research and teaching at universities. Pinquart and Bernardo note that even where there is a broad consensus regarding certain elements, this does not presume unanimity. For example, there is less cohesion about quantitative methods. Their work affirms the importance of developing global standards based on common principles that allow latitude in their operationalization.

Pandey's commentary on the Pinquart and Bernardo review of the IUPsyS survey notes that substantial work has been done in the past three decades that furthers understanding of the relationship between culture and behavioral phenomena. He concludes that the maturity of psychology requires the generation and integration of further knowledge from varied sociocultural contexts to achieve a global psychology that will benefit society. This is congruent with the ultimate aim of IUPsyS' activities concerning psychology education and training, which is to develop an initial framework that goes beyond a description of what is, toward common principles for an international standard for psychology education and training that are 'culture fair'. In other words, the establishment of a framework that is flexible enough to encompass diverse approaches to psychology. In particular, it should follow two criteria: first, the framework should subscribe to the common core of scientific psychology (which will be elaborated in subsequent steps) and the competencies required for its conduct of science and applications in service to the community. Second, the particularities of certain countries, regions or cultures have themselves to be studied and understood with the same scientific rigor.

To launch the development of common principles, a series of themes was put on the conference agenda. The first was related to existing standards (in Chapters 2 and 3 by Lunt and Bullock, respectively). Here we took the EuroPsy, a document developed by the European Federation of Psychologists Associations (EFPA), as a case in point. It prescribes basic curricular elements of a consecutive program of study in psychology, leading to an academic qualification. Nonetheless, to practice autonomously as a professional psychologist requires an additional period of practical experience accomplished under the supervision of an established psychologist. This education and training program takes six years and leads to a certificate given by EFPA and its national representatives. Currently there is still large variation across Europe in terms of length and content of prescribed qualifications, probably not only reflecting traditions in science and the professions, but also mirroring the quite diverse economic conditions.

From the experience and intense work done on the EuroPsy, Lunt's conclusions reinforce the importance of key generic principles. In particular, she recommends that an international framework for PET must include commitment to a broad understanding of academically based curriculum (especially important to generating common curricula for each component and level of education). Bullock's chapter adopts an international perspective. She suggests that an international framework would define the discipline and enhance mobility while setting the stage for aspiration to attaining standards. Both authors share a commitment to promoting competence and ethical capacity.

The section on existing standards in curricular and teaching resources is followed by one on the implications of emerging areas for psychology education and training (Chapters 4 and 5 by Fernandez-Ballesteros and Miltner). We looked for examples that reflect aspirations given the societal changes affecting large portions of the world, and for scientific innovations that are shaping the future direction of psychology. Here we took as examples the field of geropsychology, which has emerged in response to demographic changes in the North-West of the globe and to changes in the disciplinary matrix of psychology. We also looked at new topics and methodologies that have arisen in biopsychology, because of their relevance for clinical research and application. Miltner also makes the case that an international framework inclusive of neuroscience will contribute to developments in this field itself, thereby enabling a continued synergy between psychologists and other scientists working in this domain. Beelman's commentary on these chapters stresses the importance of enhanced experimental, technical and assessment skills as key requirements of the practical education and training of both applied psychologists and those pursuing a career in research. He also notes that psychology curricula need to be flexible and sensitive to societal changes to ensure high scientific standards and practically relevant education and training in psychology.

The next contributions in the book address some apparent dichotomies relevant to psychology education and training that, in actuality, reflect the challenge to find a better balance between opposing views and overcoming old attitudes. The first concerns the tension between scientific universalities and specificities in human behavior with emphasis on particular cultures (see Chapters 6, 7 and 8). We can safely start by repeating our understanding of psychology as dealing with interactions between human beings and their societal and cultural environments that necessarily vary considerably. The issue could be considered as resolved by adding that we have principles and mechanisms guiding these interactions, that the limits of generalization are an empirical question, and that this is not derived from a predetermined dogma. No one spoke in favor of a fragmented discipline. Nonetheless, certainly some, perhaps many of the principles and mechanisms established to date in relatively similar social and cultural environments need to stand the test of generalization. We cannot ignore that the issue of universality versus specificity often turns into intense dispute, sometimes pushing the boundaries of civility. This is frequently the case because it is overlaid with history. For example, powerful divisions may be rooted in colonialism of the past, which imposed religious beliefs, cultural orientations, economic regimes and systems of governance. Such histories continue to have contemporary ramifications, further imbued with political ideology. Scientific psychology is part of societies and cultures; so it is no surprise that psychology in formerly colonized regions of the world still reflects its origins. This is evident, for example, by the differences in psychological traditions between Francophone and Anglophone countries in Africa and the Americas, or between Spanish- and Portuguese-speaking countries in Central and South America. Psychology certainly risked its humanistic reputation by collaborating with the ruling oppressive powers, as in Nazi Germany and the apartheid regime in South Africa. The three contributions in this section identify such problems and use examples to show how the misperceived dichotomy between cultural universality and specificity can be overcome. As examples, in Chapter 6 Barbarin calls for greater interdependence among training institutions. Hwang (Chapter 7) emphasizes the importance of conceptualizing scientific constructs and developing universal theories while in Chapter 8 Nsamenang underscores the importance of accessing local knowledge to better understand human behavior and mental processes. Addressing the chapters in this section, Huguet's commentary notes that diversity is much broader than culture and that diversity is observed even within cultures.

Another apparent dichotomy is that between basic and applied science (Chapters 9 and 10 by Aber and de la Rey). One needs to find an adequate relationship between these two bodies of knowledge, because it is at the core of psychology's mission to respond to societal needs, often at the level of the nation.

Most often, this requires applied research particularly suited to the circumstances. Han's commentary also affirms the importance of pursuing a more universal psychology, balanced by culturally specific applications. To this, translational research must now be added to psychology's portfolio. Translational research is a unique set of endeavors that are aimed explicitly at the application of research outcomes for the guidance of social policy, such as empowering early child education, designing workplaces that encourage personality development, or establishing health services so that they help to overcome disparities within society. The broader message for psychology espoused by Aber and more generally in this book is that the education and training curriculum has to reflect partnerships with other fields, such as epidemiology and policy analysis, because needs will not otherwise be identified and consequently remain unresolved.

Whoever puts emphasis on application within a national or regional context becomes sensitized to inequalities. The recent worldwide economic shocks and their consequences are a case in point – for many individuals and countries it was just a dent in their economic functioning, but many others were hit very hard because their mere subsistence was already in jeopardy, and any further decline meant undercutting their fragile means. Equally important, and often more insidious, such circumstances can undermine the resolve to meet even the most elementary needs for healthy development and life success. Investigating the pathways through which such shocks influence human behavior requires a coalition among different disciplines for which psychologists need to be prepared (Lundberg and Wuermli, 2012).

Some countries, as de la Rey explains in the case of South Africa (Chapter 10), responded in part to the challenges faced after the end of repressive forces, such as apartheid, by investing in applied research, including psychology, because it promised to show how basic evils in society, such as racism and criminality, could be overcome. This, however, came at a price – investment in basic research was typically much less, although many of the psychology's biggest successes have come from basic research and sooner or later became drivers of widespread application. The research recognized by awarding the Nobel Prize to Kahnemann for his analyses of decision-making in ecological situations is a particularly useful illustration of the value of fundamental research.

In this book, we started by looking at curricula and standards for psychology education and training that already exist. As a profession, however, psychology also has to participate in the development and exercise of quality assurance, preferably at the global level as well as at other levels. Chapters 11 and 12 by Karandashev and Hall consider this dimension, so important to meeting internal and external accountability expectations and requirements. Credentialing is an essential means of enabling societies to ensure that the appropriate competencies are adopted and implemented by psychology education and training. The reasons are multiple; they include making it more likely that recipients of psychological services receive services of adequate quality; that applicable standards and practical requirements are articulated; and, not least, that psychologists receive adequate status and compensation for their work. In some countries and for some aspects of psychological services (mainly in the health care domain), models of quality assurance through credentialing do exist; whether they can form the basis for international regulations, thereby providing a vehicle for the mobility of psychologists, is still in question.

Karandashev notes that resistance is to be expected, probably both from within psychology and from external entities. Hall stresses the importance of a coordinated process across the multiple stages and settings of training. This becomes even more daunting at a global level. Nonetheless, as found throughout this book, means of meeting this challenge are found in national and regional contexts. In her commentary on the chapters addressing quality assurance, Thompson noted the prominent position accorded to quality in developing a culturally relevant Caribbean psychology. Indeed, she regarded this as a 'take home message' for global PET efforts. While this is promising, it is more realistic to anticipate that short- to middle-term prospects for global accomplishments lie with principles based on agreed curricula that may be operationalized differently. Hence, forward movement will require careful attention to curricula that may be delivered differentially. If this difference is nonetheless driven by common adherence to identified principles, the next step of determining functional equivalencies is made more possible.

All topics covered thus far represent a tour de force of issues related to psychology education and training. However, although we started with existing curricula, this topic does not form the core of this book. Rather, the IUPsyS survey and a blueprint of the Europsy were taken as starting points for the systematic consideration of the other essential issues: new scientific vistas with biology and other leading disciplines in cognition (mind) research, a new balance between universality and specificity (universality of principles and mechanisms moderated by cultural specificities), applied cross-disciplinary research beyond basic research, and quality assurance as a safeguard for psychology's reputation and relevance of the discipline for the pressing needs of our societies. The emerging framework is one with a common intellectual core, some shared values, and a common commitment to blending similar bodies of knowledge with those that express local and regional specificities.

Who should be charged with a review of psychology education and training across all regions of the world? As psychology has established international organizations, such as IUPsyS, it makes sense that the impetus for such work should be undertaken by them in collaboration with other focal international bodies and regional organizations. This dimension is considered in the chapters by Peiro and Maluf (Chapters 13 and 14). These contributions examine and differentiate the various roles that international organizations could assume, such as securing the cooperation of diverse systems of scientific education. In turn, these can generate productive differentiations of psychology in divergent world contexts. Moreover, the development of reference models, guiding principles and standards with which to inspire future systems of psychology education and training, requires a mandate and facilities to attract the best minds; something we expect international psychology organizations to have. Finally, one needs a platform, such as the international congresses and regional conferences that are typically organized by such institutions, to facilitate debate, analysis, dialogue, cooperation and the sharing of knowledge that is crucial to such an endeavor. In the case of IUPsys, for instance, strategic planning is used to ensure its efforts are coordinated and prioritized. Outreach to psychologists around the world is an essential part of fostering participation across the distinct cultural, economic, and social factors that are found across the world and at many levels of organized society. In her commentary on Chapters 13 and 14 Gogotishvilli notes the challenges of English as the dominant (though not exclusive) language of international science. She calls for enhanced support to reduce the linguistic barrier to scholarly and collegial exchange. A case in point for the success, as well as for obstacles to such an endeavor is the experience gained in South American, Central American and Caribbean countries when IUPsyS provided support for the establishment of national and regional psychology organizations, including the development of blueprints for adequate psychology education and training in their particular context.

A tentative synopsis

This book had a beginning. As noted earlier, its precursor, and thereby the chapters, are based on presentations at the Dornburg Conference on Psychology Education and Training, held in the Old Castle, Dornburg, Germany in 2012. They were revised in response to the discussions with the conference audience, and following exchanges with the editors. Each section of the book is accompanied by comments written by invited discussants at the conference (by Pandey, Silbereisen, Beelmann, Huguet, Han, Thompson, and Gogotishvilli). The fear of many psychologists in the majority (developing) world is that the dominance of the American–European psychology leads to a systematic underrepresentation of research and application on challenges confronting their (large) part of the globe. At the closing session, Pandey stated that the mere fact that the conference had taken place already made it a historic event. The history of the discipline is rich with declarations and reports named for the venue at which the seminal event occurred that then guided the development of psychology as a science and profession. While it would be presumptuous to present the work of the Dornburg Conference as a distinct new model for PET, this book nonetheless captures the intellectual framework generated by the participants. Equally important, they unanimously consented to have their collective work serve as the basis for IUPsyS establishing the development of international principles for PET as a strategic priority and with the same unanimity committing to a common way forward. Therefore, this book may be appropriately construed as the body of knowledge, analysis and discourse that characterizes the Dornburg Accord.

   In concluding this introduction, we want to summarize the main results as an advanced organizer for the readers of the chapters in this book. The following gives a thread of the thoughts and challenges that characterize where we are and points to where we intend to go.

First, we observe a change of the context of scientific psychology as a field of research and as a profession. In the global context, of which science is a part, economic, political and social change is generating a shift toward more influence for a large number of countries in relatively rapid states of transition, many in the Global South, though some are also found in the North-West of the globe. Globalization, which has opened borders to ideas and people, has also increased mobility and sensitivity to particular challenges that require psychological knowledge and intervention at the individual and group levels. Within science, psychology has increasingly been engaging in a new synergy that brings together cutting-edge work anchored in a broadly construed biological framework. Due to this, particular progress has been made with regard to new concepts and methods linked to the interplay of biological and related ecological approaches, and concerning new epigenetic research. The boundaries of such research are of necessity rather fluid and themselves quickly evolving. For example, how we characterize neuroscience in the early twenty-first century is already different than how we understood it in the late twentieth century. We are now well beyond the pioneering work of basic and clinical neuropsychology of only a few decades ago. In times of scarce resources and increased pressure for evidence and accountability related to investments in research, such cross-disciplinary research is an advantage. Psychology – understood as the science of the agentic individual in dynamic interaction with proximal and distal contexts – is well prepared for these new challenges. In part, this is because it becomes more and more accepted that the individual is ultimately the basic unit behind phenomena of interest for social, economic and humanistic disciplines, and that psychological knowledge supports advancements in these fields.

Second, the cornerstone for progress in any field of scientific enquiry is the education and training for the next generations. This encompasses issues such as curricular development, teaching techniques, examinations and evaluations, as well as competency attainment, accreditation of training programs and professionals, quality assurance and outcome metrics, and credentialing. The IUPsyS survey and related information in other chapters revealed many commonalities, but also differences, both of which are likely to be deeper and broader once we scrutinize them more carefully. There is also much evidence about various indigenous traditions, philosophies, opportunities, economic constraints, and cultural issues of importance for psychology. Given our understanding of scientific psychology, the interaction of individuals with such forces lies at the heart of the discipline. Hence, preparing young scholars or practitioners to deal with all types of such interactions, without prejudice, now must be high on the agenda for their training. Indeed, it is a virtue of psychology that the discipline already largely recognizes that overcoming imbalances in research activities and fields of application, thereby expressing a respect for differences, can help to overcome disadvantages in basic, applied, and translational research. Nonetheless, actually achieving symmetry in exchange, or enabling sufficient psychological contributions to social policy, or engaging in research and practice that offers evidence informed preventions and intervention is not always the reality. This is not only due to insufficient recognition of psychology's value by decision-makers, nor to the fact that they are not able to provide the necessary funding. It is also because we psychologists are not always well equipped to make such contributions, whether through basic or applied research or through science-informed practice.

Third, in this book we have not dealt much with the development of curricula concerning psychology education and training, and instead discuss a broad range of other issues, including, for instance, accreditation and quality control. This conveys the fact that psychology as a science and a profession is influenced by many factors beyond a particular body of knowledge or set of skills. Nonetheless, the next best step is to return to issues related to curricula and to engage with leaders of university programs, and with the various stakeholders, in particular employers and regulatory bodies. When thinking about experts on curricula, we are confronted with the new epistemological challenges arising from changes in the scientific foundation of the discipline. This ranges from the great questions of our times within societies and culture, and the demand for psychological expertise in the formulation of social policy. By establishing frameworks for standards from within the discipline, we maintain sovereignty over the interpretation of the psychological disciplinary matrix as well as the profile of those applications which require sound preparation in psychology. We thereby increase the likelihood that research and its applications can be carried out based on our distinct body of knowledge, anchored in a psychological intellectual framework which maintains rigor in theory-building and methodological approach, as well as adherence to psychology's ethical standards.

Fourth, all of the above underscores the role of an international organization (such as IUPsyS and its affiliates) as an enabler and broker of such a discourse. This is essential to moving the Dornburg Accord forward. It may also serve in overcoming tensions among the various branches of psychology and respective psychologists. We do not always feel that we belong to the same social group, as captured in differing world views, national needs, and disciplinary orientations. According to insights from experimental social psychology, this is not a problem as long as the various groups do not perceive unjustified differences in their chances to achieve a positive distinctiveness. While there is a risk of conflict, relevant research (Wenzel *et al.*, 2007) tells us this can be overcome by enhancing attributes that bring together various identities on a higher integrative level. In endorsing the Dornburg Accord, the role of IUPsyS is to identify variability, to search for the common ground, and to pursue this by supporting the development of flexible frameworks for psychology education and training that provide guidance for 'Diversity in Harmony', as the motto of the International Congress of Psychology 2016 in Yokohama, Japan, suggests.

Note

1 For details about the conference go to www.iupsys.net/images/secnatmembers/ga2012/dornburg-conference-report.pdf

References

Heckman, J. (2011). Effective child development strategies. In E. Zigler, Gilliam, W.S. and Barnett, W.S. (eds.), *The Pre-K Debates: Current Controversies and Issues*, pp. 2–8. Baltimore, MD: Paul H. Brookes Publishing Company.

Karel, M.J., Gatz, M. and Smyer, M.A. (2012). Aging and mental health in the decade ahead: What psychologists need to know. *American Psychologist*, 67, 184–98.

Lundberg, M.N. and Wuermli, A. (2012). *Children and youth in crisis: Protecting and promoting human development in times of economic shocks*. Washington, DC: The World Bank

Magnusson, D. (2012). The human being in society: Psychology as a scientific discipline. *European Psychologist*, 17, 21–7.

Michalski, D.S. and Kohout, J.L. (2011) The state of the psychology health service provider workforce. *American Psychologist*, 66(9), 825–34.

Perrons, D. (2004). *Globalization and social change: People and places in a divided world*. New York: Routledge

Pinquart, M. (2007). Main trends in geropsychology in Europe: Research, training and practice. In R. Fernández-Ballesteros (ed.), *GeroPsychology: European perspectives for an ageing world*, pp. 15–30. Göttingen: Hogrefe and Huber.

Silbereisen, R. K. and Chen, X. (eds.) (2010). *Social change and human development: Concepts and results*. London: Sage.

Silbereisen, R. K., Van Ijzendoorn, M., and Zhang, K. (2013). Vulnerable and resilient children after disasters: Gene-by-environment interplay. In United Nations Educational, Scientific and Cultural Organization (UNESCO) and International Social Science Council (ISSC) (eds.), *World social science report: Knowledge divides*. Paris, France: UNESCO Publishing.

Wenzel, M., Mummendey, A. and Waldzus, S. (2007). Superordinate identities and intergroup conflict: The ingroup projection model. *European Review of Social Psychology*, 18, 331–72.

Witte, E. H. and Strohmeier, C. E. (2013). Forschung in der Psychologie: Ihre disziplinäre Matrix im Vergleich zu Physik, Biologie und Sozialwissenschaft [Research in psychology: Its disciplinary matrix as compared to physics, biology, and social science]. *Psychologische Rundschau*, 64, 16–24.

Wuermli, A., Silbereisen, R.K., Lundberg, M., Lamont, M., Behrman, J.R. and Aber, L. (2012). A conceptual framework. In M. Lundberg and Wuermli, A. (eds.), *Children and youth in crisis: Protecting and promoting human development in times of economic shocks*, pp. 29–101. Washington, DC: The World Bank.

Part II
Setting the stage

1 Results of the IUPsyS survey on psychology education and training worldwide

Martin Pinquart and Allan B. I. Bernardo

Although few books have been published that aimed at providing an overview of teaching psychology internationally, authors from a small number of countries contributed their experience to that work (McCarthy *et al.*, 2007, 2009, 2012). In addition, papers on the teaching of psychology from a number of countries have been published in psychological journals (e.g., the special issue of the *International Journal of Psychology* on International Practices in the Teaching of Psychology from 2006) but their contents are difficult to compare across countries. Results from an earlier survey on psychology training from 28 members of the International Union of Psychological Science (IUPsyS) from 1990/1991 (Nixon, 1994) have become outdated because the systems of teaching psychology changed over time.

Therefore, in order to get recent information that could be compared across countries, the IUPsyS Work Group on Psychology Education and Training developed a questionnaire on psychology education and training (PET). IUPsyS national members were asked to nominate key persons who would be willing and able to complete the questionnaire. Because some IUPsyS national members did not respond, psychologists from nonresponding countries who attended international conferences were asked to answer the questions online or as a paper and pencil questionnaire. In total, responses were received from 49 countries and Hong Kong, which is a special administrative region of the People's Republic of China but also an IUPsyS member in its own right. Most of the responses came from Europe (22 countries), followed by Asia (nine countries plus Hong Kong), Middle-/South America (eight countries), Africa (six countries), North America and Australia/New Zealand (two countries each). One response came from a country that is not a national member of the IUPsyS (Kenya). Thus, we were able to use responses from 49 of the 82 National Members of the IUPsyS. As the People's Republic of China and Hong Kong are individual members of the IUPsyS with different systems of teaching psychology, we computed separate answers instead of combining them. In the case of getting more than one response from a country, we used the mean scores of these responses for the following analyses. A list of the included countries is provided in Table 1.1.

With regard to ten countries, we got responses from more than one key person, with 68 key persons responding across the assessed countries. If more than one key person of an individual country participated in our survey, we averaged their

Table 1.1 Alphabetic list of the included countries

Argentina, Armenia, Australia, Austria, Bahamas, Brazil, Bulgaria, Cameroon, Canada, Colombia, Croatia, Denmark, Estonia, Finland, France, Georgia, Germany, Great Britain, Greece, Hong Kong Special Administrative Region of the People's Republic of China, Hungary, India, Indonesia, Ireland, Italy, Japan, Kenya, Malaysia, Mexico, New Zealand, Norway, Paraguay, People's Republic of China, Philippines, Poland, Russian Federation, Singapore, Slovakia, Slovenia, South Africa, Spain, Sudan, Thailand, Turkey, Uganda, Uruguay, USA, Venezuela, Yemen, Zimbabwe

---

answers. As some of our questions may not have been very easy to answer, we asked the key persons about the sources of the information provided. Thirty-four percent of the key persons reported that they used publicly available information, 32 percent of the respondents had requested information from the national psychological society, 32 percent gathered additional information from colleagues, and 30 percent requested information from universities that offer psychological programs. Only in 13 percent of the cases did the key person report having answered only according to their own personal impression. In these cases, a larger number of questions also remained unanswered.

The questionnaire focused on the structure and content of teaching psychology courses as well on measures of quality assurance. A request for suggestions as to how the IUPsyS could help with the further development of teaching psychology in the participating countries was also included.

Structure of psychology education

The participating countries differ in whether they offer consecutive (such as Bachelor followed by Master) and/or nonconsecutive programs (such as a five-year diploma program). About 94 percent of the assessed countries offer some consecutive programs while only 26 percent offer some nonconsecutive programs. About three-quarters of the assessed countries offer exclusively consecutive programs (72 percent) compared to 8 percent of countries that offer exclusively nonconsecutive programs. Both kinds of programs exist in parallel in 20 percent of the assessed countries and most of these countries do not show a clear trend as to whether consecutive or nonconsecutive programs are the dominating form. Countries with consecutive programs typically offer two pre-doctoral levels (54 percent of all countries and 77 percent of countries offering consecutive programs) meaning that the Bachelor and Master degrees are widespread around the world.

Level 1 degree programs

The next questions covered details of level 1 degree programs (programs at the lowest academic level), including amongst other things criteria for access, financial requirements, duration and course content. With regard to criteria for access, the completion of general education at a defined level is the most frequent precondition for studying psychology (52.4 percent), but only 31.7 percent of

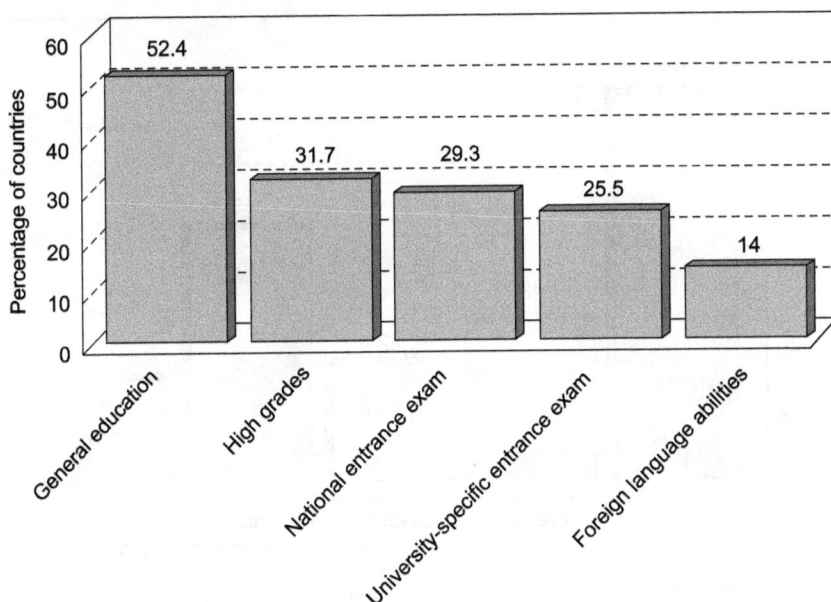

Figure 1.1 Preconditions for studying psychology at level 1 degree programs.

Note: Data from 40 countries were available.

the respondents indicated that a particular grade point average would be a precondition. National entrance examinations are preconditions for studying psychology in 29.3 percent of the assessed countries, and another 25.5 percent of the countries have university-specific entrance examinations. Other preconditions, such as fluency in foreign languages or minimal levels of mathematical abilities, were mentioned less often (Figure 1.1).

In about half of the countries, all students have to pay tuition fees (54 percent), while only about 11 percent of the countries offer exclusively feeless programs. These numbers are very similar in all consecutive programs. The average level of fees is US$5,940 ($SD = 9,017$, range 60 to 35,000). About one third of the students receive a state-funded stipend ($M = 35$ percent, $SD = 35$ percent, range 0–100 percent) while only around 4 percent of the students are estimated to receive a private or company-funded stipend ($SD = 6$ percent). Student loans at preferred rates are offered in about 37 percent of the countries ($SD = 37$ percent).

Level 1 degree programs are most often offered by public educational institutions, such as public universities (the dominant location in 82 percent of the assessed countries). Nonetheless, private institutions dominate in 18 percent of the countries. Within institutions, psychology programs are most often located in departments of social science (55 percent), although some are located in departments of arts and humanities (22 percent), natural sciences (11 percent), medicine (4 percent), or others, such as education or behavioral sciences.

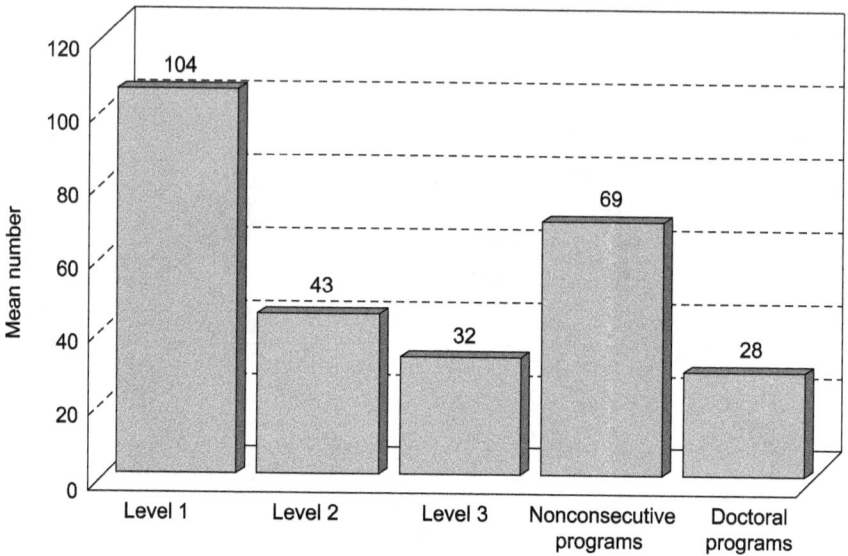

Figure 1.2 Mean number of different forms of programs per country.

The number of programs offered differs considerably across the assessed countries (from 1 to 1,367) with a mean of 104 programs per country ($SD = 245$; see Figure 1.2). Similarly, the number of students enrolled in first-level programs differs considerably with between 10 and 40,000 new students per year ($M = 6,445$, $SD = 9,712$; see Figure 1.3). The variation between countries reflects, in part, differences in the numbers of inhabitants. When totaling the number of newly enrolled students in level 1 degree programs across the 35 countries that provided estimations,[1] we come to about 227,500 students.

Across the assessed countries, psychology is more often chosen by female students. About 75 percent of first-level degree students are women ($SD = 11$) with only one country (Uganda) reporting an equal number of male and female students. About 8 percent of students in level 1 programs are non-native ($SD = 9$).

On average, students need 3.3 years to attain the level 1 degree in the field of psychology ($SD = 0.80$, range 1 to 5 years). The key persons estimated a total workload of 2,675 hours is needed for the completion of a level 1 degree, but these numbers vary considerably between the assessed countries and by the length of the program ($SD = 1,742$, range, 450 to 6,000). Overall, about three-quarters of newly enrolled students successfully finish their program of study ($M = 78.5$ percent, $SD = 18.0$), but these numbers vary widely, ranging from 25 percent (Australia) to almost 100 percent (Finland).

Most level 1 degree programs are not specialized (67.2 percent) with just 29.3 percent of respondents reporting that programs at this level progress from general to specialized content. Only one country (Venezuela) stated that level 1 degree programs in psychology are specialized from the beginning (Figure 1.4).

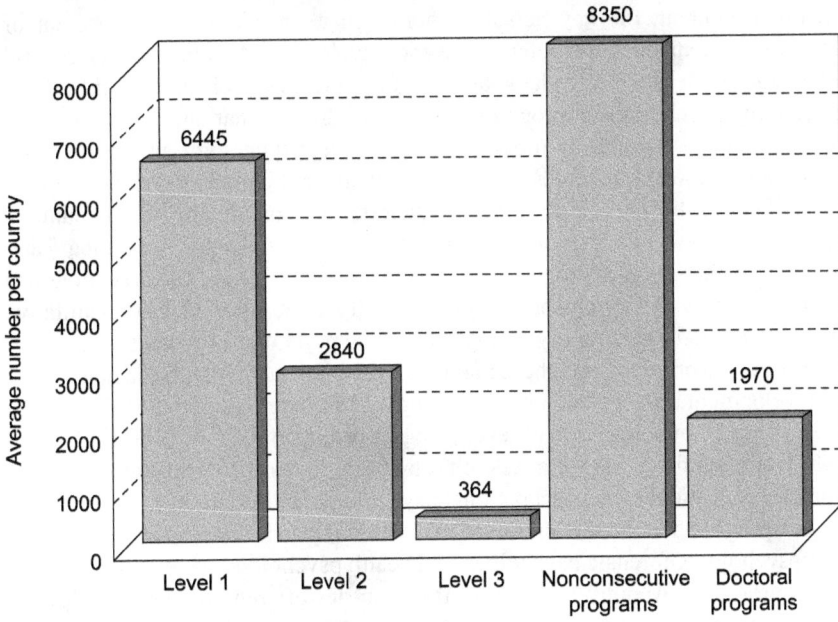

Figure 1.3 Average number of students per country in different kinds of programs.

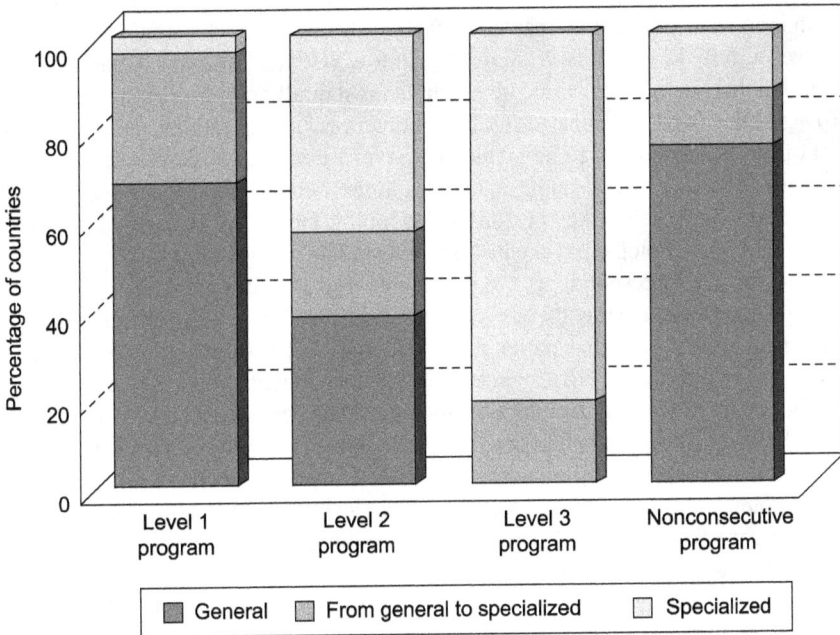

Figure 1.4 Degree of specialization of different kinds of programs.

Consistent with the notion that most level 1 degree programs are general with regard to content, the key persons reported that, on average, 20.9 percent of program content does not refer to psychology ($SD = 14.3$) but covers general education (such as a foreign language) or other sciences, such as math or biology. Regarding psychological program content, we found that the basic fields of psychology are taught in most level 1 degree psychology programs, with quantitative research methods, social psychology, and general psychology being most often taught (see Figure 1.5). Nonetheless, about one-quarter of all countries surveyed reported that quantitative research methods, social psychology and general psychology were not included in some or even all level 1 degree programs of their country. A key person from one country even reported that quantitative research methods, general psychology and social psychology are not taught in any level 1 degree program, and these numbers were higher for other basic fields, such as developmental and personality psychology. Thus, core disciplines of psychology are lacking in large numbers of level 1 degree programs.

The applied fields played a less important role in level 1 degree programs but clinical, educational, and occupational psychology is also taught in most level 1 degree programs of most countries. Cross-cultural psychology, sport psychology, geropsychology, forensic psychology and health psychology were only offered in a few programs. About 20 percent of the countries offered no courses in level 1 degree programs in geropsychology and forensic psychology, and 10 percent offered no courses in health psychology.

We also asked whether countries have a tradition of teaching national or indigenous psychology, which refers to theories or studies on phenomena specific to an individual culture that may not have (yet) become part of global psychology. However, only key persons from three countries (Croatia, Indonesia, and Russia) reported that such topics would be taught in most or all programs of their country. To assist key persons in answering these content-related questions, we included a list of topics most likely to be included in level 1 courses. We also asked them to add any topics that were taught in courses in their country but which we had not included in our list. Few key persons added topics: those that were added included community psychology, psychoanalysis and Buddhist psychology.

Almost half of respondents (48.6 percent) said that international rather than national textbooks are mostly or even exclusively used in level 1 courses. Another 33.4 percent reported that national and international textbooks are used to the same extent, and only 18.1 percent of the respondents reported that mainly textbooks in their local language were used. Forty-five percent of respondents said that all lectures are taught in a local language and another 32 percent that this would be the case with regard to most lectures. Only key persons from 6.7 percent of the countries reported that all lectures are exclusively held in a foreign language. Key persons from about 59 percent of the countries estimated that the students of their country would have good or excellent foreign language fluency when reading texts. However, only about one third reported that most students would have good or excellent abilities to speak (35.7 percent) or write (32.2 percent) in a foreign language.

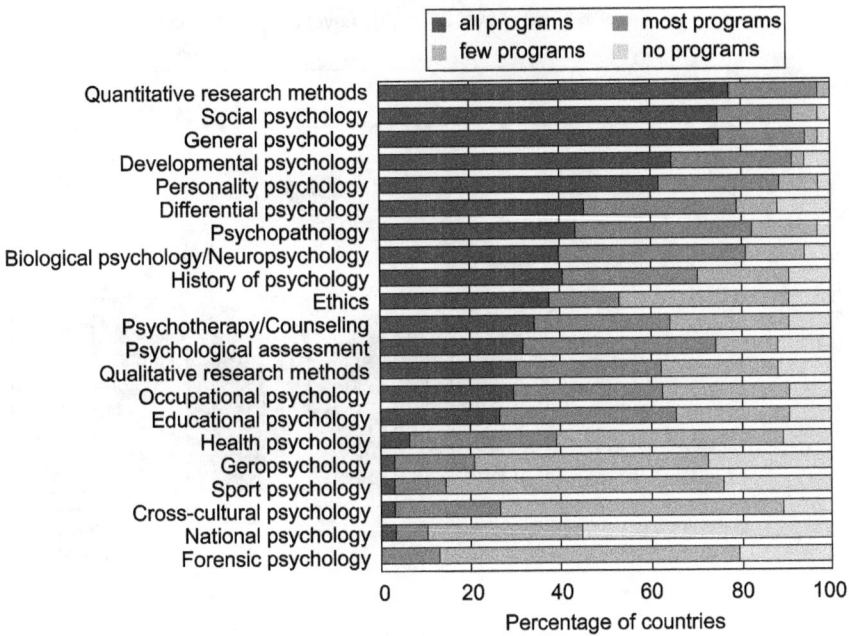

Figure 1.5 Contents of level 1 degree programs.

The dominant form of teaching at level 1 is a lecture, with more than half of all classes in 44.5 percent of the assessed countries and about half of the classes in another 36 percent of the countries being offered in this way. Only 12.5 percent of the countries reported seminars as the dominant form of teaching in most programs at level 1 (Figure 1.6). Other forms of teaching, such as online courses, are rarely used.

Regarding assessment, key persons from 69.5 percent of the countries reported written examinations with open questions/essays to be the most frequently used format; multiple choice tests are frequently used in 50 percent of the assessed countries. Research papers (37.1 percent) and oral examinations (20 percent) were less often mentioned as a frequent form of examinations in level 1 degree programs.

There is also large variability in the quality of the programs at level 1. We had asked about the percentage of programs that would have a high quality. On average, 63 percent of the programs were estimated to work at high quality (*SD* = 31). Key persons from about 42 percent of the countries reported that 80 percent or more level 1 degree programs of their country would work at high quality while 33 percent of the persons said that this would be the case for 40 percent or even fewer programs. We also took the average student–faculty ratio as an indicator of program quality. As this information was only available from 29 countries, and because the distribution was skewed, we report the median rather than the arithmetic mean. A median of 25 students per faculty member was

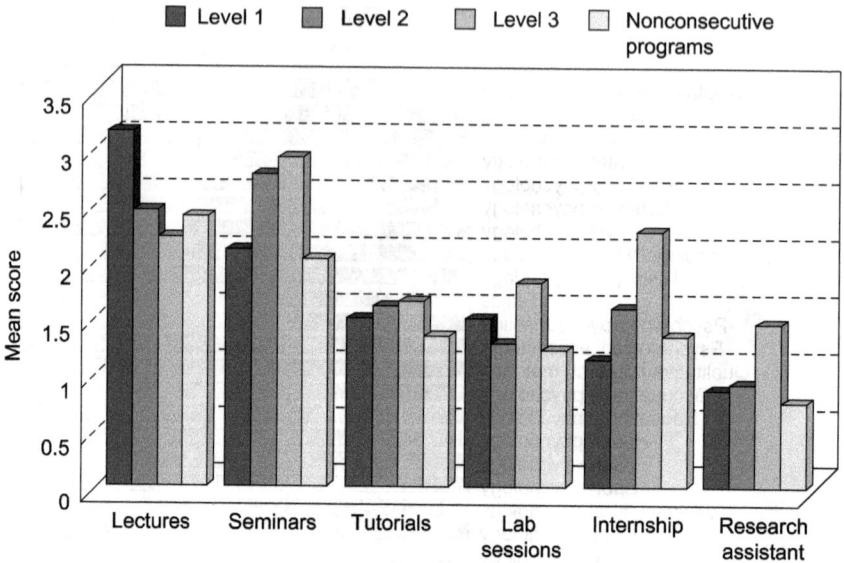

Figure 1.6 Forms of teaching that are used in most courses of the countries.

Note: 0 = not used, 1 = few courses, 2 = almost half, 3 = about half, 4 = most courses

reported, with only respondents from 6 countries reporting a student–faculty ratio lower than 20:1. Three respondents reported a ratio of 200:1 or even higher (Figure 1.7). We checked whether the student–faculty ratio would be larger in

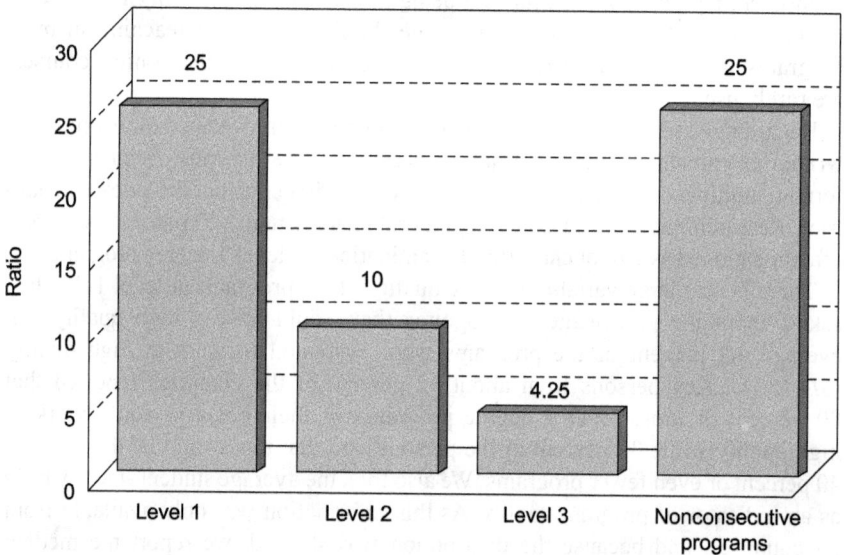

Figure 1.7 Median student–faculty ratio in different kinds of programs.

countries with larger numbers of students but did not find a significant association ($r = 0.08$).

Only about half of those successful in completing a level 1 degree were estimated to continue their study in psychology at level 2 or beyond ($M = 51.8$ percent) but there is, again, large variability between countries ($SD = 31.4$; ranging from 5 percent in Uganda to almost 100 percent in Greece, Finland, Slovenia and some other countries). As almost half of those completing a level 1 degree do not continue their studies, we were also interested in whether the completion of a level 1 degree would be sufficient for independent work as a psychologist. Only the key persons from two countries reported that the attainment of a level 1 degree would deem the person qualified for independent practice without supervision and for independent research, and only one respondent indicated that it qualifies for independent teaching at a university without supervision. Between 70 percent (independent research) and 88 percent (independent teaching) of the countries indicated that such a degree would never qualify for independent work in these fields. Thus, the completion of the lowest degree qualifies in most cases only for dependent practice with supervision (Figure 1.8).

Interestingly, we did not find a significantly higher percentage of individuals who continue their study at level 2 in those countries that offer fewer opportunities for independent work to graduates at level 1 ($r = -0.11$, n.s.). Probably other factors, such as the number of available places at level 2 degree programs or tuition fees, may be more important for the decision to continue study beyond level 1. In fact, higher tuition fees were related to lower numbers of students who continue with level 2 degree programs ($r = -0.33$, $p < 0.07$).

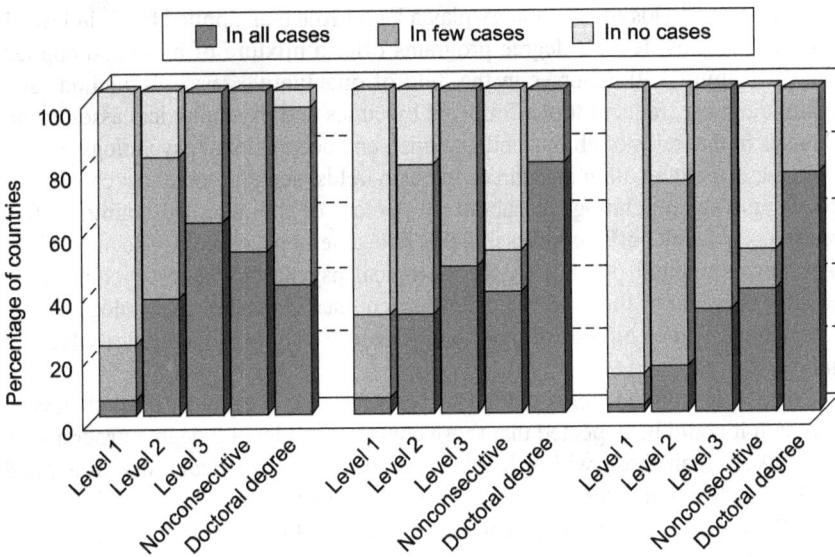

Figure 1.8 Completion of different programs as precondition for independent work.

Level 2 degree programs

Questions about level 2 degree programs were answered by representatives of 36 countries. On average, 43 universities per country offer these programs (SD = 115, see Figure 1.2), with numbers varying between 1 (Bahamas) and 652 (U.S.). The average number of newly enrolled students per country and year is 2,840 (SD = 9,936; see Figure 1.3). Again, about three-quarters of the students are young women (73 percent; SD = 13) and about 7 percent are foreign students (SD = 7). These numbers do not differ from level 1 degree programs. In most cases, students need two years to complete level 2 degree programs (M = 1.99, SD = 0.68) with variations between one and four years. The average workload for attaining the second degree was estimated to be 2,348 hours (SD = 2,151).

The programs are, again, most often located at public educational institutions (in all cases 17.6 percent, in most cases 70.6 percent). In addition to the completion of the level 1 degree in the field of psychology (80.4 percent), university-specific entrance examinations (33.3 percent) and national entrance examinations (21 percent) were reported as preconditions for participation in some of these programs.

Level 2 degree programs were more likely to be specialized from the beginning than level 1 degree programs. Nonetheless, only key persons from 44 percent of the countries reported that these programs would be specialized from the beginning; another 19 percent said that level 2 courses progress from general to specialized content (Figure 1.4). Thus, 37 percent of respondents reported that in all or in most cases these programs are general with regard to content. Compared to about 21 percent of level 1 program content, only about 8 percent (SD = 13 percent) of level 2 degree program content was estimated as not specific to psychology.

While basic fields of psychology play a larger role than applied fields in level 1 degree programs, level 2 degree programs offer a mixture of basic and applied content (Figure 1.9). Courses in the field of quantitative research methods are, again, the most frequent topic, followed by ethics and psychological assessment. Courses in the fields of clinical, educational, and occupational psychology are, on average, offered as often as courses in basic fields, such as social psychology or developmental psychology. In about 50 percent of the assessed countries, few programs at level 2 offer courses in fields like general psychology, social psychology, developmental psychology, or biological psychology/neuropsychology. In about 12 percent of the assessed countries, courses in general psychology, social psychology, and/or biological psychology/neuropsychology were totally lacking at level 2.

Courses in applied fields tended to be offered as frequently at both levels, although it could be expected that those completing a level 2 degree program are more likely than those with a level 1 degree to start practical work in applied fields. The lower frequency of courses in clinical or occupational psychology at level 2 than at level 1 may be explained by the fact that level 2 degree programs are more specialized, so that some offer only applied courses in clinical psychology,

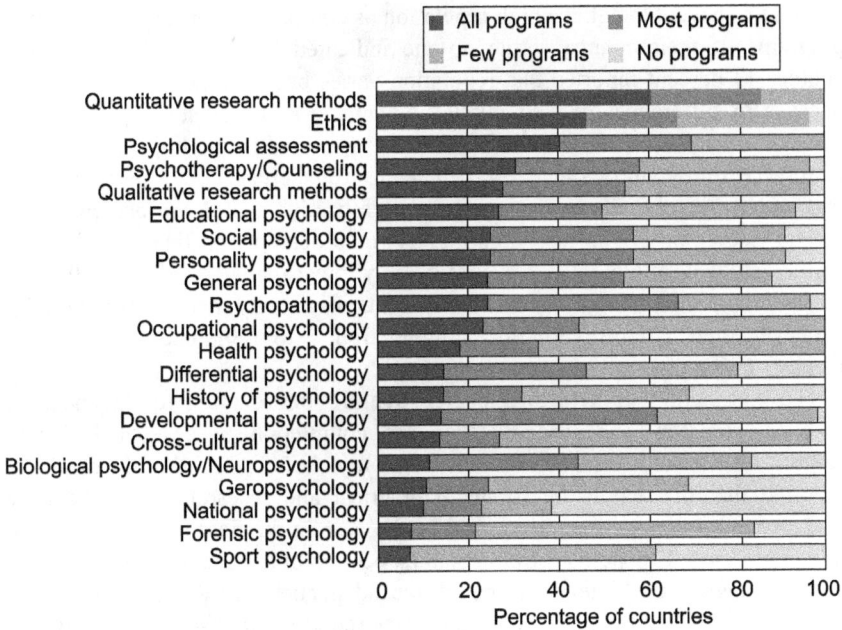

Figure 1.9 Contents of level 2 degree programs.

while others offer applied courses only in occupational or educational psychology. Similar to level 1 degree programs, cross-cultural psychology or national psychology did not play a role in most programs of the assessed countries.

The common forms of teaching differ between level 1 and level 2 degree programs (Figure 1.6). While lectures were more often offered than seminars at level 1, the reverse is true for level 2 degree programs. Nonetheless, lectures are still frequently used. Level 2 degree programs are also more likely to include an internship than programs at level 1.

A similar number of countries reported that the classes exclusively or most often held in a foreign language (39.3 percent) and in the local language (35.7 percent), and another 25 percent of countries use a mix of both languages. However, about 64 percent of the countries reported that international textbooks are mainly or exclusively used while only 5.4 percent reported that textbooks in the national language are most often or even exclusively used. The work with international textbooks is somewhat more common at level 2 than at level 1.

Similar to level 1 degree programs, most level 2 programs often use written exams with open questions (73 percent) or in multiple-choice format (70 percent). However, examinations in the form of research papers are more often held at level 2 (frequently used in 61 percent of the countries assessed) than at level 1 (37 percent). Oral examinations also tended to be used more often at level 2 than at level 1 (frequently used in 29 percent vs. 20 percent of the assessed countries).

About 46 percent of the respondents indicated that level 2 degree programs in the field of psychology have high reputation as compared to other level 2 degree programs of their country while no-one indicated low reputation. However, another 43 percent reported that reputation varies between individual programs because of differences in their quality. Nonetheless, it was suggested that, on average, 69.9 percent of level 2 degree programs would have high or very high quality (within-country range: 12 percent to 100 percent). The percentage of high-quality level 2 degree programs is slightly higher than the percentage of level 1 degree programs with high quality (62.8 percent). In line with this, the faculty–student ratio at level 2 is considerably lower than at level 1, and the key persons reported a median ratio of 10 students per faculty member (Figure 1.7). However, there is large variability ranging from 3 to 100 students per faculty member ($SD = 22$).

The completion of a level 2 degree qualifies more often for independent practice, research, and teaching than the completion of a level 1 degree (Figure 1.8). Nonetheless, key persons from only about one third of the countries reported that this would be so in all practical and research fields and only 14.3 percent indicated that this would be the case in the field of teaching at the university level. Key persons from about 20 percent of the countries reported that a level 2 degree would never be enough for independent practice or research and key persons from 29 percent of the countries reported that such a degree would not qualify for independent teaching at the university level in their country. It is estimated that about 83 percent of the students at level 2 complete their programs successfully ($SD = 15$ percent). About 18 percent ($SD = 14$ percent) of those completing a level 2 degree program are expected to continue to level 3.

Level 3 degree programs

Reports on level 3 degree programs were provided from 10 out of 49 countries. These reports often refer to Master degrees when there are two lower degrees, such as Bachelor and Bachelor with Honors or a one-year program followed by a two- or three-year Bachelor. Level 3 degree programs are, again, most often located at public educational institutions, and about 32 institutions offer these programs per country (Figure 1.2). On average, 364 students per year and country are newly enrolled in these programs (Figure 1.3). Again, the majority of students are female (72 percent) and few come from foreign countries (10 percent). The duration of these programs varies between one and four years ($M = 2.75$ years, $SD = 1.03$) and the average number of hours of lectures, seminars and other classes is 635 ($SD = 453$).

Almost all respondents reported that level 3 programs are specialized from the beginning (82 percent; Figure 1.4). Due to the high specialization, program content differs considerably within countries, and only quantitative research methods are taught in more than 50 percent of the level 3 degree programs. Level 3 degree programs have a very low student–faculty ratio with a median of 4.25 students per faculty member (Figure 1.7). Similar to level 2 degree programs, seminars/discussions are the most often used form of teaching, followed by internships and lectures. One additional difference to level 1 and level 2 programs is that students of level 3 programs are more likely to work as research assistants.

With regard to course assessment, in contrast to programs at lower levels, multiple choice exams are no longer frequently used for level 3 programs. The most common forms of exams at level 3 are the production of research papers and oral examinations.

Programs at level 3 have higher national reputation than programs at lower levels, and 73 percent of the countries indicated high reputation. Respondents from 60 percent of the countries indicated that the level 3 degree programs would show low variability within their countries. On average, 59 percent of the programs were said to show high or very high quality.

The completion of a level 3 degree is an accepted qualification – at least in some cases within each country – for independent practice, research, and teaching. Fifty-nine percent of the responses indicated that this would always be the case with regard to independent practice without supervision. Nonetheless, only 46 percent and 32 percent, respectively, of the responses indicated that this would be always the case with regard to independent research and teaching at university level (Figure 1.8).

Because only key persons from three countries reported about level 4 degree programs (such as a specialization in the field of psychotherapy) this information is not included in the present report.

Nonconsecutive programs

Detailed information about nonconsecutive programs was provided from eight countries, with five of them being located in South America and two in Eastern Europe. On average, 69 institutions offer these programs per country (Figure 1.2). The nonconsecutive programs are found in both public and private institutions. Only two countries reported a national entrance examination as a precondition for program entry. On average, these programs enroll about 8,350 new students per year ($SD = 13,787$), but the numbers vary between 75 (Slovenia) and 40,000 (Brazil; Figure 1.3). Similar to consecutive programs, the numbers of female students are high (76 percent; $SD = 8$ percent) and the numbers of foreign students are low (4 percent, $SD = 4$ percent). In all but one country, nonconsecutive programs last for five years. In Norway, six years are needed at some universities to complete a nonsonsecutive program in the field of clinical psychology. In addition, the average workload was estimated to be 3,200 hours ($SD = 590$).

Six countries with nonconsecutive programs offer mainly or exclusively general programs, while programs of one country move from general to specialized, and the programs of the remaining country are specialized from the beginning. This pattern is similar to consecutive programs at level 1 (Figure 1.4). Two basic fields of psychology – general and developmental – are topics in all nonconsecutive programs across the eight assessed countries (Figure 1.10). Similarly, ethics and psychopathology are taught in all nonconsecutive programs.

The ratio of basic and applied topics is more similar to consecutive programs at level 2 than to consecutive programs at level 1 because the classical fields of application (clinical, educational, and occupational psychology) are taught in at least some programs of each country and clinical psychology is taught as often as the basic fields. Like in consecutive programs, cross-cultural and national psychology does not play a role in most nonconsecutive programs.

Lectures and seminars are the most common form of teaching in nonconsecutive programs (Figure 1.6). Written exams with open questions are most often used, followed by research papers, oral exams, and multiple choice exams.

As only two key persons judged the overall quality of the nonconsecutive programs of their country, there was no sufficient information for analysis. However, information about the student–faculty ratio was provided from most key persons who reported on these programs. The median student–faculty ratio of nonconsecutive programs was 25 ($M = 27.4$; $SD = 17.9$) which was identical to consecutive programs at level 1 and larger than in consecutive programs at higher levels. Based on three responses, it was estimated that about 87 percent of the nonconsecutive programs per country work at high quality.

About 70 percent of the newly enrolled students complete nonconsecutive programs successfully ($SD = 23.8$ percent, range 30–95 percent). The key persons reported that in three countries the completion of a nonconsecutive program fully qualifies for independent research and teaching at the university level. This was not the case in four countries (Figure 1.8). However, the completion

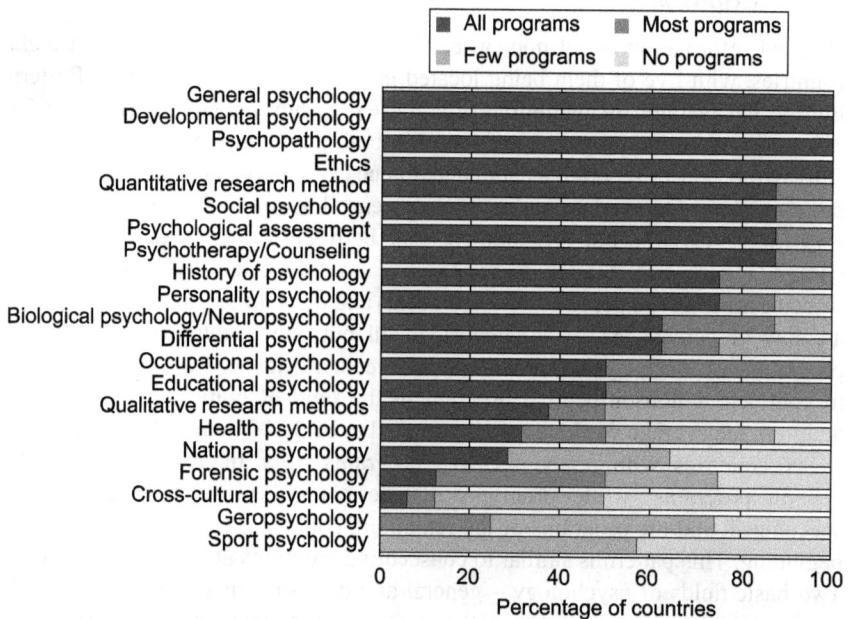

Figure 1.10 Contents of nonconsecutive programs.

of the nonconsecutive program qualifies only in half of these countries sometimes for independent practice without supervision. Thus, the opportunities for those completing nonconsecutive programs seem to be similar to those completing consecutive programs at level 2.

Doctoral programs

Forty-five of the assessed forty-nine countries offer doctoral-level programs in the field of psychology, and detailed information was provided by 36 countries. In most cases, doctoral programs are located at public educational institutions. The completion of a prior academic degree is the precondition for applying for doctoral programs in almost all cases. Only key persons from two countries reported that this would not be necessary in some programs. Key persons from five countries reported that the applicants have to pass entrance examinations, and key persons from four countries reported that high grades are necessary for getting access to these programs. However, these numbers may be higher as most key persons left this question unanswered.

On average, 28 programs are available per subset of the 36 countries, and the numbers differ considerably between 1 and 287 ($SD = 56$; Figure 1.2). On average, 1,970 students are enrolled in these programs in each country, and these numbers vary between 1 and 38,095 ($SD = 8,077$; Figure 1.3). The percentage of female students in doctoral programs is lower than in other programs ($M = 56$ percent, $SD = 14$) while the percentage of foreign students in doctoral programs is slightly higher ($M = 10.5$ percent, $SD = 18.9$). After finishing their pre-doctoral degree (e.g., master), doctoral students need, on average, 3.6 years ($SD = 0.9$; range 2–6 years) to complete the doctoral program. It is estimated that about 78 percent of the students complete the doctoral program successfully ($SD = 15$ percent, range from 30–95 percent).

We asked whether the doctoral programs are primarily focused on academic research, applied fields, or on a combination of both. The key persons estimated that 57 percent of the doctoral programs are research-only programs; while 17 percent are applied programs (mainly in the clinical field) and the remaining 25 percent have in some cases an applied focus and in other cases a research focus.

Key persons from 52 percent of the countries reported that all doctoral students have to pay tuition fees; 28 percent indicated that this would be the case for some programs or students, and 20 percent reported that doctoral programs are free. The average level of tuition fees was estimated to be US$8,960 ($SD = 11,003$, range 800 to 30,000) but this information was only available from eight countries.

With regard to financial support, only 9 percent of the 36 countries said that all doctoral students receive public funding (stipend); in 56 percent of the countries, the majority of doctoral students receive this kind of financial support. Funding by companies or foundations is available only for a minority of doctoral students. In 9 percent of the countries, participation in a doctoral program has to be financed exclusively by the student or their family. In line with this, about 30 percent of the doctoral students are estimated to be employed full time in non-academic settings and another 21 percent part time.

In only 39 percent of the countries does a doctoral degree qualify the holder for independent work without supervision in all fields of psychological work, although it qualifies for independent practice at least in some fields in almost all assessed countries (Figure 1.8). These numbers were not higher than for those holding a level 2 degree or having completed a nonconsecutive program. In other terms, having a doctoral degree does not further improve the chance for independent work outside of an academic setting. In most countries, individuals have to undergo a minimum period of supervised practice and pass a professional examination before being qualified for independent practice in all (e.g., New Zealand) or some fields of work (e.g., working as a psychotherapist in Germany).

However, compared to lower academic degrees, a doctoral degree is more likely to qualify the holder for independent research and teaching at university level. Key persons reported that this would always be the case in 77 percent of the countries with regard to independent research and in 74 percent with regard to independent teaching.

Quality control at individual level and program level

In the next part of the questionnaire, we asked how qualifications for working as a psychologist are recognized in each country. Our questions focus on registration, certification, and licensing of psychologists who demonstrate competence in approved specialty areas in professional psychology.

The *registration* of all psychologists is necessary in 32 percent of the assessed countries, and another 30 percent of the countries require a registration for some specialties, such as working as a psychotherapist (Figure 1.11). Key persons from 19 percent of the countries reported that *certification* is required for all psychologists of their country. In addition, in 41 percent of the countries this would be necessary for some specialties, such as unsupervised clinical practice. In addition, all psychologists have to be licensed in 29 percent of the assessed countries, and in another 40 percent *licensing* is necessary for some fields of work, such as when working as a psychotherapist. In addition to the completion of a specified academic degree, a minimal period of supervised practice and, in part, completion of postgraduate training and an examination are a precondition for licensing. In some countries, these procedures are carried out by the government, but in most countries a professional body, such as the national psychological society, is responsible.

Key persons from about 58 percent of the countries reported national or state-wide curricula for teaching psychology at the different levels. Key persons of about 74 percent of the countries reported that the psychology programs have to be accredited, and most of them reported a general, rather than psychology-specific accreditation. Only key persons from 26 percent of the countries did not indicate that there would be an accreditation of the programs. In 85 percent of the

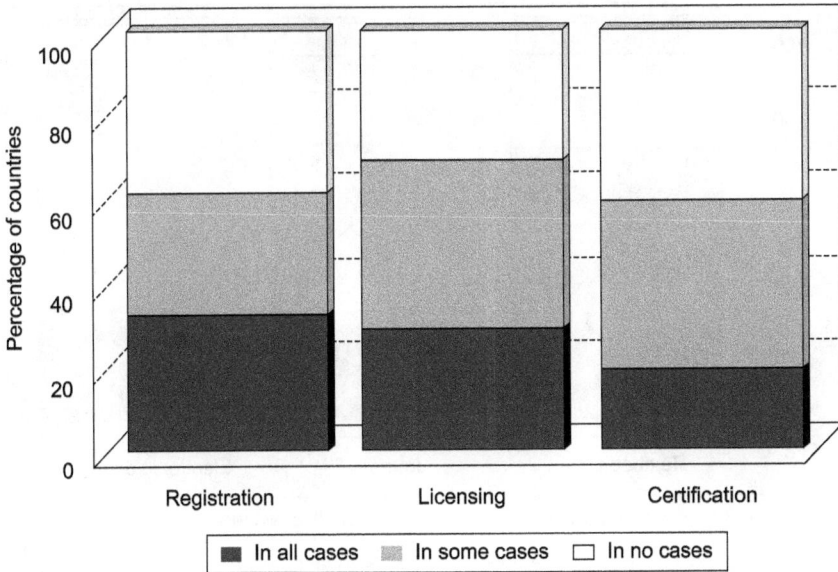

Figure 1.11 Preconditions for working as a psychologist.

countries with accreditation procedures, accreditations have to be renewed. On average, reaccreditation takes place after about five years ($SD = 1.5$), but intervals vary between one and seven years.

As additional measures for ensuring high quality of the psychology programs, respondents from 31 percent of the countries reported that there would be a national ranking of the programs and key persons from 29 percent of the countries reported that there would be a regular evaluation of the program by the students.

As a criterion of the quality of programs, we also asked whether recent international and national textbooks, scientific journals, and electronic databases would be available in the institutions that offer psychology programs. Between 36 and 46 percent of the countries reported that this would be the case with regard to almost all relevant international and national sources. Only about 8 percent of the responses indicate that few books, journals, and electronic databases would be available (Figure 1.12).

Because international exchange of faculty members and students could promote the quality of programs, we asked about whether such exchange programs would be available. It was estimated that about 13 percent of the staff members come from foreign countries but the numbers varied considerably between countries ($SD = 15$ percent, range 0–50 percent). In 30 percent of the countries, most programs have an active international staff exchange. An international exchange of students is widespread, and respondents from 46 percent of the countries reported that this would be the case in most programs. Only 9 percent and

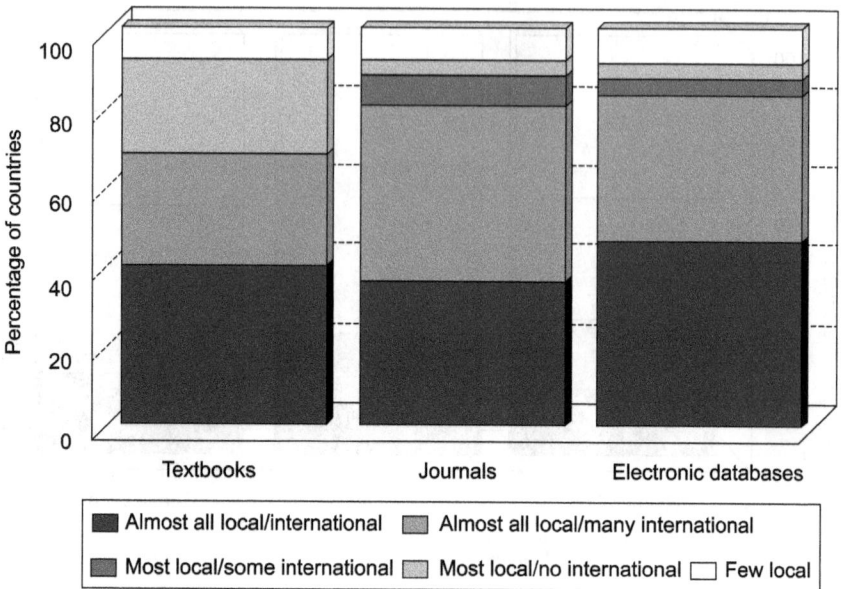

Figure 1.12 Availability of scientific books, journals, and electronic databases.

19 percent, respectively, of the assessed countries had no exchange of faculty members and/or students in any programs.

Possible measures of the IUpsyS for improving the quality of teaching psychology

Finally, we asked whether the IUPsyS could help with building and improving psychology education in their country by international exchange programs and international workshops. Key persons from about 85 percent of the assessed countries answered both questions affirmatively. By means of an open question, we also asked for comments as to how the IUpsyS could help with improving the quality of psychology programs. The answers we received referred primarily to three areas:

Improving material resources

• Allocating fund for attending international conferences and workshops.
• Waiving of registration fees for psychologists of their (developing) country.
• Increased access to online journals and other psychological resources.

Help with networking/exchange of information

• (International) training opportunities for early career psychologists
• More international exchange

- Dual degree programs
- 'We would like to improve our psychology education system through experience and good-practice in other countries'
- Helping to form international collaborations
- Collaborative workshops/seminars/symposia in specific areas in which our country is not strong enough such as forensic psychology, sport.

Logistic help/encouragement

- Help with strengthening national association and accreditation
- Assistance with building a system of licensing psychologists
- Help with increasing the standing of the national psychological organization in its relationship with the national organization of higher education
- Capacity enhancement of psychological programs
- Encouraging submissions of articles by psychologists of their country to international journals.

Comparisons of developed and developing/threshold countries

Based on information from the World Bank (2012), the participating countries were grouped as developing versus developed countries. Hong Kong could not be classified and was excluded from the following analysis. We compared the number of programs and students, indicators of the quality of programs and suggestions for support from the IUPsyS between both groups of countries. The analysis was limited to level 1 degree and doctoral programs because of the lower numbers of available answers about other programs.

Although the average number of level 1 degree programs and doctoral programs per developed country ($M = 131$ and $M = 41$, respectively) was about twice as high as in developing/threshold countries ($M = 68$ and $M = 20$) these differences did not reach statistical significance due to large variability between countries. However, a larger percentage of programs from developed countries was estimated to work at high quality (78 percent vs. 45 percent, $t = 2.96, p < 0.01$). In addition, respondents from developed countries were more likely to report that almost all international textbooks (60 percent vs. 10 percent; $t = 4.48, p < 0.001$) and journals (60 percent vs. 0 percent; $t = 3.37, p < 0.003$) as well as all relevant electronic databases (64 percent vs. 20 percent; $t = 3.15, p < 0.005$) would be available in their country's educational institutions. Developed countries were also significantly more likely to have regular international exchange programs at the faculty level (in all programs: 46 percent vs. 5 percent; $t = 2.08, p < 0.05$) and the student level (57 percent vs. 25 percent; $t = 2.59, p < 0.02$) than developing or threshold countries. Finally, we found significant differences in answers to our questions concerning whether the IUPsyS could help their country with promoting international exchange programs and offering international workshops ($t = 2.43$ and $2.25, p < 0.05$). While all representatives from developing and threshold countries answered this question affirmatively, only respondents from about 70 percent of the developed countries agreed. Similarly, suggestions stemming from our open question came almost exclusively from developing and threshold countries.

Have psychology education and training improved between the 1990/1991 and the 2011/12 survey?

This question is not easy to answer, because only 28 IUPsyS members had participated in the previous survey (Nixon, 1994), and just 20 countries participated in both surveys. In addition, the original questionnaire was no longer available so the question formulations are likely to differ. Many topics of the present paper were not included in the previous report.

Few historical differences were found with regard to the contents of teaching. A lack of some basic disciplines in some level 1 programs had already been reported in 1990/91 where 6 percent of the respondents indicated that general/experimental psychology, developmental, and social psychology would not be studied in depth in the level 1 degree programs of their country (Nixon, 1994). Biological psychology was even not studied in depth in level 1 degree programs of 44 percent of the countries in 1990/91 while in the present survey key persons from less than 20 percent of the countries indicated that this topic would be lacking in most or even all of their level 1 degree programs. The larger role of biological psychology and neuropsychology in recent programs reflects the progress that has been made in that field of research. The strongest difference between the content of level 2 degree programs refers to the higher importance of history of psychology in the early 1990s (taught in depth in 63 percent of the countries) than in 2011/12 (only included in most programs of 32 percent of the countries).

Some improvements are found with regard to the accreditation of programs. While respondents from 57 percent of the included countries had reported some kind of accreditation in 1990/1991 (Nixon, 1994), the numbers have increased to 74 percent.

While in the earlier survey only 29 percent of the key persons reported that psychology education in their country is in part or totally provided by private institutions, respondents from 74 percent of the countries of the present survey indicated that this would be the case. This reflects, in part, social change (e.g., privatization of education in Eastern Europe after the fall of communism), but we cannot evaluate the consequences of privatization for the quality of psychology education and training.

Interestingly, in the earlier survey many key persons reported that the IUPsyS could help with promoting international exchange of faculty members and students.

Starting points for improving psychology education and training

When interpreting the present results, we have to be aware that several IUPsyS members did not respond to our questionnaire, and that a large number of countries are not represented in the IUPsyS. However, as psychology education is, on average, likely to be less developed in countries that did not participate in our survey; our survey probably underestimates the need/opportunities for improving psychology education and training around the world. Furthermore, as official statistics were not available for some of the aspects of PET we assessed, many key persons had to leave some questions unanswered. We also need to consider how exact the reported numbers are. However, we received more than one response from a larger number of countries and these answers per country converged in most cases.

Despite these limitations, our survey showed that there are more similarities than differences between countries with regard to the structure and contents of programs. For example, we learned that consecutive programs are dominant in almost all regions of the globe. At level 1, almost all programs are generalized with a strong focus on basic disciplines of psychology, while programs at higher levels are more specialized. Nonetheless, we also identified important differences between and within the assessed countries that made us aware of opportunities and needs for improving psychology education and training.

First, we found that core disciplines of psychology – such as general, developmental, or social psychology – are lacking in some level 1 and level 2 degree programs, and that some level 1 degree programs do not teach quantitative methods. As already stated in the report on the earlier survey (Nixon, 1994), a set of common international standards for education and training that guide the development and accreditation of psychology programs at different levels would be helpful (see, for example, Bertram and Roe, 2005 for a definition of psychological core competences). For example, the European Federation of Psychologists' Associations (EFPA) defined a standard of education and training as part of the European Diploma in Psychology (EuroPsy): According to this standard, methods in psychology, history of psychology, general psychology, neuropsychology, psychobiology, cognitive psychology, differential psychology, social psychology, developmental psychology, personality psychology, work and organizational psychology, clinical and health psychology, educational psychology, psychopathology, and ethics should be part of level 1 degree programs. Level 2 degree programs should provide additional knowledge on topics that were already addressed during the level 1 degree programs, as well as skill development either for a future research career or a field of applied work (European Federation of Psychologists' Associations, 2011).

Second, international textbooks are widely used across the globe, but they often do not provide information as to whether the results from Western countries could be generalized to other cultures, and cross-cultural psychology, which addresses this topic, is taught in only a few programs. Thus, cross-cultural psychology needs to play a larger role in psychology education (and psychological research). Given the fact that national or indigenous psychology did not play a large role in most countries, psychology education should also put more emphasis on psychological phenomena that may be specific to a particular culture and which may not be addressed in western textbooks.

Third, we observed that, on average, only about 50 percent of those completing level 1 degree programs continued to level 2. We have to be aware that having completed a level 1 degree program in the field of psychology, some students switch to level 2 degree programs in fields other than psychology. Thus, transitional quotas from level 1 to level 2 degree programs in the field of psychology are probably lower if the educational system is permeable. Nonetheless, it has to be questioned whether the completion of a three-year program in the field of psychology is sufficient for psychological work at a high level. Limiting the work of those with only a level 1 degree to supervised rather than independent practice solves this problem in part. However, holders of the lowest degree were allowed to do unsupervised work in some fields of almost one quarter of the assessed countries. Increasing the access to level 2 degree programs and increasing the standards for qualification needed for independent practical and scientific work may help with improving the quality of psychological services in these countries.

Fourth, as more than one third of the level 1 degree programs were estimated not to work at the highest level, there is a need for increasing the number of high-quality programs within many countries. Accreditation of programs and strict quality control would be needed to improve these programs.

Fifth, there are considerable differences between countries regarding the student–faculty ratio and availability of teaching resources, such as new textbooks, scientific journals, and electronic databases. Not unexpectedly, developing and threshold countries have poorer material resources for teaching psychology than developed countries. Measures are needed to improve the quality of psychology education in many developing and threshold countries.

Sixth, our results indicate that the IUPsyS could help with improving psychology education and training in some developing and threshold countries by organizing international workshops on psychology education and by promoting international exchange programs. Some country-specific support needs were also identified, but probably not all could be met by the IUPsyS, such as free or low-cost access to online journals.

Improving quality of psychology education and training while appreciating diversity

In sum, the present survey identified some starting points for improving psychology education and training. However, we raise the issue of what 'improving' psychological education and training means in the context of diversity across countries. This issue is particularly important in the case of organizations from developing countries who are seeking assistance from IUPsyS and from more developed countries, but also in the case of more developed countries that seek to improve psychology and education globally. We discuss some of these issues in the closing sections of this paper.

First, does improvement mean to make psychology education and training of developing and threshold countries more North American or more European? This is implied when we speak of better access to journals, psychological resources, and international conferences that are now largely dominated by North American and European psychologists. Thus, the flow of resources and ideas would seem to be from developed to developing and threshold countries. But we can consider the need to support and to sustain a more multidirectional (although perhaps asymmetrical) flow of resources. That is, the improvement of psychology education and training would involve the sharing of ideas from all possible sources, with the assumption that we all can learn from each other's experiences, even if these experiences come from less developed circumstances. For example, Western psychology would benefit from knowing whether particular results that have been found in North America and Europe could be generalized to non-Western countries or whether different results are found under other cultural conditions. The possibility we raise is of course constrained by various mindsets within the different national psychology education communities. It may also be constrained by the fact that psychological science seems to be moving more resolutely towards levels of analysis that require more advanced technologies available mostly to more developed countries. Nevertheless, psychologists from developing and threshold countries should be confident about what they can share in terms of psychological knowledge and methods of analysis, as psychologists from developed countries should be open to insights coming from psychology communities from other parts of the world.

Second, we need to ask whether all countries seek to develop and improve their psychology education and training systems in the same way, or towards the same goals. Perhaps countries define distinct goals for psychologists in their national and societal development, and as such, they might have different sets of aspirations for the psychology education system in their respective countries. It is important to note that the survey does not assume a common goal for psychology education and training for all countries. Indeed, we can assume that the psychology education system in each country may be 'functional' within the structures of the educational and professional systems of each country. These structures, in turn, are likely to have been shaped by historical, economic, and even political movement within the country or a region of the world; in some cases, this socio-historical environment has strong colonial ties with countries that now have strong psychology education systems. If we probe further, we might even realize that specific psychology discourses are shaped by long-standing epistemological and intellectual traditions and conventions (Yang, 2000).

Third, as we affirm the diverse aspirations and contexts of psychology education across countries and regions, we should also realize that amidst globalization there are now common goals emerging, such as the need for mutual recognition of credentials of psychology graduates, and the need for mutual recognition of qualifications of psychologists in the growing global workplace for psychologists. Indeed, it is becoming increasingly difficult to imagine any national psychology education system being isolated from global developments. But as international psychology bodies begin to signal international standards, benchmarks, and best practices in psychology education, we should be careful about imposing these standards in ways that disregard the specific aspirations and contexts of many countries, particularly those in the developing world. Indeed, a strong push for common global or even regional standards may invite resistance, and even withdrawal. As such, the international psychology community would need to explore varied forms of engaging and interacting with diverse forms of education and training in the field of psychology that affirm the functionality and value of each national psychology and education system. We believe that the results of the current survey provide a very good foundation upon which we can begin the difficult but necessary task of improving psychology education and training while appreciating and maintaining diversity.

Acknowledgement

We want to thank all key persons who helped with collecting information about psychology education in their country. We also thank the work group members for their help with developing the questionnaire and collecting data.

Note

1 No information was available from Argentina, Austria, Brazil, Cameroon, Canada, Indonesia, Paraguay, Poland, Slovakia, Slovenia, Uruguay, Venezuela, Yemen, and Zimbabwe.

References

Bartram, D. and Roe, R.A. (2005). Definition and assessment of competences in the context of the European diploma in psychology. *European Psychologist*, 10, 93–102.

European Association of Psychologists' Associations (2011). *EuroPsy: European Certificate in Psychology EFPA Regulations on EuroPsy and Appendices*. Available online at htpp://europsy.de/dokumente/Europsy.pdf (retrieved 8 August 2012).

McCarthy, S., Dickson, K.L., Cranney, J. Trapp, A. and Karandashev, V. (eds.) (2012). *Teaching psychology around the world*, vol. 3. Newcastle: Cambridge Scholars Publishing.

McCarthy, S., Karandashev, V., Stevens, M. Thatcher, A., Jaafar, J., Moore, K., Trapp, A. and Brewer, C. (eds.) (2009). *Teaching psychology around the world*, vol. 2. Newcastle: Cambridge Scholars Publishing.

McCarthy, S., Newstead, S., Karandashev, V., Prandini, C., Hutz, C. and Gomes, W. (eds.) (2007). *Teaching psychology around the world*, vol. 1. Newcastle: Cambridge Scholars Publishing.

Nixon, M. (1994). Practices and needs in psychological training: A survey of 28 countries. *Australian Psychologist*, 29, 166–73.

World Bank. (2012). *Country and lending groups*. Available at http://data.worldbank.org/about/country-classifications/country-and-lending-groups (retrieved 1 April 2012).

Yang, K.-S. (2000). Monocultural and cross-cultural indigenous approaches: The royal road to the development of a balanced global psychology. *Asian Journal of Social Psychology*, 3, 241–263.

Commentary on 'Setting the stage'

Janak Pandey

The International Union of Psychological Sciences (IUPsyS) aims to develop programs of action to raise the quality of education and training of psychologists worldwide to ensure the advancement of science as well as quality psychological services rendered to individuals and collectives. In accordance with these objectives, the Work Group for Psychology Education and Training (PET) was constituted as a part of the IUPsyS strategic plan adopted in 2008, with the initial task of a comprehensive stock-take of systems and structures of education highlighting commonalities and differences internationally across countries. Issues relating to the content and specialization of academic programs at various levels required the collection of information, particularly from member countries of IUPsyS. The earlier IUPsyS survey of 1990–91, with responses from 28 countries (Nixon, 1994), was considered outdated, necessitating a new survey. Chapter 1 by Pinquart and Bernardo reports the results of responses from 49 countries to the 2011–12 IUPsyS survey on psychology education and training.

The IUPsyS recognizes the importance of variations in the history and development of psychology across regions (e.g. Europe), countries (e.g. developed and developing) and within a country (e.g. institutions) in shaping education, training and practice. The survey questionnaire was developed during its pilot stage by incorporating suggestions and comments received from a number of experts from different countries. The primary objective of the survey was to collect information on the structure and contents of psychology education at various degree levels and also accreditation/regulatory systems, if any.

The national societies/organizations members of the Union were approached and asked to nominate a knowledgeable person to serve as country respondent and to be the person who would complete the questionnaire, which required national-level information. This made the task difficult at times because of the lack of such data. The results reported and discussed are partly based on impressionistic information, particularly in the case of those respondents who were from countries without available data on education and training. The results of the survey, therefore, provide at best some valuable insights about the state of affairs of psychology education and training in the countries covered in the survey.

The survey results suggest that the structure of education in psychology generally consists of three consecutive levels: the Bachelor degree (level 1), Masters degree (level 2) and Doctoral degree (level 3), with the two lower degrees being the most common around the world. The uniform five-year program is most prevalent in South American and Eastern European countries and offers general courses to begin with and a gradual movement toward specialization. Doctoral-level programs aim to prepare independent researchers, teachers, and practitioners. Of course, a doctoral program may not put equal emphasis on all three and variations in emphasis (research, teaching, practice) may exist in programs across institutions. Thus the survey results present a broad comparative picture of structure and systems of education, training, courses taught, and quality control across the countries of respondents.

A number of other relevant issues not included in the survey but discussed in a substantial way are: syllabus and contents of various courses; pedagogy; quality and appropriateness of textbooks and journals; availability of literature in native language; contextualization of psychology; development of indigenous concepts; quality and acceptability of psychological services; recognition and applications of psychology in larger society; the role played by professional organizations of psychology in determining national policy; so on and so forth. It would be too much to expect in-depth analysis of all of the above using results of any single questionnaire survey. The first approach should probably be understanding psychology education at a national level. The work group considered that a national-level report should be prepared by each national member society of the IUPsyS, but this could not be accomplished.

In the last three decades, there has been an enormous development in under-standing the relationship between culture and behavioral phenomena, questioning the universality of psychological theories and laws. One prevalent view is that US- and Europe-based Western psychology has little relevance in the majority world, and that the emergence of an indigenous psychology approach has become visible, particularly in developing countries.

It is strongly suggested, therefore, by many leading psychologists of both developed and developing countries that a goal should be the development of a global psychology which is valid and relevant across cultures. This goal could be achieved by the development of indigenous psychologies in distinct societies and by pulling together and integrating the findings of these psychologies in creating a truly universal psychology. Progress has been made in the development of indigenous psychologies across countries but has yet to be assessed systematically.

A future survey by IUPsyS might tackle assessing the development of indigenous psychologies and the use of sociocultural variables in understanding psychological phenomena in many parts of the world, and the possible integration of such findings in global psychology. Thus the maturity of global psychology requires the generation of knowledge in varied sociocultural contexts and the integration of such knowledge in a global psychology that would be acceptable and useful to people worldwide.

Reference

Nixon, M.C. (1994) Practices and needs in psychological training: a survey of 28 countries. *Australian Psychologist*, 29(3): 166–73.

Part III

International framework for psychology education and training (PET)

2 International frameworks for psychology education and training

A European perspective

Ingrid Lunt

Introduction

Among the challenges of the twenty-first century for psychology is its need to 'internationalize' both its base of scientific knowledge and the nature of its professional or applied practice, while at the same time respecting its diversity. Psychology has a relatively short history which is well-known. Originating with what is frequently referred to as the first psychological laboratory established by Wilhelm Wundt in 1879 in Leipzig, Germany, psychology developed and diversified through the twentieth century during which it was dominated to a considerable extent by the USA, and to a lesser extent by UK and other western-European countries. The present century has brought a greater awareness of the salience of wider economic, societal, cultural and professional demands which require a more international discipline. As Karandashev (2009: 12) suggests, 'by the second half of the 20th century three worlds of psychology had been formed in relative isolation from each other' (the USA, developed countries of Europe, and developing countries). It is timely now to consider ways in which these three 'worlds' might be integrated, or at the least inform each other, in order to meet the challenges of an increasingly globalized, and mobile, world. A further aspect of the history of psychology, again well-known, is the emergence and enormous growth following World War II, of applied psychology, in particular clinical psychology.

This history is reflected in the professionalization of psychology through national and international associations. It should be noted here that academic psychology has from the start had an international perspective, whereas applied or professional psychology has tended to develop a more national focus. We note that the earliest national psychological associations, e.g. the American Psychological Association (APA) founded in 1892, and Société Française de Psychologie (SFP) and British Psychological Society (BPS) inaugurated in 1901 had an academic and pure scientific focus and functioned as learned societies. Their purpose was mainly to arrange scientific meetings, predominantly national, but also to support participation in international meetings and interactions with scholars from other countries. From the start, these early scholars tended to take an international perspective on the discipline, and the first international congress of psychology was held in Paris in 1889. The early part of the twentieth century saw the creation of a number of national psychology associations across Western European countries which tended to focus on more academic psychology. On the other hand, national associations formed more recently and since World War II, have adopted a more professional practitioner orientation, dominated substantially by the practice and requirements of clinical psychology. Given the constraints of a local (national) context, cultural and linguistic differences, and national conditions of employment and practice, it is understandable that psychology practice took on a more national identity.

The education and training for psychology has reflected these historical and national trends. As mentioned earlier, from its beginnings scientific psychology has had an international dimension. Wundt's laboratory attracted students and scholars from many countries. International associations, such as the International Association of Applied Psychology (IAAP), formed in 1920, and the International Union of Psychological Science (IUPSyS), formed in 1951, brought scholars together for scientific meetings and scholarly exchange. This implied a common understanding of the concepts, language and methods of psychology and its different scientific branches, and indeed the PhD degree as an academic qualification has long had an international currency for purposes of study and post-doctoral opportunities in psychology in countries across the world. So why the need for an international framework for psychology education and training? And what are some of the possible elements of such a framework?

One aim of this chapter is to begin to address these questions. The first section presents some of the features of the current context for psychology and psychologists, both in universities and in professional practice. The second section describes some trends towards greater regionalization, including mutual recognition arrangements. We then move on to present an example of a regional development of a framework for psychology education and training within Europe, the EuroPsy. In the final section, propositions are put forward for a more international framework which features flexibility and respect for important cultural differences.

Context

We live in a world with a global higher education system, resultant international competitiveness, rankings and league tables, and international comparisons initiated by organisations such as the Organization for Economic Co-operation and Development (OECD) and others. International competitiveness, predicated on an international knowledge-based economy, is leading to demands for greater transparency in terms of the outcomes of university education, and their relevance to the demands of the labour market. One example of this growing competitiveness is the AHELO (Assessment of Higher Education Learning Outcomes), currently at the stage of a feasibility study, through which OECD aims to develop measures to evaluate student performance and compare higher education institutions across countries, along similar lines to the PISA (Programme for International Student

Assessment) evaluations of high school students that have achieved widespread influence and significance. AHELO currently involves 17 countries engaged in evaluating the feasibility of carrying out an international assessment of higher education learning outcomes at the end of a Bachelor's degree program. This involves developing measures which will be global and valid across different cultures and languages and which will evaluate students' performance in higher education, through testing the learning outcomes, i.e. what they know and can do, at graduation at Bachelor degree level. The feasibility study at this stage is developing assessment instruments looking at generic skills (critical thinking, analytical reasoning, problem-solving and written communication), and discipline specific skills in the two disciplines of engineering and economics. Of particular interest here are (i) the goal to measure and compare student performance at the international level and (ii) the focus on learning outcomes as a measure of performance.

A second feature of this context is the pressure for greater comparability and transparency created by international league tables and university rankings, and therefore a demand for greater comparability of degree structures as a baseline. This has led to the development of 'qualification frameworks' which are intended to produce a means to compare and to ensure comparability of qualifications, at national, and in some cases at regional, level. These frameworks provide qualification descriptors which set out the generic outcomes and attributes expected for the award of different qualifications, e.g. Bachelor, Masters, PhD. The 'level descriptors' are generic statements of learning outcomes for different degrees which seek to make transparent and comparable different degree systems across different institutions and different countries. National and regional examples of frameworks include the Qualifications Framework of the European Higher Education Area (QF-EHEA) (www.bologna-bergen2005.no/Docs/00-Main_doc/050218_QF_EHEA.pdf), the UK Framework for higher education qualifications (FHEQ) (QAA 2008), and the Australian Qualifications Framework (see www.aqf.edu.au). These frameworks all rely on 'level descriptors' with statements of learning outcomes of different degrees.

This shift has been described in the QF-EHEA as follows:

> There are different ways to express and measure study programmes, including time-based (years) approaches, credit points, identification of learning outcomes and competencies, qualifications and level indicators, subject benchmarks.
>
> Traditional models and methods of expressing qualifications structures are giving way to systems based on explicit reference points using learning outcomes and competencies, levels and level indicator, subject benchmarks and qualification descriptors. These devices provide more precision and accuracy and facilitate transparency and comparison.

A major practical example of the use of the level descriptors and qualification frameworks is the so-called Tuning project (http://unideusto.org/tuningeu/) which was an initiative launched in Europe in 2000. *Tuning Educational Structures in Europe* has been developed as a university-driven project which provides reference points for common curricula on the basis of agreed learning outcomes for each cycle. It focuses on educational structures at the three levels of degree (Bachelor, Masters, Doctorate) and seeks to build on the qualification frameworks and to develop reference points for different subject areas. Significant here is the involvement of subject teams from different European countries such that the reference points are based on agreed learning outcomes and descriptors within each discipline field. *Tuning* reference points have now been developed for most content areas (see Lunt *et al.* 2011, for psychology reference points) and provide a European framework for common curricula on the basis of agreed learning outcomes and cycle level descriptors. The *Tuning* approach has been extended beyond Europe to include Latin American and Caribbean countries, as well as a number of states of the USA.

A third feature of our current world is a demand for increasing accountability and a greater focus on client protection and consumer rights. This manifests itself in a number of ways: increased transparency of qualification systems, more frequent public recourse to codes of conduct and ethics, and to litigation, and a growth of legislation which is intended to protect the consumer. Demands for accountability and the rights of consumers may be interpreted by professionals, including psychologists, as a requirement for quality. And quality (and consumer protection) forms an important aspect of the claims by psychologists for legal regulation and recognition. The public needs to be able to trust the professional, and the professional needs to show evidence of the quality of education and training and competence to practise. These developments are both national and international, and are increasingly moving into concerns for compatibility and transparency of qualifications, and debates on the 'value for money' of qualifications.

Finally, our world is also a mobile world. While the world of academic psychology has a long history of international collaboration, it is only relatively recently that this has extended to the world of professional practice, driven in part by the demands of students, and in part by developments fostered by governmental and quasi-governmental bodies. Initiatives include academic mobility programs such as those organized within the NAFTA (North American Free Trade Agreement) and the EU (European Union) free trade zones (see Corbett 2003; Crespo 2000). In Europe the Erasmus program has enabled over two million students from European countries to study abroad in its 25-year history, while the Erasmus Mundus programme has extended this mobility and co-operation to include countries outside the EU/EFTA. In similar vein the Program for North American Mobility (PNAM) encourages and supports mobility across the NAFTA region. At governmental level cross-border mobility is supported by professional mobility directives such as those developed within Europe over the past 25 years.

Regionalization

Such developments have contributed to what has been termed a 'new regionalism' (Hettne *et al.* 1999; Söderbaum and Shaw 2003). New regionalism develops from an acknowledgment of the close and complex relationship between globalization and regionalization, and the complex patterns of interactions and reactions at local, national, regional and global levels. 'New regionalism' has resulted in regional collaborations in many regions around the world, such as Association of Southeast Asian Nations (ASEAN), African Union (AU), European Union (EU), MERCOSUR (Mercado Común del Sur), NAFTA, SAARC (South Asian Association for Regional Collaboration) and so on. These initiatives have had a strong influence on regional collaboration in higher education, and in the professional domain have led to attempts to create mutual recognition arrangements (see Hall and Lunt 2005; Hall and Altmaier 2008).

> International mobility is not unattainable, and limited progress toward a definition of global education and training standards has occurred in certain regions of the world. However, there is no global consensus on the educational level required for psychologists.
>
> (Hall and Lunt 2005: 712)

Regional developments have tended to seek to establish mutual recognition agreements or reciprocity agreements across the countries of the region, in order to facilitate mobility and recognition of equivalence of qualifications so that psychologists may practise in a different country from the one in which they were educated and trained. Examples include the NAFTA collaboration between the United States, Canada and Mexico, and the commitment among psychological associations of 35 European countries to the standard of EuroPsy.

Education and training in psychology

When we consider the different patterns of university education and training in psychology across the world, we see differences in degree structure, degree title and organization, variations in departmental location of psychology within a university, and disparity in the conceptualization of psychology as a discipline. While most of the Anglophone world (including its former colonial regions) has adopted an organization of degree programs progressing through Bachelor, Masters, Doctoral degrees, and an accompanying notion of undergraduate and postgraduate study, other countries with long national traditions of higher education have organized psychology study (particularly the professional qualifications) through titles such as 'diplom', 'license', 'laurea', 'ptychion', 'licenciado', titles which do not map onto undergraduate/postgraduate distinctions. These differences are reflected in terms of nomenclature of degrees, organization of programs and in terms of content of the curriculum. A psychology department may be located within a faculty of arts, humanities, social sciences, medical sciences or even natural (basic) sciences, reflecting the way in which it is conceptualized by the university. A recent survey of national regulations in different countries and length of university education required in order to be able to practise as a psychologist revealed a range of three years to over six years.

Yet there has been a widespread agreement across the Western world that a foundation of basic (theoretical) psychology is required to underpin both subsequent research activity and professional practice. There is also widespread commitment across this region to the 'scientist practitioner' model of professional psychology, originating from the Boulder Conference on Graduate Education in Clinical Psychology in 1949 (Raimy 1950; Benjamin and Baker 2000) which called for psychologists to be trained both as scientists (researchers) and as practitioners. More recently this has been accompanied by a growing call for 'evidence-based' practice. These developments have been reflected in changes in requirements of the Bachelor degree in psychology, and a general understanding of the comparability of the PhD. More challenging have been very different national and regional conceptualizations and practices in education and training for professional practice, and different national requirements of curricula and competencies.

A number of attempts to compare psychology teaching and curricula (for example, see Newstead and Makinen 1997; McCarthy *et al.* 2009) suggest broad agreement in subdivisions of psychology at undergraduate level, or basic level. Based on their comparison across western European countries Newstead and Makinen (1997: 7) comment 'perhaps the most striking aspect is the similarity between the curricula in different countries', perhaps unsurprising since the main headings in psychology textbooks (dominated by those written and published in the USA) 'have remained largely unchanged for 100 years or so' (ibid.). In reaction to this dominance and in recognition of the questionable applicability of Euro-American paradigms of psychology to the developing world, there have been significant and at times vociferous calls to redress the imbalance created by what is claimed to be Western intellectual domination (Allwood and Berry 2006). It is by no means obvious that the psychology curriculum and competencies as defined by Western/Northern frameworks are immediately applicable to the context, traditions and understandings of the whole world. Regional and national differences in cultural and linguistic contexts and economic, demographic and political situations have given rise to very different conceptualizations of psychology as an explanatory discipline and a therapeutic intervention.

A European standard for education and training in psychology

In the light of this context and recent developments, an awareness of the challenges created by the substantial differences in psychology qualifications across the different countries of Europe led to a project which sought initially to develop a European framework for education and training of psychologists (Lunt 2002). The project, which began in 1998, was supported for four years by funding from the EU under its Leonardo da Vinci program, and was influenced by European initiatives of the time, such as the European Directive on professional qualifications which aimed to facilitate mobility, and the so-called Bologna Agreement, signed in 1999, which has led to an ever more powerful process of greater convergence in higher education (see Lunt and Peiro 2012). It should be noted that these initiatives in Europe provided a supportive, and indeed fertile, context for the project, which culminated in the development of EuroPsy as a benchmark or standard of psychology agreed across the psychological associations of 35 European countries. It is also worth noting that the project required the work of a team of experts drawn from 14 European countries, and consulting with a wide range of national and European stakeholders, over a period of about 10 years to reach agreement on a common framework for the education and training of psychologists (see Lunt 2002, 2011).

The project pursued two main aims:

- to explore the commonalities and differences in curricula and training requirements both within and between countries;
- to develop a framework of minimum standards for education and training that would provide the basis for assessing equivalence of qualifications across Europe.

It worked to three general objectives:

- to develop procedures to facilitate mobility of students and qualified psychologists within Europe;
- to increase the exposure of individual members countries to the education and training practices of others;
- to increase communication and spread best practice in professional training between European countries.

The initial 'scoping' of the field involved a detailed comparison of national education and training in psychology along various dimensions: structure (and duration) of university education, title of degree(s), curriculum content, learning outcomes (where available), and legislation for professional practice. Although the EuroPsy project itself may be seen as an example of a 'bottom-up' activity, it was substantially supported by the 'top-down' initiatives mentioned above. This is significant, because Europe provides an example of the most powerful regionalization/regionalism, strongly driven by political and economic imperatives and supported by a strong political and financial infrastructure; the EuroPsy initiative benefitted from the European context in which it developed, and indeed was supported through being funded by the EU for its first two phases.

At the start of the project in 1998, evaluation of qualifications and mobility between European countries constituted a major challenge. Attempts by the EU to create mutual recognition systems had proved cumbersome, unwieldy and ultimately unsuccessful. Despite directives mandating mobility instruments, psychologists carrying out similar tasks and activities yet trained in different countries were not able to move and practise in another country, and patterns of education and regulation remained the explicit purview of national governments.

Considerable effort, negotiation, compromise and debate culminated in a formal agreement, ratified at the General Assembly of the European Federation of Psychologists Associations (EFPA) and involving psychological associations of 35 European countries, for a Framework for Education and Training of Psychologists in Europe (EuroPsyT) in 2001, summarized below.

Summary of EuroPsyT

Key role of the professional psychologist defined as: 'to develop and apply psychological principles, knowledge, models and methods in an ethical and scientific way in order to promote the development, well-being and effectiveness of individuals, groups, organisations and society'.[1]

A common framework for education and training of psychologists with duration of six years, covering three phases: a three-year first phase leading to a Bachelor degree or equivalent qualification, a two-year second phase leading to a Master's degree or equivalent qualification, a one-year period of supervised practice.

The first phase offers a basic education and introduction to major theories and techniques in psychology. It has a broadly specified core curriculum content with a focus on individuals, groups, society, and covering the different subfields of psychology. The first phase is of three years duration.

The second phase aims to prepare the students for independent practice as a psychologist. There are two routes in this phase: one route leads to PhD training and a research career, the second route covers professional training in one of the major professional fields, clinical and health; educational; work and organizational psychology. The second phase is of two years duration.

The third phase (though not necessarily consequent in time) is the year (or equivalent) of supervised practice.

EuroPsyT includes a broad framework for a curriculum in psychology.

In 2005, the European Certificate in Psychology (EuroPsy) was formally agreed at the General Assembly of EFPA as a benchmark or standard for European countries, and is summarized below.

EuroPsy

EuroPsy Regulations define: the Register of EuroPsy Psychologists and a definition of eligibility for entry (five years' recognized academic study, one year supervised practice, commitment to abide by the EFPA Meta-code of Ethics and the national code of the country of practice); the notion of revalidation and the requirement to renew EuroPsy after seven years; the related notion of continuing professional development and maintenance of competence; EuroPsy limitations to one field of practice (clinical and health, educational, work and organizational, or 'other'); loss of EuroPsy validity after date of expiry, or ethical infringement

EuroPsy also includes appendices defining the Framework and minimal standards for the education and training of psychologists; competences and competence profiling; supervised practice; continuing professional development.

Development of these commitments into a European system for mutual recognition now constitutes a central goal in the strategic plan of EFPA, which is now an important and relatively powerful body which has taken on the practical implementation of the system. Strategic work within EFPA is accompanied by political dialogue with organs within the European Union with a view to using EuroPsy to facilitate mobility and mutual recognition at the governmental level.

A key feature of the EuroPsy Certificate is the use of competences, and the concept of learning by doing under supervision. According to Poortinga and Lunt (1997) 'the moral justification for the professional activities of psychologists is invariably based on their competence in psychology' (p. 294); this competence is based on scientific education in psychology, professional training and experience.[2] Roe (2002) presents a competence model which serves as a base for the development of competence profiles (Figure 2.1) and which proved useful in the development of the EuroPsy standard.

Importantly EuroPsy combines an 'input' model of education (specifying the knowledge and understanding gained through academic curricula which reflect the consensus of academic psychologists) with an 'output' model (identifying the competences which are gained through training at the university and through learning by doing under supervision in a period of supervised practice). It is these competences which are related to the learning outcomes described earlier in this chapter, both as constituting the level descriptors, as used by the *Tuning* initiative, and as proposed for evaluation of student performance in AHELO measures. We note that *Tuning* makes the useful distinction between 'learning outcomes' (desired learning outcomes as statements of what a learner is expected to know, understand and/or be able to demonstrate after completion of learning, and as

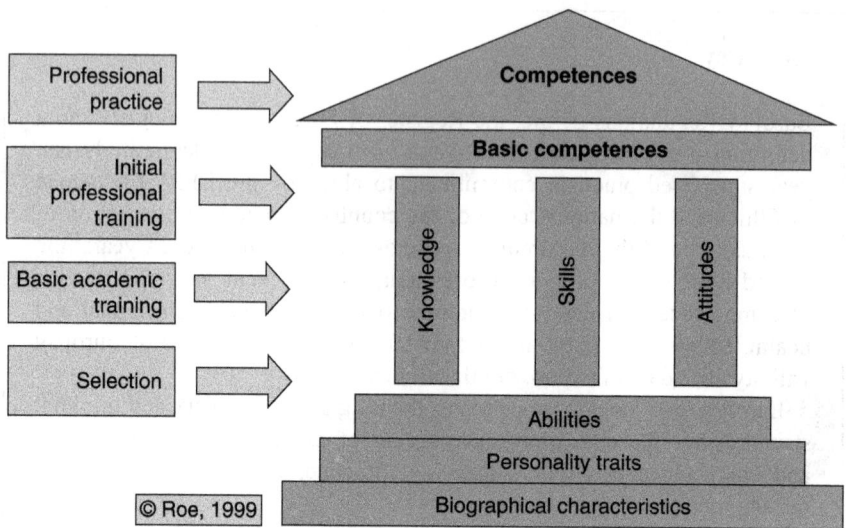

Figure 2.1 A model of competences (Roe, 2002).

formulated by academic staff) and 'competences' (as a dynamic combination of knowledge, skills, understanding and abilities that the student develops during the process of learning in a period of study).

While it was clear during the development of EuroPsy that the use of competences as part of education and training was unfamiliar to a number of countries and a number of universities, it was also evident that international developments were leading in this direction, and that the use of competences as part of the assessment of learning outcomes and as a significant element of university education and training was becoming more widespread. The EuroPsy model provides a detailed specification of competences which are used to provide the basis for both the structure and evaluation of supervised practice, and for the evaluation of professional competence in the award of the EuroPsy Certificate. These competences served as a useful tool in the formulation of standards for the European benchmark. It remains to be seen how far these may be adaptable to other parts of the world.

Finally, it is worth considering the guiding principles which were drawn up to underpin the European Certificate in Psychology in which the European standard is embedded. These principles aim to:

1   Promote the availability of adequate psychological services across Europe. Every citizen and any institution should be able to obtain psychological services from a competent and qualified professional, and the system should help to achieve this objective.
2   Protect consumers and citizens in Europe through the assurance of quality and protect the public against unqualified providers of services.

3　Contribute to mechanisms to promote the mobility of psychologists by enabling them to practise anywhere in Europe, provided that they have the proper qualifications.

4　Ensure that the EuroPsy is awarded on the basis of: (a) demonstrated completion of an academic curriculum in psychology of sufficient scope; (b) demonstrated competence in the performance of professional roles during supervised practice; (c) endorsement of European (as well as national) ethical standards for psychologists.

5　Ensure that the EuroPsy system is fair and avoids favouring or disfavouring psychologists on the basis of national or other differences in educational or professional background, and that it recognizes high service quality as a prevailing principle. This implies that the EuroPsy will not pose specific requirements concerning the structure or format of the academic education, or the nature and organisation of the internship for professional practice.

6　Guarantee the qualification for psychological practice at an entry level to the profession as well as beyond.

7　Endorse a commitment to the active maintenance of competence. For this reason the EuroPsy is awarded for a limited time period, and shall be renewed, again for a limited period of time, on the basis of evidence of continuing professional practice and professional development.

8　Respect national regulations for psychologists which are already in place.

These principles, which were debated at length, may provide a starting point for a more international framework for psychology education and training, such as that provided by the Universal Declaration of Ethical Principles for Psychologists which was adopted by the IUPsyS and the IAAP in 2008.

Elements of a more international framework for education and training in psychology

An extension of the fourth principle above might look something like this:

> To ensure that *an international framework provides*: (a) a broad specification of an academic curriculum in psychology of sufficient scope; (b) demonstrated competence in the performance of professional roles; (c) endorsement of international (as well as national) ethical standards for psychologists.

The first point (a) above implies a broad understanding of the nature of the discipline of psychology, which respects both its unity and diversity, and its universality and cultural specificity. It also implies some idea of scope, i.e. duration of university study, and breadth and depth of curriculum. While earlier comparisons of curricula in psychology have tended to be based on higher education in the developed world, it is important to take into account the understanding of psychology as promoted by other parts of the world. Reference points such as those provided by the *Tuning* project provide a useful starting point, and a useful point of comparison.

The second point (b) implies a commitment to the principle of competence, increasingly defined through competencies or learning outcomes (which are mandated in a growing number of jurisdictions by national or regional higher education qualifications frameworks). Competences also provide evidence of the 'fitness to practise' required by ethical codes, be this practice as a professional or as a researcher. And, as mentioned earlier, the use of competences and the specification of learning outcomes are becoming increasingly widespread in use by governmental and non-governmental bodies such as quality assurance agencies, and qualifications frameworks.

The final point (c) implies an ethical commitment. This has been facilitated by the work already carried out for the Universal Declaration of Ethical Principles which has been supported by international bodies (IUPSyS, IAAP, IACCP) and by national associations through membership of international organisations.

Conclusion

This chapter has presented some aspects of the current context within society and higher education internationally which support, and indeed endorse the need for, the development of an international framework for psychology education and training. However, although it is no longer sufficient or appropriate that psychologists define their work within a solely national context, the local context is of major importance in determining the relevance of an international framework. The pressures of regionalization and of globalization, and the growth of the profession of psychology require a more international framework, though one that is able to respect cultural differences and to acknowledge different epistemological and value positions within the discipline of psychology. The question of what could be some of the elements or principles of such a framework is more complicated. As suggested by Roe (2002) 'developing and maintaining the professional qualifications of ... psychologists is not merely an issue of standardizing educational input or performance output' and goes on to suggest that 'psychologists devote more research to their own professional role and work activities, before taking efforts toward standardization too far' (p. 201). It is in this spirit that the development of an international framework might proceed: involvement of a wider community of psychologists across the world, widespread consultation (such as that used in the development of the Universal Declaration of Ethical Principles) and international and local trialling. It is clear that the use of competences provides a useful tool for defining the knowledge, skills and qualities required for the competent practice of psychology, be this as a researcher or as a practitioner. It is possible to define competencies at a number of different levels: generic and higher-level abstraction to specific and very concrete tasks. The challenge will be to develop an international framework which is sufficiently robust and generic to be widely applicable, yet provides clear standards for the quality and integrity of the discipline worldwide.

Notes

1 This definition was originally used by the British Psychological Society (1998) in its National Occupational Standards in Applied Psychology and was adopted by the EuroPsy Team in its final report.
2 We follow the broadly accepted convention that uses the term 'competence' to refer to an ability based on work tasks or job outputs, while the term 'competency' refers to abilities based on behavior (Whiddett and Hollyforde 1999).

References

Allwood, C.A. and Berry, J.W. (2006) Origins and development of indigenous psychologies: an international analysis. *International Journal of Psychology* 41, 4, 243–68.

Benjamin, L.T. and Baker, D. B. (2000) History of psychology: the Boulder Conference. *American Psychologist* 55, 233–54.

Corbett, A. (2003) Ideas, institutions and policy entrepreneurs: towards a new history of higher education in the European Community. *European Journal of Education* 38, 3, 315–30.

Crespo, M. (2000) Managing regional collaboration in higher education: the case of the North American Free Trade Agreement (NAFTA). *Higher Education Management* 12, 1, 23–39.

Hall, J. and Altmaier, E. M. (2008) *Global Promise. Quality Assurance and Accountability in Professional Psychology.* Oxford: Oxford University Press.

Hall, J. and Lunt, I. (2005) Global mobility for psychologists: the role of psychology organizations in the United States, Canada, Europe and other regions. *American Psychologist* 60, 712–26.

Hettne, B., Inotai, A. and Sunkel, O. (1999) *Globalism and the New Regionalism.* Basingstoke: Palgrave Macmillan.

Karandashev, V. (2009) The internationalization of psychology teaching around the world, in S. McCarthy, V. Karandashev, M. Stevens, A. Thatcher, J. Jaafar, K. Moore, A. Trapp and C. Brewer (eds.), *Teaching Psychology Around the World*, vol. 2, pp. 1–38. Newcastle upon Tyne: Cambridge Scholars Publishing.

Lunt, I. (2002) A common framework for the training of psychologists in Europe. *European Psychologist* 7, 3, 180–191.

Lunt, I. (2011) EuroPsy: the development of standards for high quality professional education in psychology. *European Psychologist* 16, 2, 104–09.

Lunt, I., Job, R., Lecuyer, R., Peiró, J.M. with Gorbeña, S. (2011) *Tuning-EuroPsy: Reference Points for the Design and Delivery of Degree Programmes in Psychology.* Bilbao: Publicaciones de la Universidad de Deusto.

Lunt, I. and Peiró, J.M. (2012) The Bologna process, education and assessment in psychology, in Dana S. Dunn, Suzanne C. Baker, Chandra Mehrotra, Eric Landrum and Janie C. Wilson (eds.), *Assessing Teaching and Learning in Psychology: Current and Future Perspectives*, pp. 172–89. Belmont CA: Wadsworth Publishing

McCarthy, S., Karandashev, V., Stevens, M., Thatcher, A., Jaafar, J., Moore, K., Trapp, A. and Brewer C. (eds.) (2009) *Teaching Psychology Around the World*, vol. 2. Newcastle upon Tyne: Cambridge Scholars Publishing.

Newstead, S. E. and Makinen, S. (1997) Psychology Teaching in Europe. *European Psychologist* 2, 1, 3–10.

Poortinga, Y. and Lunt, I. (1997) Defining the competence of psychologists with a view to accountability. *European Psychologist* 2, 4, 293–300.

QAA (Quality Assurance Agency for Higher Education) (2008) *The Framework for Higher Education Qualifications in England, Wales and Northern Ireland*. Gloucester: QAA.

Raimy, V. (ed.) (1950) *Training in Clinical Psychology*. New York: Prentice Hall.

Roe, R. (2002) What makes a competent psychologist? *European Psychologist* 7, 3, 192–202.

Sinha, D. (1994) Origins and development of psychology in India: outgrowing the alien framework. *International Journal of Psychology* 29, 695–705.

Söderbaum, F. and Shaw, T.M. (2003) *Theories of New Regionalism*. Basingstoke: Palgrave Macmillan.

3 International frameworks for psychology education and training

Overarching issues and principles

Merry Bullock

Introduction

Around the world there are well over 4,000 psychology education and training programs in colleges, universities and professional schools. These programs exist in faculties, schools, departments, and sub-departments, and are categorized within their larger institutional structure as arts, humanities, social sciences, educational sciences, human sciences, business or medicine.[1] Programs offer degrees with a multitude of names, specialties and implied scope, and prepare students for entry-level research, practice and application in schools, universities, labs, communities and businesses.

This diversity underscores enormous variability in what psychology is called, where it is housed, and how it is taught. There is also variability in levels of psychology education deemed appropriate for independent activities in science and application. This variability makes it difficult to know if psychology, as taught around the world, reflects a coherent discipline or one that varies on a national, regional or international level. Certainly, psychology as a discipline is categorized differently in different countries – as a humanities, as a science, social, natural, human, science, technology, engineering and mathematics (STEM), as an educational or business tool, or as a health profession, and psychologists' activities vary with national priorities and resources.

Amid such variability there are strong pressures to reach an understanding about commonalities in psychology, and to articulate a framework or scaffolding to allow comparison and harmonization across what psychologists do and who they are around the world. In an increasingly global and mobile world, these pressures become practical and logistically oriented, as psychologists want to work, collaborate, learn and educate across borders.

The goal of this chapter is to lay some of the groundwork for discussion of what is required to develop an international framework, what issues those proposing an international framework need to consider, and even whether such a framework is possible.

In preparation for this chapter, I asked a number of colleagues what a universal framework for psychology education might look like. Some answered straight away that it would be a set of competencies, and procedures for how to teach and assess them. Others focused on standards, guidelines, curricula, or simply said this was an impossible task because there is no identifiable, common, global psychology.

There are many reasons for articulating an international framework for psychology education and training, including defining the discipline, enhancing mobility, providing minimal standards and providing aspirational standards. The goal of this chapter is to promote productive discussion about these goals, and about the scope, content and relevance of an international framework for psychology education and training.

Grounding principles

Developing an international framework is based on three grounding principles that address coherence to the discipline, and processes for defining and expanding that coherence.

Coherence to the discipline

Although psychology and psychology education are immensely varied in their scope, details, level of development, context, and local applications, there is an underlying coherence to the discipline based on a core, 'psychological' perspective that refers to a set of reference phenomena, models and processes.[2]

A first aspect of this perspective is the unit of analysis – for most psychologists the central unit of analysis is an individual or an individual in context. Of course, the range of psychological inquiry extends to smaller units (e.g., brain functioning and behavior; sensory systems) and to larger units (e.g., families, groups, societies). But psychology generally is not focused at the cellular level, and generally is not focused at the macro-societal level. This means that the phenomena studied by psychology, the literature accessed to understand those phenomena, and kinds of data routinely collected by psychologists are mutually understood across the field. Psychologists generally understand each other's metrics, measurements and analyses. They share a common vocabulary and set of constructs.

A second aspect of a shared coherence is adoption of a scientific perspective. This includes skepticism about statements of psychological fact or models of psychological functioning, and ways to express this skepticism through hypothesis-testing and data-gathering to confirm or deny the statements or models. Whether in the lab or the clinic, this is a feature that distinguishes psychologists from allied professions – and does, or should, trace back to training in metrics, methods of analysis, the use of data to test ideas, and critical thinking. Across the discipline there is lively discussion about which methods and which forms of hypothesis testing are valid or relevant or productive, but there is general agreement that psychology is a science of behavior, not simply an explanatory system.

A corollary aspect of a scientific perspective is receptiveness to new perspectives and approaches. As Carl Sagan wrote of science in general:

> At the heart of science is an essential balance between two seemingly contradictory attitudes – an openness to new ideas, no matter how bizarre or counterintuitive, and the most ruthlessly skeptical scrutiny of all ideas, old and new. This is how deep truths are winnowed from deep nonsense.
>
> (1996, p. 304)

Developing a framework requires identifying the coherence in psychology

Finding what is coherent and general across psychology is essential to developing a framework for psychology education. Despite much controversy in the literature about whether psychology is a coherent or unified discipline (e.g., Goertzen, 2011; Henriques and Sternberg, 2004; Kimble, 1994; Sternberg, 2005), there is and has been a good deal of effort to articulate consensus about the kinds of knowledge included within psychology's purview (e.g., through the development of curriculum guidelines, sample curricula, and textbooks), and the kinds of skills that psychology education and training should produce (e.g., in the definition of competencies, requirements for publication, or mastery of the research process).

Finding this coherence is not simple and requires mechanisms for generating inclusive, discipline-wide input, such as workshops, summits, publication series, conferences and the adoption of common definitions, models, frameworks or guidelines. Many countries have developed such documents: nationally accredited curricula for psychology (Mexico), model curricular guidelines (e.g., undergraduate curricula guidelines in the United States, see APA, 2002, 2004), consensus models (e.g., the 'Boulder model', Peterson and Park, 2005), or the many competencies, proficiencies and specialty guidelines (e.g., Psychology Board of Australia, 2011; National Rehabilitation Council of India, 2012; Commission for the Recognition of Specialties and Proficiencies in Professional Psychology, 1996–2010).

Developing an international framework requires even more attention to inclusion

Because of the enormous diversity in the scope, timing, naming and structure of psychology education around the world, developing an international framework for psychology education and teaching requires even more attention to inclusion.

First, it is important to ensure that traditional visibility and leadership in terms of the demographics of psychology, measured as power or numbers or level of development, does not outweigh voices from smaller or newer or less visible or less resource-rich communities of psychologists. Setting the conditions for international consensus poses a communications challenge to be sure to identify those who are knowledgeable and effective in representing the education and training of the community of psychologists in a specific region. Important issues to address include language and resources to participate. Any discussion that assumes that a specific solution to how psychology education and training is delivered will fail to provide a framework in which international consensus can develop.

Developing an international framework also requires addressing the relation of psychology within countries or regions to their own, specific history, context and needs. For example, discussion of the indigenization of psychology often focuses on relevance of psychology within non-North American/European countries to the local perspectives, traditions and needs of the country (Cheung *et al.*, 2011; Marsella, 2007; Moghaddam *et al.*, 2007; Paranjpe, 2006). Within this context, it is also important to understand that every approach to psychology is in fact indigenous to somewhere. That is, there is no 'neutral' cultural lens. Exploring the implications of this perspective is important for developing an international framework that can be inclusive, rigorous, and relevant to both global science and local needs.

Steps to developing an international framework

International frameworks, like national frameworks, can take a variety of structures. Some may articulate the topics, tools, and assessments that constitute basic education in a discipline, by developing model curricula or texts. This kind of framework would be likely to issue guidelines for psychology education and training, defining core content areas, or specifying necessary skills. Others, in contrast, may articulate the more aspirational principles that education in a profession should include, such as scientific rigor, learner orientation, multicultural awareness, culture of service.

In the following, some of the orienting issues important for developing an international PET framework are outlined. The points raised span a number of overlapping and complementary areas, including what we need to know about the current status of psychology education and training, the scope and nature of possible frameworks, whether a framework for science and a framework for practice will be compatible, how local perspectives and needs can be incorporated, and the purpose and audience for an international framework.

What do we already know or can we already know?

A first step in developing an international framework is scoping the 'lay of the land' – performing a 'PET scan', as it were. Different approaches to this are addressed throughout other chapters in this volume, including analyses of the questionnaire sent to colleagues in a broad number of countries, and the report on psychology in Latin America. There are many kinds of information that are important for understanding the landscape: the kinds of education offered, degree names and content, scope of areas taught, areas considered 'core' areas, status of research and research training, placement of psychology within the educational institution and within the educational system, the mix of private and public universities, as well as the prevalence of non-university venues, focused on professional training. It is also important to know the resources available at the local and national level for higher education in general, for psychology, for research, and for professional training, as well as issues in quality assurance.

Such a survey of available educational models, guidelines and curricula would provide information on the understanding of psychology as an academic research discipline, a health profession or an applied science. Articulating these different models will provide information relevant to finding a balance between universal and local needs and drawing out common principles underlying any education in psychology.

Does a framework need to articulate content, standards or principles?

There are examples of frameworks that range from broad, general statements to specific procedural details. Articulating the kind of structure is important to guide its development. The following are examples.

Competencies and skills: one kind of framework would outline a set of core content knowledge, core tools, and core characteristics that constitute an 'educated' professional. This kind of framework might also be seen as a set of standards or guidelines for the development and evaluation of psychology education. Within psychology there are countless such standards covering psychology education from high school through to the PhD. Most statements of this kind address professional psychology, rather than research competence. Examples of such frameworks are the EuroPsy (Lunt, 2011), the APA curriculum guidelines (APA, 2007), Australian School Competency Framework (Australia Department of Education, 2010), and specialty guidelines for education in many areas of applied psychology. These frameworks provide benchmarks.

Policy statements, principles: another kind of framework might articulate the general purpose and goals of psychology education, and set out guiding, aspirational principles. One example of such a framework in psychology (although not for education) is the Universal Declaration for Ethics in Psychology (Gauthier et al., 2010). Another is the APA's *Principles for Quality Undergraduate Education in Psychology* (APA, 2011), although this is not directed toward training to be a psychologist, but rather to broad undergraduate education in psychology. Other disciplines have statements for education practice (e.g., pharmacy, see FIP, 2008, 2009). These are aspirational, and intended to be used as a guide to develop more detailed action oriented documents and guidance.

Other formats may include curriculum templates or examples, operating procedures or processes, or articulation of competencies. Each of these may overlap somewhat with standards or principles.

Can a single framework encompass psychological science and professional psychology education?

Historically, psychology has always encompassed scientific and applied aspects, explicitly articulated in the 'scientist-practitioner' model for professional psychology and in calls for broad relevance in research arenas. Although this model still underlies training in many university settings, psychology is increasingly being taught as a 'learned profession' in settings outside of traditional university settings. In many countries there are separate tracks for scientists and practitioners, with different degree names, courses of study and regulations; in others, psychology is taught solely as an applied profession with few or no resources for research. A psychology education and training framework would need to address these issues.

A central issue is whether the competencies or skills of a researcher are the same as those of a practitioner (e.g., Belar, 2000; Raimy, 1950). Within psychology, the answer has generally been yes at a basic knowledge level (including a scientific attitude, data-gathering, hypothesis-testing, and critical thinking), but then mute on the question for advanced training. Certainly, when one is active as a researcher or practitioner, the evaluative and regulatory mechanisms are different. For a scientist, evaluation is based on peer review and publications, which is intended to regulate the quality of ideas and research; the conduct of research is regulated by ethical codes and for many, research ethical review boards. For practitioners, regulation, when it exists, is generally focused on meeting educational and experiential and ethical requirements that attest to a level of competence to perform services, and continuing education to maintain these. There is no clear discipline-wide system for evaluation.

It may be that it is possible to identify core knowledge or skills that span both areas, that would constitute a first level framework, but, at least for most countries, this would need to be supplemented with additional considerations more relevant to application and professional services. In any case, the question of whether a framework for education for psychological science can be the same as a framework for education for professional practice or the same as a framework for applied psychology will need to be addressed (see Belar, 2006; Henriques and Sternberg, 2004; Norcross *et al.*, 2010; Ral, 2006).

How can a framework be articulated to encompass universal principles or standards and address a defining role for local perspectives and needs?

Addressing the level of generality of a PET framework and ensuring that it will be relevant and usable across countries touches on some of the most controversial issues in efforts to reconcile psychology around the world. These include the extent to which it is possible to articulate 'a' discipline of psychology as opposed to multiple psychologies, and the extent to which psychology itself forms a coherent discipline. The considerable literature on this (mostly from Western authors) points to the dimensions that must be considered (methodologies, treatment of extra-scientific belief systems, basic definitions for psychological constructs). To address coherence issues, any PET framework must further acknowledge the importance of local relevance – that is, the local, regional and national contexts in which psychology is taught and practiced, as well as a mandate to address the needs and conditions of specific countries, cultures and groups.

From an international perspective such grounding is essential to any framework as a central aspect. This means that any consensus on a 'universal core' or core competencies must be sufficiently general or flexible to allow local application. This issue has been addressed in several ways within psychology – in articulation of principles of multicultural awareness; in calls for cultural competence; and in discussion of the indigenization of psychology.

The challenge to a PET framework is to identify the core that describes psychology in such a way that it will both carve out a common disciplinary identity and be sufficiently broad to include international variation. At the same time, any PET framework will likely also meet demands to foster the development of a psychology that is knowledgeable about and able to collaborate in multidisciplinary and interprofessional contexts.

What is the perceived role of an international PET framework? Who is the audience? Who are the 'stakeholders'?

A framework for education can be used in many ways: as internal guidance for the development of programs and degrees; as support for the development of psychology programs, degrees and institutions within a larger institution; as support for regulatory activities in quality assurance or legal recognition; as a guide to broad priority setting; as a statement of the core features of a discipline. Which of these is emphasized will vary with the intended audience of an international framework.

Development of a framework will require attention to the categories of audiences or 'stakeholders' that need to be included in development, review and consensus-building. Examples are researchers; educators, practitioners; users of psychological knowledge and practice; regulators; in universities, the academy, applied areas; health settings; educational settings, and more.

'Placing a framework' – content and process

Table 3.1 summarizes some of the issues discussed as a way of organizing the several dimensions and questions for discussion about the nature, form and scope of an international framework for psychology education and training, organized as a chart listing 'Steps to a PET framework'. This is not a linear process, and answers in one row do not affect the answers in subsequent rows (that is, the columns do not reflect unitary constructs). As the table suggests, building a framework requires outreach, resources, consensus-building, and leadership and infrastructure development.

Table 3.1 Steps to a PET framework

Tasks in developing PET

Tasks in developing PET		
	Principles	*Standards/guidelines*
• Identify goals of PET framework: principles, standards, guidelines	Aspirational; address content, learning process, learning outcomes	Basis for regulatory systems; basis for curriculum development
	Educators	*Students*	*Researchers*	*Regulators/policy*
• Identify stakeholders	Program development; curriculum development, scope, depth, interdisciplinarity	Identify needs; workforce analysis	Scope of content; diversity of research tools	Basis for quality assurance; Basis for workforce analysis and prediction
	Information	*Consensus building*	*Developing outcomes*
• Develop mechanisms for broad international inclusion	PET scan	Mechanisms for international representation of multiple groups of stakeholders (funding, access)	Dissemination (languages)
	Research	*Practice*
• Identify special issues relevant to psychological science and psychological practice	Multiple methods; ethics of international collaboration; cultural awareness; dissemination practices	Scope of practice; competencies; evidence-based practice in international context
	Information	*Resources*		
• Develop comprehensive 'PET scan'	Map 'lay of the land'	Develop curriculum bank; open access texts and data sets	Develop education leaders; Develop education infrastructure	

This is a propitious time for psychology to gather itself and develop a PET framework. Changed workforce conditions require psychology both to define itself as a coherent discipline, and to position itself as part of multidisciplinary, transprofessional teams to address complex challenges. As workforce demands increase in places where the need for psychological services far outstrips the number of trained professionals, or where the demand for teaching and research is greater than the available educators, or as they decrease in other places where there is an oversupply of psychologists in some areas, it will be important for the discipline to endogenously decide what it is, what it encompasses, and how its students need to be educated to bring the power of a psychological perspective to science, service and society.

Notes

1 Estimate based on entries for "Institutions of Psychology" for each of the 193 countries listed in *Psychology Resources Around the World* (www.psychology-resources.org). These are primarily psychology department in academic settings.
2 Note that the existence of this coherence does not preclude broad support for interdisciplinary training or research. The point is that if one is to understand PET internationally, this coherence can offer some organizing principles.

References

APA (American Psychological Association) Task Force on Undergraduate Major Competencies. (2002). *Undergraduate psychology major learning goals and outcomes: A report.* Washington, DC: Psychological Association, available at www.apa.org/ed/pcue/taskforcereport2.pdf

APA (American Psychological Association). (2004). *Developing and evaluating standards and guidelines related to education and training in psychology: Context, procedures, criteria, and format.* Washington, DC: American Psychological Association, available at www.apa.org/education/grad/beaguidelines- 04final.pdf

APA (American Psychological Association). (2007). *APA guidelines for the undergraduate psychology major.* Washington, DC: American Psychological Association, available at www.apa.org/ed/resources.html.

APA (American Psychological Association). (2011). *Principles for quality undergraduate education in psychology.* Washington, DC: American Psychological Association, available at www.apa.org/education/undergrad/principles.aspx

Australia Department of Education (2010). *Competency Framework for School Psychologists.* Available at http://det.wa.edu.au/studentsupport/behaviourandwellbeing/detcms/school-support-programs/behaviour-and-wellbeing/behaviour/school-psychology-services/public-content/competency-framework-for-school-psychologists. en?oid=com.arsdigita.cms.contenttypes.FileStorageItem-id-11395549

Belar, C. (2000). Scientist-practitioner ≠ science + practice: Boulder is bolder. *American Psychologist*, 55, 249–50.

Belar, C. (2006). Graduate education in clinical psychology: 'We're not in Kansas anymore'. *Training and Education in Professional Psychology*, vol. S, 69–79 (reprinted from 1998, *American Psychologist*, 53, 456–64).

Cheung, F. M., Van de Vijver, F. J. R. and Leong, F. T. L. (2011). Toward a new approach to the study of personality in culture. *American Psychologist*, 66(7), 593–603. doi: 10.1037/a0022389

Commission for the Recognition of Specialties and Proficiencies in Professional Psychology. (1996–2010). *Recognized specialties and proficiencies in professional psychology*, available at www.apa.org/ed/graduate/specialize/recognized.aspx.

FIP (2009). *FIP statement of policy. Quality assurance of pharmacy education*, available at www.fip.org/www/uploads/database_file.php?id=302&table_id=, accessed 5 August 2013.

FIP (International Forum for Quality Assurance of Pharmacy Education) (2008). *A global framework for quality assurance of pharmacy education*. Accessed www.fip.org/files/fip/PharmacyEducation/Global%20Framework%20Final%20Draft.pdf August 5, 2013.

Gauthier, J., Pettifor, J. and Ferrero, A. (2010). The universal declaration of ethical principles for psychologists: A culture-sensitive model for creating and reviewing a code of ethics. *Ethics and Behavior*, 20, 179–96.

Goertzen, J. R. (2011). Further problematizing the potential for a more unified experimental, scientific psychology: A comment on Mandler. *Journal of Theoretical and Philosophical Psychology*, 31(4), 247–9.

Henriques, G. R. and Sternberg, R. J. (2004). Unified professional psychology: Implications for the combined-integrated model of doctoral training. *Journal of Clinical Psychology*, 60, 1051–63.

Kimble, G. (1994). A frame of reference for psychology. *American Psychologist*, 49, 510–19.

Lunt, I. (2011). EuroPsy: The development of standards for high-quality professional education in psychology. *European Psychologist*, 16, 104–10.

Marsella, A. J. (2007). Education and training for a global psychology: Foundations, issues and actions. In M. J. Stevens and U. Gielen (Eds.), *Toward a global psychology: Theory, research, intervention and pedagogy*, pp. 333–61. Mahwah, NJ: Erlbaum.

Moghaddam, F., Erneling, C., Montero, M. and Lee, N. (2007). Toward a conceptual foundation for a global psychology. In M. J. Stevens and U. P. Gielen (Eds.), *Toward a global psychology: Theory, research, intervention, and pedagogy*, pp. 179–206. Mahwah, NJ: Lawrence Erlbaum Associates.

National Rehabilitation Council of India (2012). *Examination for Certifying Clinical Competency (EC3) in Psychology*, available at www.rehabcouncil.nic.in/exam/ec3_guidelines.pdf

Norcross, J., Ellis, J. and Sayette, M. (2010). Getting in and getting money: A comparative analysis of admission standards, acceptance rates, and financial assistance across the research–practice continuum in clinical psychology programs. *Training and Education in Professional Psychology*, 4, 99–104.

Paranjpe, A. C. (2006). From tradition through colonialism to globalization: Reflections on the history of psychology in India. In A. C. Brock (Ed.), *Internationalizing the history of psychology*, pp. 56–74. New York: New York University Press.

Peterson, C. and Park, N. (2005). The enduring value of the Boulder Model: 'Upon this rock we will build'. *Journal of Clinical Psychology*, 61, 1147–50.

Psychology Board of Australia (2011). *Guidelines on Psychology Areas of Practice Endorsements*, available at www.psychologyboard.gov.au/Standards-and-Guidelines/Codes-Guidelines-Policies.aspx

Raimy, V. C. (1950). *Training in clinical psychology*. New York: Prentice Hall.

Ral, J. M. T. (2006). The unity and diversity of psychology. *Psychology in Spain*, 10, 110–16.

Sagan, C. (1996). *The Demon-Haunted World: Science as a Candle in the Dark* (pp. 304–306).

Sternberg, R. (Ed.) (2005). *Unity in psychology: Possibility or pipedream?* Washington, DC: American Psychological Association.

Commentary on 'International frameworks for psychology education and training'

Rainer K. Silbereisen

When psychology as an academic science came into existence in the late nineteenth century, it was almost instantaneously international. For example, people from various countries across the world went to study under Wilhelm Wundt at his institute in Germany, so that when they returned home, a social network had been established. This process of collaboration enabled further internationalization through congresses held in different countries that brought together the elite of the discipline. A short time later, however, especially with the emergence of applied psychology, it became clear that psychology is embedded in cultural traditions and needs related to economy and welfare; a view that promoted an emphasis on the national context. A distinction in the traditions between basic and applied psychology can still be seen today in publication patterns – more international, in English, in basic science vs. more national, in the heritage language, among applied psychologists. Note, however, that some international psychology organizations, such as the International Association for Applied Psychology, were founded in the early 1900s, indicating that the wish to communicate across borders existed in all branches of classical psychology.

Today we are confronted with a new push for internationalization through globalization, while interestingly also being encouraged towards regionalization. The globalized world is characterized by increased competitiveness and this according to Lunt (Chapter 2) led to the need to evaluate Bachelor students' performance, to make degrees of higher education more transparent, to harmonize them across countries, and to protect the consumers of psychological services by offering clear benchmarks. For psychology, this means to guarantee the quality of education and training, and in exchange to receive recognition and gain legal regulation for the discipline.

An internationally approved framework for PET would help to increase the mobility of scientists and professionals, provided the framework is not only an agreement among psychology organizations but also part of official, multinational government regulations. In this regard, Lunt discusses the process that led to the EuroPsy, a standard or benchmark for independent practice in psychology. It defines the role of a psychologist and provides a common framework for education and training covering six years, including supervised practice. It distinguishes between a first phase (Bachelor), which is devoted to a common basic education and the introduction to major theories and techniques in psychology, and a second phase that leads either to Ph.D. training in preparation for a research career, or to professional training in one of the major fields of psychology (clinical and health, educational, work and organizational psychology).

The major drivers behind this development were political attempts at the level of the European Union to increase mobility among professions across Europe. To date, the EuroPsy has been taken up by many European psychology organizations, but it is yet to be recognized as a government-approved instrument of mutual recognition within the EU. It is nevertheless a great achievement. Work over ten years among experts from various countries (also funded by European research monies) was required to identify commonalities and differences in PET, and in all aspects of quality control and recognition management. The means to find a consensus was the identification of competences (dynamic combinations of knowledge, skills, understanding, and abilities gained through an academic program) that someone attending a psychology program for independent practice should have developed over the full course of study, including supervised practice.

While this is indeed a wonderful accomplishment, it also shows that even within a rather homogenous region such as Europe, there are remarkable differences in the length and quality of PET and in many other aspects of the discipline. Achieving a consensus requires an impartial and systematic search for differences and commonalities (a PET scan, so to speak, as Bullock called it in Chapter 3), and the group in charge of such a program needs to be as inclusive as possible concerning all branches of psychology in the region.

This brings me to the most intriguing issue of how an international framework for psychology education and training can be achieved. It would seem that the psychology in countries that have been dominating the field in terms of research productivity and scientific publication (mainly those of North America and Europe) is as influenced and shaped by its cultural background as any other 'indigenous' psychology around the globe. This was not well recognized by the field for a long time, and it needed a long debate initiated by cultural psychologists to increase awareness. Nevertheless, as Bullock explains, we certainly have a shared core understanding of the discipline (the individual as unit of analysis, the methodological skepticism of confronting theories with data, and the principle of openness to innovative perspectives) around the globe. Further, we may have many more universals in the biologically-based mechanisms leading to behavior, although even here context and culture play a role. Nevertheless, there are concepts of and approaches to psychology unique to particular regions of the world, which often have a long history because they may represent adaptation to the specific cultural and national context, and they deserve our attention.

The important point is that all such traditions possibly belong to psychology, presuming that they share the core features of the discipline as described. So, when developing a regional framework for PET in Europe required a decade without the ultimate aim of achieving regulation of the profession by appropriate legislation on the European level being achieved, we need to ensure the inclusion of the many viewpoints about psychology, fresh research on our own role as psychologists in all corners of the world, and patience for consultation with all stakeholders (academic institutions, professional organizations, employers, national and regional governmental bodies) involved. We should not rush things and come up with benchmarks for PET competences and policies prematurely, but rather allow things to emerge in their own time. That is not to say, however, that developing benchmarks should not be done with activity and passion. In addition, it would be a mistake to think that all differences in concepts of psychology and its education and training need to be leveled; many are worthwhile to maintain. It is also an open question as to whether ultimately there should be the same framework for PET concerning psychology as a science or a profession, or how large the overlap between the two may be; this balance may also differ as a function of the cultural and national context. The assumption of a coherent discipline of psychology is not in contradiction to regional specificities, as long as there is no stereotypical valuation of the one approach over the other in terms of scientific dignity and professional viability.

The discipline of psychology itself is in dynamic flux, being particularly influenced by two poles that in my view have come together in recent cutting-edge research. At one extreme, social science research on the massive economic, social and ecological transitions and transformations of the last two decades has demonstrated that humans respond with resistance and adaptation during their own lifetime. At the other extreme, biological research has demonstrated that such environmental pressures leave lasting and rather stable marks on the basic genomic and physiological processes that, in turn, influence the development of motivation and cognition. In other words, research on social change and research on gene–environment interplay have given new insights into the basis of psychological processes and thus the understanding of the discipline, and have brought new perspectives that need to be reflected in psychology education and training.

Chapters 2 and 3 by Lunt and Bullock are strong in illuminating why we need frameworks for PET, on suggesting how we can establish them, and in detailing what the likely result may be – a coherent discipline of human behavior-in-context, with scholars and professionals educated and trained to be flexible and sensitive to the range of scientific approaches found around the globe, and well prepared to realize the necessary quality of psychological services, based on legal regulation of the profession and on evidence provided by basic, applied, and translational science.

Part IV

Implications of emerging areas for psychology education and training

4 Implications of emerging areas for psychology education and training

The case of geropsychology

Rocío Fernández-Ballesteros

Introduction

Rapid population growth among older adults around the world means there is an increased need for psychologists to apply their scientific knowledge about ageing, age, and the aged (Birren, 1996a), with the principal objective of increasing quality of life and well-being throughout the life cycle.

When psychology first emerged as a scientific discipline, in the late nineteenth century, in Western societies (or developed countries), life expectancy was around 40 years, fertility rate was close to 5 children per women, the population of over-65s was about 5 percent, and the percentage of children under 15 was 30 percent. Today, however, we live in an ageing world in which life expectancy is closer to 80 years, the over-65's account for almost 20 percent, fertility rate is close to 1.5 children per woman, and the percentage of under 15s is lower than 20 percent. Most importantly, this specific demographic pattern is being globalized: the proportion of persons aged 60 years and older around the world is expected to double between 2000 and 2050 from 10 to 21 percent, whereas the proportion of children is projected to drop by a third, from 30 to 21 percent (United Nations, 2002).

In the early days, age-related applied psychology focused on child and adolescent development and context of application: school psychology. Although Galton studied individual differences (including age) in sensory, perceptual and motor processes, at that time most research on the study of basic psychological functions and structures was based on young adults' functioning. Perhaps the first author to highlight the importance of ageing for psychology was the developmental psychologist G.S. Hall (1922) in his book *Senescence. The second half of life*:

> As a psychologist I am convinced that the psychic states of old people have great significance. Senescence, like adolescence, has its own feeling, thought, and will, as well as its own psychology, and the regime is important, as well that of the body. Individual differences here are probably greater than in youth.
>
> (1922, p. 100)

Geropsychology (gerontopsychology or geropsy) is a relatively new area in the field of psychology, having emerged at the interface of psychology and gerontology. Gerontology is defined as the science devoted to the study of ageing and elderly people. According to Webster's dictionary, it is the comprehensive study of aging and the problems of the aged, while the Medical Webster's defines it as 'the scientific study of the biological, psychological, and sociological phenomena associated with old age and ageing'(Webster New World, 2008).

As pointed out by Birren and Schroots (2006), geropsychology is a basic subdiscipline of psychology devoted to the scientific study of ageing, age and the aged. According to Qualls *et al.* (2005) geropsychology can be considered a mature field of study whose aim is to improve the wellbeing and quality of life of older adults throughout the lifespan, and should therefore be taught as a specialized field of psychology.

Obviously, the psychology of ageing is one of its basic corpuses of knowledge, but the study of ageing, age and the aged, and the application of such study cannot be reduced to the psychology of ageing or the psychology of the lifespan; it must embrace many other types of knowledge, skills and competences that may derive from other branches of psychology, including social and environmental psychology, psychopathology, neuropsychology, methodology and assessment or clinical and health, or work and educational psychology. The first part of Figure 4.1 shows how psychology constitutes an important part of gerontology as a multidisciplinary science, while the second part illustrates how geropsychology is supported by the psychology of ageing as its main pillar, but also embraces other psychological areas from a diversity of subdisciplines.

Geropsychology as an education and training discipline

It is not easy to identify the starting point of geropsychology as a potential subject field for psychologists. For Hinrichsen and Zweig (2005), it was Robert

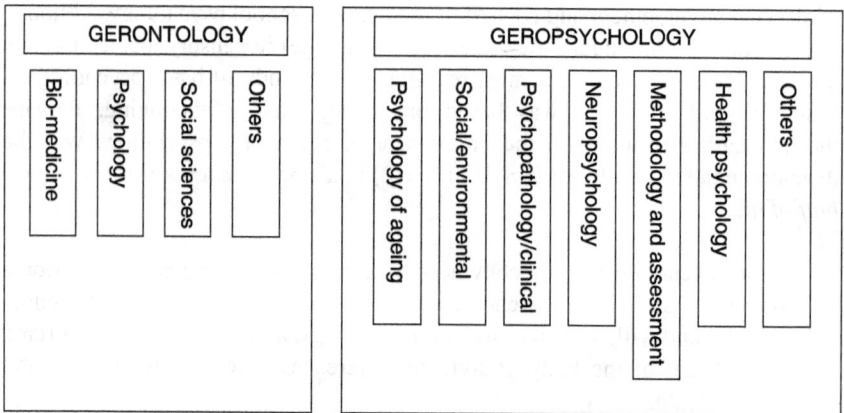

Figure 4.1 Multidisciplinarity of gerontology and psychological disciplines involved in geropsychology.

Kastenbaum who introduced geropsychology as a professional field around 1950, when he encouraged psychologists to work in this area because 'working with older adults is professionally challenging, intellectually fascinating, and personally fulfilling'(p. 19).

With regard to geropsychology as a field of education and training, it was at the first conference on Training Psychologists for Work in Aging, organized in 1981 by the American Psychological Association (APA), that the importance of geropsychology was established, with the main goal of defining its core knowledge, outlining a model for curricula at undergraduate and graduate levels, and highlighting the importance of specialty tracks at Masters or PhD level and in continuing education. Moreover, a national network of Psychologists in Long-Term Care (PLTC) was set up in 1983, one of whose functions was to develop, with input from colleagues and consumers, standards for psychological practice in long-term care facilities. These standards address provider characteristics, methods of referral, assessment practices, treatment, and ethical issues (see Parr and Gallagher-Thompson, 1998).

Without doubt, from that point on, the APA can be considered the leading institution working on matters of education and training in geropsychology. In 1998, the Commission for the Recognition of Specialities and Proficiencies in Professional Psychology recognized geropsychology as an area of practice. Finally, in 2010, professional geropsychology was recognized as a specialty by the APA.

Five primary issues emerged for geropsychology, as described by Knight *et al.* (1995), and which have guided the discipline to date:

1   the improvement and expansion of the psychology of ageing and training in that area;
2   the inclusion of complex and multiple problematic issues of ageing;
3   training that addresses both normal and abnormal ageing;
4   the importance of taking into account short-term and long-term care; and finally,
5   the importance of the provision of additional skills in geropsychology for professionals working in this field.

Since these important events for the constitution of geropsychology as a field of education and training, special emphasis has increasingly been placed on the clinical aspects of ageing, age and the aged, though without taking into account non-clinical but important issues.

Demands of geropsychology

A speciality program does not emerge simply because the science/s in question reach a certain level of maturity (in our case, both gerontology and psychology), or because of social demands (in our case, an ageing population). As Qualls *et al.* (2005) point out, before setting up a new field of education and training, it is important to consider client demands, which in this case have two aspects: demands for geropsychologists' services and psychologists' demands for education and training.

It is difficult to calculate the need for gerontological services in a given country without recourse to reliable records. Gatz and Smyer (2001) propose an estimation that involves multiplying the number of older adults by the percentage that needs mental health services (around 20–28 percent), but this proposal is based on the assumption that 'mental health problems' constitute the only source of needs for psychological services. There are, however, other needs in many other fields, as pointed out in the survey conducted by Pinquart *et al.* (2007; see also Fernández-Ballesteros *et al.*, 2007) among European psychologists, as described below. For example, lifelong learning is a right throughout the life cycle and that includes older adults; preparation for retirement, working prolongation or non-mandatory retirement could be considered as important needs emerging in the work setting; promoting healthy and active ageing is one of the extended policies at international, regional, national and local levels; social participation and intergenerational solidarity are important social psychology issues; several person–environment fit theories emerge from psychology of ageing within environmental psychology; highlighting an important source of needs emerging from home, community, residential and senior citizen center contexts is an emerging issue in the field of educational psychology. All such aspects, and others besides, are relevant to education and training in geropsychology. Table 4.1 shows some examples of the needs of different target populations addressed by psychologists.

In sum, the demands (or needs) of the target population cannot be reduced to mental health prevalence; rather, a broader perspective must be taken, as stressed by Witkin (1984), who suggested taking the followings types into account: normative needs (national and international recommendations), perceived needs (from survey data on the relevant populations), expressed needs (demographic data, utilization of existing services) and relative needs (services dispensed to similar populations). For example, the Madrid International Plan of Action on Aging (United Nations, 2002), approved by 162 countries, declared, 'the need for training of care providers and health professionals with the main objective of the provision of improved information and training for health professionals and para- professionals on the needs of older persons'(p. 35).

Another source of information concerning psychologists' needs for education and training comes from potential providers of services for older adults. Qualls et al. (2002) conducted a representative survey of 1,227 practitioner members of the APA who provided information about patterns of practice with older adults, sources of training in geropsychology, perceived needs for continuing education and type of training format. Although only 3 percent reported providing services exclusively to older patients, the majority of respondents (69 percent) provide some type of psychological services to older adults (most notably psychotherapy and assessment). Two kinds of training must be increased: formal training (e.g., internships, postgraduate and postdoctoral training) and continuing education for experienced practitioners on the following topics: depression, adjusting to

Table 4.1 Examples of needs of an ageing society addressed by psychologists

Target	Examples of needs in relation to ageing, age, and the aged
General population	Educate lay public about the process of ageing, teach how to age well.
	Educate the lay public about common mental disorders in later life.
Ageing population	Promote active and healthy ageing.
	Provide education in health promotion and illness prevention.
	Promote self-care strategies.
	Prevent the most prevalent mental and physical illnesses.
Caregiver population	Promote strategies for coping with stress.
	Provide training in enhancement of activities of daily living.
Other professions involved (medical doctors, nurses, policy-makers, etc.)	Encourage professional organizations to offer certification in disciplines related to ageing to promote increased knowledge of specialists within their field (Halpain *et al.*, 1999).
Psychologists' organizations	Expand the core curriculum on ageing at undergraduate level.
	Diversify training and education levels (Masters, PhD and continuing education).
	Increase incentives for individuals who seek specialty training in geropsychology at all levels.
	Introduce geropsychological issues in other specialties (at different levels), such as clinical, work, education or environmental psychology programs.
	Promote, among policy-makers, the necessity to proceed to assess older population needs within their settings.
	Promote, among policy-makers, funding for geropsychology research, education and training.
	Improve information technology for translating results from research centers into practice.

medical illnesses, dementia, bereavement and grief, psychotherapy, caregiver stress, anxiety, positive psychological growth, psychological assessment, marital/ family difficulties, health promotion/maintenance, neuropsychology, substance abuse, psychoeducational intervention, personality disorders, staff training/ supervision and chronic mental health. Finally, the teaching and learning format would be distance learning.

Also in the USA, Gordon (1997) investigated factors influencing a trainee's pursuit of geropsychology training, in an effort to identify ways of attracting students to this relatively new field of applied psychology emerging as a result of social linked to worldwide increases in the older adult population (United Nations, 2002). Gordon's study examined the influence of a trainee's personal experiences, previous clinical training, coursework on ageing, knowledge about ageing and mental health, attitudes toward older adults, and interest in field on their pursuit of geropsychology training at the internship level. This was done through an Internet survey of 409 psychology trainees who were either (a) completing internship in the 2005–2006 training year (*interns*; *n* = 238) or (b) registered to begin internship in 2006–2007 (*prospective interns; n* = 171). No significant differences were found between any of the variables considered, with the exception of geropsychology education – that is, previous training in the area of ageing had the greatest influence on interest in being trained in geropsychology and in working with older adults in the future. Greater clinical training, greater knowledge of ageing and mental health, and greater interest in geropsychology were predictive of completing more ageing-related training at the internship level. The results also indicated that training experiences with older adults through both academic coursework and clinical training enhanced interest, knowledge, and attitudes. It is important to stress that offering more educational opportunities at undergraduate level is a significant way of increasing the numbers of those taking geropsychology training specialization courses at postgraduate level.

In Australia, Koder and Helmes (2008) carried out an extensive survey of practicing psychologists, finding that average ratings of confidence in working with older adults were very low, and only 6 percent of psychologists surveyed specialized in working with older adults. Indeed, 40 percent of psychologists reported no contact at all with older adults.

Recently, Pachana (2012) reported some international data indicating, among other things, that the situation for psychologists interested in working with older people in Brazil would appear to be similar to the scenario described in Australia (see later in this chapter). Thus, the Brazilian Society of Geriatrics and Gerontology reported that the number of psychologists certified in gerontology is 120. As reported by Knebel (2011), Brazil's population is a young one, with just 9 percent (21 million people) over 60. Even so, the projected figure for the year 2050 is 30 percent, with a life expectancy of 81.

Regarding Japan, Pachana (2012) reported that specialized training opportunities in geropsychology are rare. A survey conducted in 2007 revealed that only 50 clinical psychologists were working with older adults in care facilities for the elderly, representing just 0.5 percent of all clinical psychologists in that country.

In sum, the need for education and training in geropsychology is derived from an ageing world and demographic projections, while normative needs promoted by international organizations should also be taken into account. Nevertheless, we must admit that surveys among psychologists do not indicate a strong interest in this specialization.

Geropsychology education and training programs

Level of education and training

The extent of training in geropsychology depends upon the level at which it is implemented. Authors in this area have referred to the following levels: psychology graduate programs; postgraduate studies (Masters or PhD) at specific (geropsychology) and non-specific levels (clinical psychology, generalist, neuropsychology) (see DeVries, 2005); practicum (and/or internship); and, finally, postdoctoral and continuing education.

Although we have tried to take a global overview, the information available comes mostly from North America (USA and Canada), Australia (APPIC, 1993) and Europe, though there was also a non-systematic survey carried out in Latin American countries (Cohen and Cooley, 1983; Fernández-Ballesteros, 2007; Fernández-Ballesteros *et al.*, 2007; Gallagher-Thompson and Thompson, 1995; Hinrichsen and Zweig, 2005; Hinrichsen *et al.*, 2000; Kneebone, 1996; Knight *et al.*, 2009; Pachana *et al.*, 2010; Pinquart *et al.*, 2007; Pinquart, 2007; Siegler *et al.*, 1979).

Comparisons between the USA, Canada and Australia

Pachana *et al.* (2010) carried out a survey of geropsychology education and training in university-based clinical and counseling psychology training programs in 2007 in Australia, Canada, and the USA. As it is shown in Table 4.2, both clinical/counseling programs and internship/practicum placements were surveyed with regard to didactic content, staffing, and training opportunities.

Table 4.2 Geropsychology graduate programs in the USA, Australia, and Canada: geropsychology faculty and practium opportunities (modified from Pachana *et al.*, 2010)

	Australia *n = 25%*	*Canada* *n = 22%*	*USA* *n = 46%*
Contents			
Psychopathology	88.0	81.0	63.0
Assessment and diagnosis	92.0	72.7	58.7
Psychotherapy (individual, family, couples, group)	72.0	57.1	52.2
Ethics	58.3	68.2	45.7
Research methodology	32.0	25.0	28.3
Lifespan development	56.0	50.0	63.0
Other	8.3	9.1	4.3
Faculties involved	*Mean (SD)*	*Mean (SD)*	*Mean (SD)*
Total clinical/counseling faculty	7.56 (4.4)	9.75 (5.05)	10.06 (6,7)
Faculty with clinical geropsychology as primary research interest	0.40 (0.60)	0.64 (0.79)	0.41 (0.75)
Faculty with clinical geropsychology as secondary research interest	0.88 (1.0)	0.59 (0.73)	0.54 (0.94)
Faculty who provide research supervision to students on an age-related topic	1.5 (1.5)	1.59 (1.92)	1.70 (1.90)
Faculty who provide clinical supervision to students working with older adults	1.16 (1.7)	1.00 (1.23)	1.60 (2.00)

(Continued)

Table 4.2 (Continued)

	Australia n = 25%	Canada n = 22%	USA n = 46%
Faculty who work clinically with older adults	0.88 (1.2)	1.27 (1.35)	1.27 (1.80)
Faculty with specialized clinical geropsychology training	0.36 (0.6)	0.63 (0.73)	0.54 (0.80)
Number of practicum sites that provide a training experience working primarily with older adults	2.5 (2.0)	1.10 (1.14)	1.2 (1.3)
Number of practicum sites that provide some exposure to working with older adults	5.39 (6.2)	3.51 (1.96)	3.7 (2.9)
Number of practicum supervisors who have speciality training with older adults	1.89 (1.7)	2.60 (1.95)	1.9 (2.3)
Practicum/internship			
Number of psychologists affiliated with internship (USA) or externship (Australia)	29.1 (30.2)	19.21 (14.16)	14.5 (12)
Number of psychologists who work clinically with older adults	5.4 (6.0)	6.0 (6.49)	4.8 (5.6)
Number of psychologists who have specialized training in working with older adults	1.0 (1.2)	1.8 (1.88)	1.3 (1.8)

Survey response rates ranged from 15 percent in the USA ($n = 46$) to 70 percent in Australia ($n = 25$) to 91.5 percent in Canada ($n = 22$). Data from the USA and Australia revealed the existence of specialization courses in geropsychology within graduate clinical psychology training programmes. More assessment and psychopathology courses in these three countries were cited as having ageing content than psychotherapy courses. Many non-specialist programs offered course work in geropsychology, and many had staff specialized in working clinically with an older population. Interest in expanding ageing courses and placements was cited at several sites where there was geropsychology training. Recruiting staff and finding appropriate placement opportunities with older adult populations were cited as barriers to expanding geropsychology provisions.

In the light of their results, they concluded with a discussion about innovative means of engaging students with ageing content/populations, and suggestions for overcoming staffing and placement shortcomings, referring to the Pikes Peak model as a potential tool for improving and homogenizing training in geropsychology in the three countries in question, namely the USA, Australia and Canada.

European data from the European Federation of Psychologists' Associations

Data from Europe come from the European Federation of Psychologists' Associations (EFPA) who, in 2003, set up a Task Force (TF) in geropsychology (see also Fernández-Ballesteros and Pinquart, 2011; Fernández-Ballesteros *et al.*, 2007; Pinquart *et al.*, 2007; Pinquart, 2007). The TF identified 5 key persons in each of 30 European countries and surveyed them concerning research, teaching and practice on ageing. Regarding teaching, they were asked to provide an overview of whether – and if so which – ageing-related topics were part of regular undergraduate and graduate student training in the field of psychology, and whether there were specialist courses or even postgraduate programs for those wanting to specialize in work with older adults.

To assist in completing the questionnaire, the key persons received a list of eight topics potentially involved in teaching geropsychology on undergraduate or graduate courses, based on published recommendations about the knowledge and skills required by psychologists working with older adults (Molinari *et al.*, 2003).

The topic most frequently found in training courses was lifespan development and psychological development in old age, which was taught at all institutions in 6 of the 30 countries, and was totally absent from the training of psychologists in only one country. Psychopathology in old age (covering issues such as depression or dementia) was the second most important topic, followed by psychological assessment of older adults, psychotherapy and counseling with older clients, social services for older adults, life-long learning, and environmental issues. Psychological aspects of work and retirement were also mentioned in some countries and institutions. Nonetheless, three or more of these topics were missing from teaching programs in half of the countries surveyed.

The highest levels of teaching in geropsychology were reported in Sweden, Norway and Austria, and the lowest levels in Belarus, Serbia-Montenegro, Turkey, Finland, Portugal and Israel. In this latter group of countries, ageing-related topics only played a role in courses on developmental psychology at a few institutions or departments, or as part of courses on psychopathology or social services. Postgraduate programs on geropsychology or gerontology (with the inclusion of psychological topics) were reported to be available in 47 percent of the countries assessed (Austria, Bulgaria, Czech Republic, Denmark, France, Germany, Greece, Israel, the Netherlands, Norway, Spain, Switzerland, Sweden and the United Kingdom); two-thirds of the programs were mainly academic, one-third practical. The availability of postgraduate programs in Europe was probably somewhat overestimated.

About 30 percent of the key persons reported that geropsychology was a regular topic at postgraduate level in clinical psychology or psychotherapy in their country: nevertheless, these programs are mainly professional (77 percent). The length of time (number of hours) of postgraduate training in geropsychology varied considerably between countries, ranging from about 15 (Austria, Germany, Spain) to 500 (Luxembourg; Mean = 127).

The most prominent geropsychology topics for clinical psychologists were psychological assessment of older adults (63 percent), psychotherapy with older clients (63 percent), and psychological disorders in old age (50 percent). Prevention of mental health problems of older adults (12.5 percent), and evaluation of interventions with older adults (12.5 percent) did not play a prominent role in these programs.

Geropsychological topics were included in a few nonclinical postgraduate programs, such as in the fields of neuropsychology (10 percent), cognitive psychology (7 percent), developmental psychology (3 percent) and community psychology (3 percent), with 15 to 60 hours of training in geropsychology topics. These programs provided information about environment–behavior transactions of older adults, caregiver interventions, prevalence of cognitive problems in old age, and psychological research with older adults. We should also point out that at the European level there is a European Masters Programme in Gerontology (EuMaG), in which geropsychology is one of five core modules.

With regard to teaching, the number of full professors in the field of geropsychology is quite low in Europe when compared to US standards. On average, only 2.3 full professors were reported per country (the highest number being in France, $n = 20$), and a total of 69 people were teaching geropsychology in the 30 countries.

Concerning geropsychology practice, according to the key persons surveyed, geropsychology was most often applied in the clinical field (70 percent of the countries studied). About 60 percent of the key persons reported the social field as one of the most significant application contexts. Geropsychology applied in the prevention of health problems and in health promotion was reported by 40 percent of the respondents, and in adult education by 33 percent. However, only 17 percent of the key persons reported geropsychology being widely applied in the field of work and retirement.

Finally, the key persons were asked about future fields of application in geropsychology. Here, promotion of healthy ageing and illness prevention were most often reported (33 percent), followed by work/retirement (27 percent), life-long learning/adult education (20 percent), social issues (20 percent), psycho-therapy (7 percent), liaison with primary somatic units (7 percent), caregiving (7 percent), traffic psychology (3 percent), successful ageing (3 percent), and health economics (3 percent). (Figures 4.2 and 4.3 present data on geropsychology taken from research, teaching, and practice in 30 European countries.)

In sum, the situation in Europe is highly heterogeneous from all perspectives: level of education and training, number of teaching courses, faculties offering training courses, research carried out, etc.

A glance at Latin America

Finally, we asked 205 Latin American professionals working in the field of gerontology in 11 countries of South and Central America, whether, in their respective countries, there were training programs on geropsychology. There are some programs in geropsychology at different training levels in the following countries: Chile,[1] Argentina,[2] Uruguay,[3] and Colombia.[4] Mexico and Cuba have training in psychogeriatrics linked to the schools of medicine: finally, other countries have specialization in gerontology and within them geropsychology as a subdiscipline. It is important to mention that those Southern America countries (such as Chile, Argentina and Uruguay) with highest population rates and with

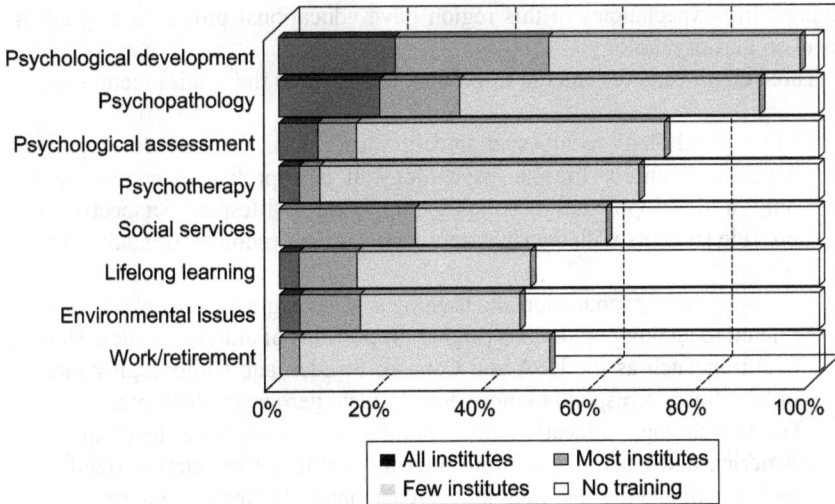

Figure 4.2 Main contents in teaching European geropsychology.

Source: From Pinquart (2007): reproduced with permission from *GeroPsychology*, ISBN 978-0-88937-340-2, p. 23 © 2007 Hogrefe & Huber Publishers, www.hogrefe.com.

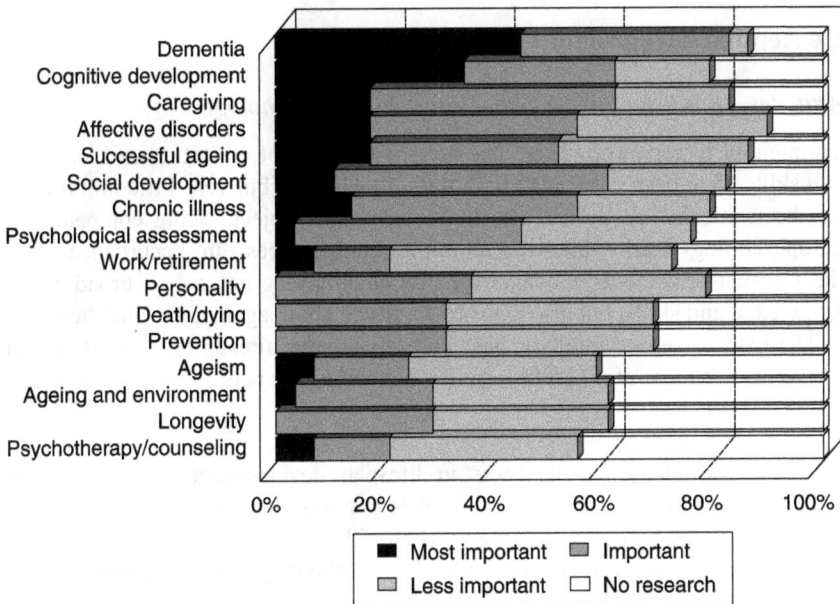

Figure 4.3 Topics of research in European geropsychology.

Source: Pinquart, 2007. Reproduced with permission from *GeroPsychology* ISBN 978-0-88937-340–2, p. 17 4 © 2007 Hogrefe & Huber Publishers, www.hogrefe.com.

highest life expectancies in this region have educational programs at graduate level on geropsychology.

Three characteristics emerge from the findings of all the studies mentioned:

1   Most psychology courses at undergraduate level include developmental psychology and/or lifespan psychology. It is important to emphasize that only a developmental psychology applying a lifespan perspective will provide students with the right approach to the psychology of adulthood and old age.
2   Geropsychology education and training at the postgraduate level appear to be related to ageing populations (higher proportions of elderly people). Thus, in countries such as the USA and Canada, Sweden and Chile, higher rates of older adults correspond to more postgraduate geropsychology programs.
3   Geropsychology education and training at postgraduate level in North America and Australia have a much more clinical orientation (tending to include clinical geropsychology content) than in European countries.

In our opinion, it must be said: to reduce geropsychology to clinical geropsychology is to perpetuate the stereotype that ageing and old age concerns only psychopathology and illness. Background in geropsychology must take into account a broad picture of ageing.

Conceptual background

Attitudes, knowledge, skills: competences in geropsychology

Throughout history, knowledge has been at the core of education and learning, and skills have been associated with training abilities, but very little importance has been attached to attitudes to the educational subject. Being competent in geropsychology tasks involves multiple competences, in accordance with the scientist-practitioner model, which requires having not only a broad set of knowledge and skills, but also a positive attitude about ageing, age and the aged.

The field of geropsychology, based on the surveys already mentioned and on the work of Knight *et al.* (2009), can be defined in terms of the following major aspects:

1   Geropsychology has its roots in lifespan developmental psychology in adulthood and old age. Therefore, it is important to understand 'normal' or usual ageing before attempting to work with older adults.
2   Geropsychology requires positive attitudes about ageing and knowledge and skills relevant to later life.
3   Geropsychology is also associated with psychopathological conditions, with a very common presence of chronic medical illnesses, so that it is important to understand health in later life and its impact on both medical and psychological conditions.

4   Geropsychology cannot be reduced only to clinical conditions. In fact, services and programs for older adults have emerged from other subdisciplines of scientific psychology, such as work psychology, educational psychology and health psychology (see Figure 4.1).
5   The person–environment relationship is particularly important in the assessment of and intervention with older adults.
6   Given that geropsychologists' competences should be compatible with a scientist-practitioner model, assessment instruments and methodological design and procedures must be appropriately taught and updated.

Based on this conceptual approach, a set of attitudes, knowledge and skills or competences has been proposed, which we shall describe here. The most extensive list of attitudes, knowledge and skills or competences in relation to geropsychology training was set down in the Pikes Peak model as described in Knight *et al.* (2009). The Council of Professional Geropsychology Training Programs (CoPGTP) is an international organization of graduate, internship, postdoctoral, and postgraduate programs that provide geropsychology training consistent with the Pikes Peak Model for Training in Professional Geropsychology, and also welcomes international members. Since it is international in scope, let us look further at this model, which is the most complete one for education and practice in geropsychology.

The model includes a total of 50 items reflecting 9 competences related to the following attitudes, types of knowledge, and types of skills:

- *Four attitudes*: for example, psychologists are encouraged to work with older adults within their scope of competence, to recognize that their attitudes and beliefs may be relevant for their work, to expand their awareness of the diversity of the process of ageing and to continuing education;
- *Four types of knowledge*:
    (a) General knowledge about adult development, ageing and the older adult population (for example: theoretical models and research methodologies for understanding the process of ageing; demographics of ageing; normal and 'usual' ageing; biology, psychology and social dynamic of ageing; awareness of the diversity in the ageing process.
    (b) Foundation of clinical practice with older adults (e.g. the neuroscience of ageing, cognition, and their implications for clinical interventions with older adults; the salience of functional changes in later adulthood; awareness of the concept of person–environment interaction; psychopathology in middle and later adulthood; knowledge of common medical illnesses in late life).
    (c) Foundations of the assessment of older adults (for example: theory and research informing about psychological assessment of older adults; limits of using assessment instruments created for younger persons with older adults without adequate standardization; contextual issues in the assessment of older adults).

(d) Foundations of intervention, consultation and other service provision (for example: theory, research, and practice related to various methods of intervention with older adults, including their efficacy and effectiveness; health, illness, and pharmacology as related to assessment and treatment of late-life mental health problems; knowledge of ageing services in the local community (e.g., day care, transportation, residential); prevention and health promotion services; awareness of the broad array of potential clients, models and methods of interdisciplinary collaboration; knowledge of ethical and legal standards).

• *Five types of skills or competences*:

(a) The functioning of professional geropsychology (for example: understanding and applying ethical and legal standards, with particular attention to ageing-specific issues; understanding cultural and individual diversity as relevant to assessment, intervention and consultation; addressing complex biopsychosocial issues; practicing self-reflection and self-assessment; relating effectively and empathically with older adult clients, their families and other stakeholders; applying scientific knowledge to geropsychology practice and policy advocacy; practicing appropriate documentation/billing/reimbursement procedures, and defending clients' needs).

(b) Assessment (for example: conducting clinical assessment leading to DSM diagnoses and other clinically relevant problems; formulation of treatment plans, using psychometrically sound screening instruments; referring to neuropsychological, neurological, psychiatric, medical or other evaluations as indicated; using cognitive assessments and/or neuro-psychological reports to clarify clinical issues and inform treatment planning; evaluating decision-making and functional capacities; assessing risk; adapting instruments and tailoring assessments to accommodate older adults' specific characteristics and contexts, and communicating assessment results to various stakeholders with relevant, practical, and clearly understandable recommendations).

(c) Intervention skills (for example: applying individual, group, and family interventions to older adults using appropriate modifications; using available evidence-based treatments for older adults; developing psychotherapeutic interventions; being proficient in using commonly employed late-life knowledge; and demonstrating an ability to intervene in settings involving older adults and their family members).

(d) Consultation and training skills (for example: consulting families, professionals, programs, health-care facilities, legal systems, and other agencies/organizations that serve older adults; providing training in geropsychological issues; participating in inter-professional teams that serve older adults; communicating psychological conceptualizations to medical and other professionals in a concise and useful manner;

implementing strategies for systems analysis and change in organizations and facilities that serve older adults; designing and participating in different models of ageing services delivery; collaborating and coordinating with other agencies and professionals that serve older adults, and recognizing and negotiating multiple roles in older adult consultation settings).

(e) Skills for service delivery in different settings (for example: outpatient mental health services; outpatient primary care/medical settings; in-patient medical services; inpatient psychiatric services; long-term care settings; rehabilitation settings; hospices; community-based programs; forensic settings; home-delivered psychological services; and research settings).

- Finally, the reader may wish to refer to the Guidelines for psychological practice with older adults published by the APA (2004).

Recently, delegates at a conference acknowledged that skills in supervision/ teaching, research/evaluation, and management/administration are also crucial for geropsychology practice in many settings, as well as for the further development of professional geropsychology as a scientific field.

Assessing level of expertise and assessment tools

The CoPGTP sets out a series of different education and training levels: undergraduate, postdoctoral fellowship, internship and postgraduate. At the same time, Karel *et al.*, (2012) describe a new tool with which to evaluate the development of geropsychology competences in trainees.

The CoPGTP Geropsychology Competency Evaluation Task Force also developed a tool for appropriate evaluation by supervisors and for self-evaluation by trainees and professionals. First of all, the 50 Pikes Peak types of knowledge and skills were operationalized through detailed behavioral items. As the authors claim, 'our goal, therefore, was to develop a tool with detailed behavioral anchors of reach competency to help trainees and psychologists review their competences at varying levels of training' (Karel *et al.* 2011, p. 112).

The anchor range has five levels:

1 *Novice*, possesses entry-level skills, needs intensive supervision;
2 *Intermediate*, has background of some exposure and experience, ongoing supervision is needed;
3 *Advanced*, has solid experience, handles typical situations well, requires supervision for unusual or complex situations;
4 *Proficient*, autonomously functioning, knows limits of ability, seeks supervision or consultation as needed; and
5 *Expert*, serves as resource consultant to others, is recognized as having expertise (see www.copgtp.org).

Table 4.3 Examples of Pikes Peak geropsychology knowledge and skills and level of expertise assessment tool (version 1.2; Karel *et al.*, 2011) *1. Models of ageing*

	N	I	A	P	E
a. Development as a lifelong process encompassing early to late life, and encompassing both gains and losses.					
b. Different theories of late-life development and adaptation.					
c. Biopsychosocial perspective for understanding an individual's physical and psychological development within the sociocultural context.					
d. Concept of, and variables associated with, positive or successful ageing.					
e. Relevant research on adult development and ageing, including methodological considerations in cross-sectional and longitudinal research.					

Note: Key: N = Novice, I = Intermediate, A = Advanced, P = Proficient, E = Expert.

Fulfilment of objectives and level of expertise can be assessed through an assessment tool. Table 4.3 shows examples of one of the topics present in *general knowledge*: Models of ageing.

Karel *et al.* (2012) carried out an online survey among geropsychologists and geropsychology trainees involved in geropsychology practice, with the aim of examining the utility and viability of the Pikes Peak geropsychology knowledge and skills assessment tool. A total of 109 individuals participated in this study: 75 doctoral-level psychologists and 34 trainees.

The mean scores for psychologists and trainees on the nine rating scales ranged from 3.48 to 3.99 (advanced to proficient range) for psychologists and 1.86 to 2.51 (novice to intermediate range) for trainees. Significant differences were found between the two groups. The overall competence score for psychologists was predicted by the extent of clinical training and proportion of practice devoted to older adults. As regards utility of the tool, this was generally positive, with 64.2 percent of the sample finding the tool very or extremely useful, and more than 50 percent stating that they were very or extremely likely to recommend that other colleagues/programs use the tool. Comments regarding the tool's utility included that it was 'excellent', 'comprehensive', and 'helpful to identify areas of weakness'.

Preliminary results of this study suggest that formal training – as compared to continuing education – is a critical contributor to self-perceived geropsychology competence. Research has concluded that the geropsychology field is expanding opportunities for continuing education; however, there remain few options for more formal training at postgraduate levels. The contribution of the Pikes Peak training model would seem to be as an innovative strategy for continuing education and training in geropsychology.

Conclusions

- Populations are ageing throughout the world, so that more and more countries have higher relative or absolute numbers of older adults. This has given rise to the need for a new specialization field for psychology and psychologists, geropsychology being an emerging field for education and training.
- Geropsycology is a subdiscipline of scientific psychology emerging from developmental psychology, psychology of ageing and psychology of the lifespan. However, since its main purpose is to contribute to the wellbeing and quality of life of the older population, there is a demand for other knowledge, skills and competences from other areas of psychology (general, social and environmental psychology, psychopathology, neuropsychology, methodology and assessment, clinical and health psychology, educational psychology, work psychology etc.).
- Geropsychology programs originally emerged from the field of clinical psychology and counseling, and in some countries, such as the USA and Canada, it would be better called 'clinical geropsychology'. Since gerontology is devoted to the study of age, ageing, and the aged (see Birren, 1996b), it cannot refer exclusively to clinical (pathological) ageing; in doing so it would be reinforcing the common stereotype about the equivalence between ageing and illness.
- European countries appear to have a broader conceptualization of geropsychology as a scientific subdiscipline of psychology, as a field of practice and as an area of education and training.
- Many institutions, such as the American Psychological Association, who are leaders in this field, have developed strategies for regulating education and training in geropsychology and developed an important corpus (knowledge and skills, principles for best practice, etc.) for developing education and training.
- In sum, geropsychology is an emerging field of specialization across the psychology discipline, and is mainly developed and taught in the contexts of postgraduate training (Masters and PhD levels) and continuing education in those countries with higher rates of population ageing.

Notes

1 Catholic University: www.paginasprodigy.com/psisofia/page3.html
2 Maimonides University: http://gerontologia.maimonides.edu/escuela-de-ciencias-del-envejecimiento
3 University La República: www.psico.edu.uy/ensenanza/postgrado/diplomatura-en-psicogerontolog%C3%AD
4 Quindio University: www.uniquindio.edu.co/uniquindio/presentacion_portafolio/archivos/index.htm.

References

American Psychological Association (2004). Guidelines for psychological practice with older adults. *American Psychologist*, 59, 236–60.

APPIC (1993). *APPIC Directory of Internship and Postdoctoral Programs in Professional Psychology: 1993–1994*. Washington, DC: Association of Psychology Postdoctoral and Internship Center.

Birren, J. E. (1961). A brief history of the psychology of aging, Part II, *The Gerontologist* 1(3): 127–34.

Birren, J. (Ed.) (1996). *The Encyclopedia of Gerontology: Ageing, age and the aged*. New York: Pergamon Press.

Birren, J. (1996). History of gerontology. In J. Birren (Ed.), *The Encyclopedia of Gerontology: Ageing, age and the aged*, pp. 655–64. New York: Pergamon Press.

Birren, J. E. and Schroots, J. J. F. (2001). The history of geropsychology. In J. E. Birren and K. W. Schaie (Eds.), *Handbook of the Psychology of Aging*, 5th edn, pp. 3–28. San Diego, CA: Academic Press.

Cohen, L. D. and Cooley, S. G. (1983). Psychology training: programs for direct services to the aging. *Professional Psychology: Research and Practice*, 14, 720–8.

DeVries, H. M. (2005). Clinical geropsychology training in generalist doctoral programs. *Gerontology and Geriatrics Education, 25*(4): 5–20.

Fernández-Ballesteros, R. (2007). *Report from the Task Force of Geropsychology*. Prague: European Federation of Psychologists Associations (EFPA).

Fernández-Ballesteros, R., Pinquart, M. and Torpdhal, P. (2007). Geropsychology: demographic, sociopolitical and historical background. In R. Fernandez-Ballesteros (Ed.), *Geropsychology: European perspective for an aging world*, pp 1–14. Gottingën, Germany: Hogrefeand Huber Publishing.

Fernández-Ballesteros, R. and Pinquart, M. (2011). Applied geropsychology. In P. Martin, F. Cheung, M. Kyrios, L. Littlefield, M. K. Knowles, J. M. Prieto and J. B. Overmier (Eds.), *Handbook of Applied Psychology*, pp. 413–39. London: Wiley-Blackwell-Andrew McAleer.

Gallagher-Thompson, D. and Thompson, L. W. (1995). Issues in geropsychology training at the intership level. In B. G. Knight, L. Teri, P. Wohlford and J. Santos (eds.), *Mental Health Services for Older Adults. Implications for training and practice in geropsychology*, pp. 129–42. Washington, DC: American Pychological Association.

Gatz, M. and Smyer, M. A. (2001). Mental health and aging at the outset of the twenty-first century. In J. Birren and and K. W. Schaie (Eds.), *Handbook of Psychology of Aging*, 5th edn, pp. 523–546. San Diego, CA: Academic Press

Gordon, B. H. (1997). *Geropsychology Training: A national survey of psychology trainees*. Ann Arbor, MI: ProQuest Information and Learning.

Hall, G. S. (1922). *Senescence. The second half of life*. New York: Appleton and Co.

Halpain, M. C., Harris, M. J., McClure, F. S. and Jeste, M. D. (1999). Training geriaric mental health: Needs and strategies. *Psychiatric Services*, 50(9). http://journals.psychiatryonline.org/article.aspx?articleid=83369

Hinrichsen G. A. and Zweig, R. (2005). Models of training in clinical geropsychology. *Gerontology and Geriatrics Education*, 25: 1–4.

Hinrichsen, G. A., Myers, D. S. and Stewart, D. (2000). Doctoral internship training opportunities in clinical geropsychology. *Professional Psychology: Research and Practice*, 31: 88–92.

Karel, M. J., Holley, C. K., Whitbourn, S. K., Segal, D. L., Tazeau, Y. N., Emery, E. E. Molinary,V., Yang, J. and Zweig, R.A. (2012). Preliminary validation of a tool to assess competencies for professional geropsychology practice. *Professional Psychology: Research and Practice*, 43(2): 110–17.

Knebel, P. (2011). Brazil: The young country is aging. *Infosur Hoy*, 23/02/11. http://infosurhoy.com/ cocoon/saii/xhtml/ en_GB/features/ saii/features/society/ 2011/02/23/ feature-02.

Kneebone, I. (1996). Teaching about ageing: the new challenge for Australian clinical psychology. *Australian Psychologist*, 31: 124–6.

Knight, B. G., Santos, J., Teri, L. and Lawton, M. P. (1995). Introduction: The development of training in clinical geropsychology. In B. G. Knight, L. Teri, P. Wohlford and J. Santos (Eds.), *Mental Health Services for Older Adults: Implications for training and practice in geropsychology*, pp. 1–8. New York: American Psychological Association.

Knight, B. G., Karel, M. J., Hinrichsen, G.A., Qualls, S. H. and Duffy, M. (2009) Pikes Peak model for training in professional geropsychology. *American Psychologist*, 64: 205–14.

Koder, D.A. and Helmes, E. (2008). Predictors of interest in working with older adults: a survey of postgraduate trainee psychologists. *Gerontology and Geriatrics Education*, 29: 158–71.

Molinari, V., Karel, M., Jones S., Zeiss, A., Cooley, S. G., Wray, L., Brown, E. and Gallagher-Thompson, D. (2003). Recommendations about the knowledge and skills required of psychologists working with older adults. *Professional Psychology: Research and Practice*, 34: 435–43.

Pachana, N., Emery, R., Konnert, C. A., Woodhead, E. and Edelstein, B. (2010). Geropsychology content in clinical programs: a comparison of Australian, Canadian and US data. *International Psychogeriatrics*, 22: 909–18.

Pachana, N. (2012) *Geropsychology Workforce Crisis: An International Perspective.* International Psychogeriatric Association. Available at www.ipa-online.org/ ipaonlinev4/ main/homepagearticles/gwc.html.

Pelham, A., Schafer, P., Abbott, D. and Estes, C. (2012). Professionalizing gerontology. *Gerontology and Geriatrics Education*, 33: 6–19.

Pinquart, M., Fernández-Ballesteros, R. and Torpdahl, P. (2007). Teaching, research, and application of geropsychology in Europe. *European Psychologist*, 12: 229–34.

Pinquart, M. (2007). Main trends in geropsychology in Europe. In R. Fernández-Ballesteros (Ed.), *Geropsychology. European perspectives for an aging world*, pp. 15–31. Gottingën: Hogrefe.

Qualls, S. H., Segal, D. L., Norman, S., Niederehe, G. and Gallagher-Thompson, D. (2002). Psychologists in practice with older adults: Current patterns, sources of training, and need for continuing education. *Professional Psychology: Research and Practice*, 33(5): 435–42.

Qualls, S. H., Segal, D. L., Benight, C. C. and Kenny, M. P. (2005). Geropsychology training in a specialist geropsychology doctoral program. *Gerontology and Geriatrics Education,* 25(4): 21–40.

Schroots, J. J. F. (1995). Psychological models of aging. *Canadian Journal of Gerontology*, 14: 64–7.

Schroots, J. J. F. (1996). Theories of aging: psychological. In J. Birren (Ed.), *The Encyclopedia of Gerontology: Ageing, age and the aged*, pp. 557–68. New York: Pergamon Press.

Siegler, I. C., Gentry, W. D. and Edwards, C. D. (1979). Training in geropsychology: a survey of graduate and internship training programs. *Professional Psychology*, 10: 390–5.

United Nations (2002). *Second World Assembly on Ageing. Political Declaration and Madrid International Plan of Action on Ageing.* New York: United Nations.

Webster New World Medical Dictionary (2008) 3rd Edition. N. J. Wiley

Witkin, B. R. (1984). *Assessing Needs in Educational and Social Programs.* San Francisco, CA: SAGE.

5 Implications of emerging areas for psychology education and training

The case of neuroscience, psychophysiology, and biological psychology

Wolfgang H. R. Miltner

Introduction

While theories on cognition, emotion, and action have been the main domain of philosophy for hundreds of years, most contemporary concepts and theories on these central human functions have emerged from psychological experimental and empirical research in countries where modern psychological laboratories became established during the last 150 years.

Within this relatively short period, psychology has become the prime discipline for human attention, learning, thinking, problem-solving, reasoning, decision-making, action, and action control, for emotion and emotional control, motivation and many more such areas of human capabilities. During the past 20 to 30 years, however, there has been a significant decrease in the degree to which psychology is viewed as the central science of these human functions. Instead, as a careful check of the major journals on cognition, emotion, and behavior, and of those with the highest impact on the reception of new ideas, like *Science*, *Nature* and *PNAS*[1] will show, there has been a significant shift towards other sciences, broadly subsumed under the term 'neuroscience', that have increasingly been involved in the investigation of these central psychological subjects. In addition, a simple check on the research fields of authors whose ideas are picked up most frequently and systematically in contemporary publications on cognition, emotion, and behavior, shows that the most cited papers in these classical areas of psychology come from systems and molecular biology, neurophysiology, cognitive, and affective neurology, psychiatry, computer science, biochemistry, endocrinology, and genetics. This suggests that these disciplines are about to take over the lead in theory development in many of the fields that have customarily been the province of basic psychology: i.e., in human development, maturation, attention, learning and memory, decision-making, emotion and emotion regulation, action and action control, and social interaction just to mention a few. Therefore, if psychology does not want to lose its leading role in these fields, its academic curricula must incorporate teaching about the biological foundations of such human functions and about the methodologies and instruments used in their investigations. And this has to happen in all academic institutions where psychology is taught.

Additionally, psychology should remind itself that the current attraction of neuroscientific studies in no way indicates that psychology has become superfluous and best replaced by neuroscience and its many facets, i.e., by systems neuroscience, cognitive neuroscience, affective neuroscience, or social neuroscience. As John Kihlstrom (2012) put it so perfectly,

> there is no need to incorporate 'neuroscience' or 'brain science' into psychology because it is already there: psychology is the science of mental life, but everyone understands that the brain is the physical basis of mind, and so psychology is naturally interested in the biological substrates of mental structures and functions ... [Replacing or] appending 'neuroscience' to psychology also suggests that, somehow, psychology needs neuroscience in order to complete its task of understanding mental life. But this gets the whole thing backwards. Neuroscience depends on psychology to characterize the mental functions that are performed by the brain. As I put it ... psychology without neuroscience is still the science of mental life, but neuroscience without psychology is just the science of neurons.

Within this framework, I will argue that observations based on neuroscientific methods and concepts can only throw additional and sometimes new light on some theoretical concepts and research findings that would not be available through pure behavioral observation or subjective inquiries and that they therefore can help to refine our psychological theories and concepts.

Examples of how neuroscience can inform psychology

The following examples are drawn from the field of hypnosis, biofeedback or brain–computer interface, and psychopathology.

Hypnosis

Hypnosis is applied with great success in many fields of psychotherapy and medicine, such as anesthesia, surgery, cancer therapy, bone marrow transplantation, stroke rehabilitation, and hypnotic analgesia, i.e., the reduction or even obviation of pain by specific hypnotic suggestion, represents one of the most impressive but yet unsolved enigmas of the human mind and its impact on the sensory and affective processing of painful and other threatening stimuli and on motor behavior of humans (see, for example, Al-Harasi *et al.*, 2010; Bongartz *et al.*, 2002; Cyna *et al.*, 2004; de Jong *et al.*, 2007; Ginestet, 2006; Hammond, 2010; Hauser, 2003; Hilgard and Hilgard, 1983; Jensen, 2009; Jones *et al.*, 2012; King *et al.*, 2001; Michaux, 2008; Montgomery *et al.*, 2000; Patterson and Jensen, 2003; Porter and Keefe, 2011; Serebro *et al.*, 1988; Wobst, 2007; Wood and Bioy, 2008). Indeed, examples such as cataract surgery in an elderly woman or the implantation of artificial teeth into the jawbone of a young man without any analgesic agent pose the question of how a human being is able to accept such a dramatic nociceptive experience and tolerate such procedures without any terrifying response of pain, rage, or despair.

Many theories have addressed this human capacity of pain control, but so far, no single explanation is available that would provide a satisfactory answer to resolve this enigma. One group of psychological explanations has considered the painless mastery of such situations of an individual to be the result of a takeover of the social role suggested by the hypnotist (Spanos, 1982; Wagstaff, 1995). In fact, *role-taking theory of hypnosis* has become one of the most accepted theories of why subjects are able to master such painful experiences. Others have considered the hypnotic control of pain as a consequence of attention (*attention theory of hypnosis*), i.e., subjects under hypnosis focus their attention onto the suggestions of the hypnotist, which narrows or even blocks the processing of the noxious input and prevents the generation of pain (Crawford, 1994; Crawford *et al.*, 1998). Alternatively, Ernest Hilgard and Kenneth Bowers and colleagues have provided experimental evidence that such hypnotic mastery is not an expression of a role-taking but rather the consequence of a dissociation of several independent functions of the human mind (*neo-dissociation theory of hypnosis*) that normally orchestrate the sensory processing of noxious stimuli, its affective concomitants, its personal meaning and autobiographic significance, and the reflexive and deliberate behaviors that follow in response to painful input (Bowers, 1989; Bowers and Brennenman, 1981; Bowers and Lebaron, 1986; Hilgard, 1973, 1974, 1994; Hilgard and Hilgard, 1983).

The conception that hypnotic analgesia is based on attentional mechanisms has been challenged by a number of recent studies (Friederich *et al.*, 2001; Miltner *et al.*, 1992; Miltner and Weiss, 2007; Schuler *et al.*, 1996). In these studies, highly suggestible subjects were stimulated with painful stimuli while exposed in a counterbalanced sequence to a control condition without any intervention, a condition with suggestions of hypnotic analgesia, and a condition where the subject's attention was distracted from the stimulation. After each block of stimulus presentations, subjects were requested to rate the intensity and aversiveness of pain in response to the stimuli on a visual analog scale. During the control condition, subjects were asked to relax quietly while exposed to the noxious stimulation. In the hypnotic analgesia condition, subjects received suggestions that they would wear an anesthetic glove that causes the sensations of their middle finger tip to become absolutely numb and totally insensitive to any kind of noxious input. During the distraction condition, subjects had to find words out of a conglomerate of letters organized in crossword-puzzle style. In addition to the recording of subjects' pain ratings, subjects' somatosensory evoked potentials (SEP) of the brain were recorded from a dense array of electrodes mounted on subjects' scalp. In response to noxious stimuli, the magnitude of late components of SEPs were found to be significantly correlated with the physical intensity of the stimulus applied and even more with subjects' reports on the intensity and aversiveness of stimulation (e.g. Flor *et al.*, 1992). The stronger the physical stimulus is perceived, the larger the magnitudes of late SEP components. When pharmacological pain treatments or psychological interventions are effective, a number of studies have shown that these peak-to-peak-amplitudes become smaller than during the action of placebos or other control treatments (for reviews see Bromm and Lorenz, 1998; or Miltner and Weiss, 2007).

When subjects of the Friederich *et al.*'s (2001) experiment were exposed to suggestions of hypnotic analgesia as compared to the control condition, pain intensity and aversiveness ratings were significantly reduced with values partially below the pain threshold. Similarly, pain ratings were also significantly lower during the distraction instruction as compared to the control condition. However, no significant difference for pain intensity ratings was found between the hypnosis and the distraction condition, indicating that both instructions affected subjects' pain intensity similarly. The peak amplitude of the positive going brain electrical activity around 260ms post stimulus was significantly lower during distraction as compared to hypnotic analgesia and control condition, but no significant differences were found between hypnotic analgesia and the control condition. Results of this study clearly indicate that suggestions of hypnotic analgesia and distraction of attention significantly reduces subjects' pain to painful electrical stimuli and thus confirms earlier reports that hypnotic analgesia (Halliday and Mason, 1964; Hilgard and Hilgard, 1983; Peter, 1998; Revenstorf, 1993; Revenstorf and Peter, 2008; Friederich *et al.*, 2001) and distraction of attention (Friederich *et al.*, 2001; Johnson *et al.*, 1991; Miltner *et al.*, 1989) represent effective methods for the control of acute experimentally induced pain.

However, SEP amplitudes also show that there is a significant difference of the brain's response to painful stimuli during the hypnotic state and the distraction condition. While SEP amplitudes to painful stimuli were significantly smaller during distraction as compared to the control condition of resting, there was no difference in SEP magnitude between hypnosis and the control condition. Obviously, filters at thalamic and thalamo-cortical levels are activated during distraction so as to prevent or to protect the somatosensory cortices from noxious input. However, while under hypnosis the somatosensory cortex still receives full information about the noxious input. While hypnosis and distraction abolish pain on the subjective level in similar ways, hypnotic analgesia and distraction seem to have different impacts on the brain. During hypnotic analgesia, the processing of somatosensory stimulus aspects and its subjective meaning obviously are dissociated from each other as proposed by Hilgard and Hilgard's (1983) dissociation account of hypnosis. While the somatosensory features of noxious stimuli are still evaluated properly during hypnosis by the brain as they are in the non-hypnotic control condition, the output of this somatosensory processing is, it seems, not being communicated appropriately to other brain areas that complete the evaluation of these stimuli as being painful and that organize the affective response to noxious stimuli and proper behaviors to pain. However, it is not known how the brain organizes this dissociation between the processing of somatosensory, affective, and intensity-related aspects of pain during hypnosis.

Based on research on the effects of anesthesia on the brain, where a breakdown of coherence of neural oscillations (also called binding) between different areas of the brain was postulated as the major reason for the loss of consciousness, we reinvestigated the data of the Friederich *et al.* study (2001) and examined whether such a breakdown might also account for hypnotic analgesia as compared to the control condition. The analysis of coherence of neural activities within the so-called gamma band between frontal brain areas that are known to be critical for the intensity evaluation and affective aspects of painful stimuli and areas of the brain that process the somatosensory aspects of such stimuli in fact indicated a significant breakdown of coherence within the gamma band between somatosensory and frontal sites of the brain while subjects were hypnotized as compared to the control condition. Based on this analysis, we suggested that hypnosis represents a dissociative brain state that dissociates integrative functions of the brain between subunits that are responsible for the formation of conscious experience (Trippe *et al.*, 2004).

The investigation of such brain activities thus has provided additional evidence that Hilgard and Hilgard's concept of hypnosis as a state of brain dissociation might represent a proper theory of hypnotic analgesia. However, whether Hilgard's concept of dissociation is also valid for other hypnotic phenomena like hypnotic-induced deafness, amnesia, or post-hypnotic commands has still to be shown.

Brain–computer interface for completely disabled individuals

Another challenging example of the value of neuroscientific methods and concepts for psychology is represented in some new applications for brain–computer interfaces (Birbaumer, 2009; Birbaumer *et al.*, 2009; Birbaumer, 2006; Kuebler and Kotchoubey, 2007). Whenever a subject is observed in a so-called 'locked-in' state during a late period of the disease called amyotrophic lateral sclerosis (ALS) – also referred to as motor neuron disease or as Lou Gehrig's disease – it could be thought that such a state is horrible and life as such not worth living. ALS is a very a debilitating disease whereby subjects with complete ALS cannot speak, move any body part, their eyes or eyelids; they can't breathe without the assistance of a respirator (Birbaumer, 2006). From the outside, they appear as if dead, without any chance to communicate with the outside world. Surveys with relatives and significant others indicate that these people consider these patients to be in agony and many would approve their release (Birbaumer, 2006).

However, based on studies on the self-control of brain electrical activities by means of biofeedback procedures, Birbaumer and his colleagues (Birbaumer, 2009; Birbaumer, 2006, Birbaumer *et al.*, 2009; Hinterberger *et al.*, 2005; Kotchoubey *et al.*, 2002; Kuebler and Kotchoubey, 2007) have shown that the brains of many ALS patients are still functioning well enough so that the control of its electrical activity could be used as a communication device.

The communication device was constituted by recording the brain electrical activity called the contingent negative variation (CNV, among others) and by using the magnitude of this CNV for the selection of letters from the alphabet in order to compose written messages (words, sentences of words etc.) presented onto a video monitor for other people. The CNV represents an electrical brain activity that emerges in the human electroencephalogram during the time interval whenever one expects a second, imperative stimulus after processing a warning signal. In other words, whenever you are waiting in your car for a traffic light to turn from red (warning stimulus: 'Wait!') to green (imperative stimulus: 'Go!') a change in the brain's electrical activity is observed, going from a more positive to a more negative voltage in the EEG recording.

Birbaumer and his coworkers enabled some of these patients to control the amplitude of this CNV by either increasing or decreasing its magnitude while they observed a rocket that slowly moved from the left border of a video screen into one of two goals that were placed at the right border of the screen. By voluntarily increasing the negativity of the brain's CNV amplitude, i.e., its negative voltage, during the rocket's flight from the right to the left side of the screen, subjects could navigate whether the rocket flew into either the upper or lower goal. When they managed to navigate the rocket into the upper goal, their CNV amplitude was more negative while when the rocket landed in the lower goal the CNV was more positive.

So trained, patients got self-control of a simple binary brain response that enabled them to express a 'Yes' or 'No' through their brain without verbal language. The researchers then used this mechanism to select single letters from the alphabet in order to express their wishes, needs, emotions, pains, and concerns in response to questions and to communicate with more complex written statements to their environment.

From these studies, information was obtained on how these patients perceived and evaluated their current state. Somewhat surprisingly, not all ALS patients rated their current life as miserable and negative as we would expect. Some of them considered their current status as worth living and were far from asking for release and euthanasia. From a mere observational perspective of such a distressing status, no one would have expected such an evaluation. This not only makes us examine our convictions about the validity of observations but also brings another perspective to the current debate about euthanasia and the problem of declarations about a person's last will in the context of medical treatment.

Can we really foresee our evaluations of a medical disorder and intervention and what condition and treatment we would tolerate or not while we are healthy and mentally fit, i.e., before we actually have experienced the condition, or will our actual experience of even the most miserable condition lead us to a completely opposing evaluation about the situation when we are experiencing it? What burden do we put on others when they have to decide about us based on poor and restricted observational evidence in such a condition when we cannot express ourselves? Again, Birbaumer's studies provide clear evidence that we would miss profound knowledge of the status of such patients and even would be threatened with misinterpreting their current status. This additional information that is only accessible through the use of neuroscientific approaches significantly improved our information on ALS and the range of putative interventions.

The brain in complicated grief

My third example is drawn from studies on complicated grief (Stroebe *et al.*, 2012). Complicated grief is a complex psychological condition of bereavement following the loss of a loved other. While people with complicated grief know that their loved one is gone, they don't want to believe it and often show strong yearning or longing for the lost person for many months following the loss (Rynearson *et al.*, 2012; Shear *et al.*, 2006, 2011; Stroebe *et al.*, 2012; Toblin *et al.*, 2012). Thoughts and memories about the deceased person completely absorb the grieving person, induce feelings of bitterness or anger about the death, and many complicated grievers often are convinced that a life without the deceased person is meaningless and not worth living (Kristensen *et al.*, 2012). Many of such individuals have great difficulties becoming engaged in new social relationships and show resistance to visit places and situations that formerly were shared with the lost person (Morina, 2011; Morina *et al.*, 2010).

Behavioral studies mainly associated complications of adaption to bereavement with cognitive and emotional factors and emphasized that negative thoughts about the loss changed with positive thoughts about the lost person (for review see Stroebe *et al.*, 2012).

Whether the change between the positive and negative memories and emotions occurs in a sequential order, with the positive memories and emotions preceding the negative ones or vice versa, is not known. When such a sequential order of both memories would be the normal case, one would have to expect two alternative consequences for the time course of grieving: where negative memories and emotions frequently precede the positive ones, one would expect a conditioned extension of negative memories and emotions about the loss due to the reinforcing effect of the positive memories and emotions on the grieving person. Due to that, the memories should become dominated gradually mainly by negative cognitions about the lost person and the adaptation should turn into an increase of yearning over time. If the opposite were the case, then positive thoughts and emotions about the loss should become punished by the negative thoughts and emotions about the lost person. Therefore, positive thoughts about the lost person should become reduced and grieving should become dominated by mainly negative thoughts and emotions about the lost person. However, both responses seem to be less typical in complicated grief.

A recent study, which hypothesized that complicated grieving is the consequence of a *concurrence of positive and negative cognitions and emotions* (O'Connor, 2012) offers an alternative view. In this study, functional magnetoencephalographic imaging (fMRI) was used in 11 women who suffered from complicated grief, and 12 women without complicated grief, all of whom had experienced the death of a mother or sister due to breast cancer within the preceding five years. Each of these participants was exposed to photographs of strangers and of the lost person and to words that reflected aspects of the death event and further grief-related idiographic words and to neutral words, both groups of words superimposed on the image of the strangers and the lost person. Subjects were requested to focus on any thoughts, feelings, or memories that came to mind while watching the photos and the words, and to focus on feelings that emerged while watching the stimuli.

Analysis of the fMRI data revealed greater phasic reward activity of the nucleus accumbens (NA) and simultaneously also stronger tonic activity of the amygdala (A) and the anterior insula (AI) in response to grief-related versus neutral words that was significantly greater in subjects of the complicated grief group than in subjects of the noncomplicated grief group. While the NA always is engaged and significantly activated for very brief moments when stimuli with positive valence or reinforcing stimuli are processed, activity of A takes longer and is regularly associated with stimuli that are rated as negative and are evaluated as punishing. Furthermore, activity of the AI is commonly strong when stimuli induce strong sympathetic arousal that subjects evaluate as distressing. In contrast, both groups show similar activity in brain areas that mirror neurophysiological activation in response to sadness feelings. To clarify, the functional role of NA activity in grief correlational analyses with parameter estimates of activity in NA further correlated significantly with more self-reported yearning for the deceased, that was independent of the length of time since the death, participant age, or general positive or negative affect (O'Connor, 2012).

These findings indicate that subjects with complicated grief and those with normal grief felt sadness in response to the grief-related stimuli, but only those with complicated grief also activated simultaneously an area important for reward processing when viewing cues of the deceased. The reward-relevant aspect of this neural response may help to explain why it is hard for some subjects to accustom themselves to the loss of a loved one. The short, phasic simultaneous emergence of positive emotions about the deceased and the more tonic activation of structures that become engaged when negative emotions are present, might thus reinforce yearning and prevent these subjects from adjusting to the loss and hinder the fading of yearning. Behavioral data did not show this sensitivity of simultaneous but opposing emotional neurobiological processes, or to differentiation between complicated and noncomplicated grief, whereas the observation of brain areas critical for reinforcement provided new insights as to why some subjects develop complicated grief and others do not.

Consequences for the curricula in psychological education and training

The three examples just given illuminate the importance of neuroscientific methods in deepening current psychological concepts on cognition, emotion and behavior. If psychology education wants to profit from such new methods of investigation, psychology education and training curricula have to be extended to include the neurobiological foundations of our psychological capacities and the methods by which such foundations can be observed, assessed, and evaluated.

A suggestion for core curricular areas to improve psychologists' competence in biological aspects of cognition, emotion and behavior might include lectures and seminars on the following basic anatomy and physiology and functions of the central and autonomic nervous systems:

- neurons, and neural networks;
- the communication and plastical adaptations of neural networks during maturation and in light of changing environments;
- basic information about the genetic and biochemical basics of neural functioning;
- principles and functions of the human perceptual and motor systems;
- the emotional and motivational systems;
- systems organizing attention, learning and memory;
- systems that constitute our capacity to use language;
- systems for cognitive functioning, like reasoning, decision-making, moral and ethical actions, action and emotional control.

Furthermore, information about the following might be important:

- autonomous, endocrinological and immune functions;
- the cardiovascular system and systems for energy delivering and gastrointestinal systems, the reproductive system and sexual functions;
- the hormonal and immunological systems and their regulational functions and interactions with the central nervous system (CNS) and autonomic nervous system (ANS).

Besides that, curricula should include the basics of and new development in genetics and epigenetics and their role in maturation and adaption to changing environments.

In order to investigate all these functions, a broad array of methods should be taught to students, including information about the physics of neural/muscular electrical activities – electroencephalograpy (EEG), magnetoencephalograpy (MEG), electromyography, (EMG), electrocardiography (ECG), apparatus for electrodermal activity (EDA) recording, for transcranial magnetic stimulation (TMS) and magnetic resonance imaging (MRI), positron emission tomography (PET), optical imaging, diffusion tensor imaging, real time MRI and the analysis of hormones, genes, epigenetic structures, immunological compounds and basics about its instrumentations. For data analysis, teaching methods should include presentations of basic theories of time series analysis, concepts and methods of time sampling and event-related analysis, source analysis, coherence analysis, and causal modeling.

Instruction about methods is also indispensable, as is instrumentation of stimulus presentation, cognitive, behavioral and emotional assessment, experimental control etc. using MATLab and other software packages (Presentation, E-Prime etc.), methods of data-handling and analysis (software programs like EEGlab, Brain Recorder, Brain Vision, Statistical Parametric Mapping [SPM], Brain Voyager, and many more). Finally, the well-educated student should receive training in data presentation and visualization and receive basic information about the physics and operation of biosignal amplifiers (multi-channel EEG, MEG, EMG, ECG, EDA, TMS and so on), data sampling instrumentation (computers, A/D converters, navigation instrumentation), the operation and underlying physics of magnetic resonance imaging techniques and scanners, and other imaging techniques like PET scanners, instrumentation for genetic analyses and analyzers for immunological and hormonal parameters.

All these requirements will impose strong financial pressure on most psychological departments to secure teaching of these concepts, methods, and techniques. Additionally, it requires a broadening of the personnel of departments by engaging experts for research and teaching from many different faculties, including physicists, engineers, biochemists, computer specialists, software programmers and other technical staff who can instruct and train students to get the most out of these concepts, methods and instrumentation. Many special scientific societies have set up teaching curricula and overviews about the costs of such instrumentation and the implementations of such laboratories and are supportive in setting up the basic steps for its implementation into the curricula of its Bachelor and Masters programs (see, for example, the Society for Psychophysiological Research, www.sprweb.org/).

Note

1 *Proceedings of the National Academy of Sciences of the United States of America.*

References

Al-Harasi, S., Ashley, P. F., Moles, D. R., Parekh, S. and Walters, V. (2010). Hypnosis for children undergoing dental treatment. *Cochrane Database of Systematic Reviews*, 8. doi: 10.1002/14651858.CD007154.pub2.

Birbaumer, N. (2009). Brain–computer interfaces (bci) in criminal psychopaths. *Psychophysiology*, 46, S23–S23.

Birbaumer, N., Murguialday, A. R., Weber, C. and Montoya, P. (2009). Neurofeedback and brain–computer interface: clinical applications. In L. Rossini, D. Izzo and L. Summerer (Eds.), *Brain Machine Interfaces for Space Applications: Enhancing astronaut capabilities*, pp. 107–117. London, New York, San Diego, CA: Academic Press.

Birbaumer, N. (2006). Breaking the silence: Brain–computer interfaces (BCI) for communication and motor control. *Psychophysiology*, 43, 517–32.

Bongartz, W., Flammer, E. and Schwonke, R. (2002). Efficiency of hypnosis. A meta-analytic study. *Psychotherapeut*, 47(2), 67–76.

Bowers, K. S. (1989). Dissociation in hypnosis and multiple personality-disorder. Paper presented at the 40th Annual Meeting of the Society for Clinical and Experimental Hypnosis, St Louis, MO, November.

Bowers, K. S. and Brennenman, H. A. (1981). Hypnotic dissociation, dichotic-listening, and active versus passive-modes of attention. *Journal of Abnormal Psychology*, 90(1), 55–67.

Bowers, K. S. and Lebaron, S. (1986). Hypnosis and hypnotizability – implications for clinical intervention. *Hospital and Community Psychiatry*, 37(5), 457–67.

Bromm, B. and Lorenz, J. (1998). Neurophysiological evaluation of pain. *Electroencephalography and Clinical Neurophysiology*, 107(4), 227–53.

Crawford, H. J. (1994). Brain dynamics and hypnosis: attentional and disattentional processes. *The International Journal of Clinical and Experimental Hypnosis*, 42(3), 204–32.

Crawford, H. J., Knebel, T. and Vendemia, J. M. C. (1998). The nature of hypnotic analgesia: Neurophysiological foundation and evidence. *Contemporary Hypnosis*, 15(1), 22–33.

Cyna, A. M., McAuliffe, G. L. and Andrew, M. I. (2004). Hypnosis for pain relief in labour and childbirth: a systematic review. *British Journal of Anaesthesia*, 93(4), 505–11.

de Jong, A. E. E., Middelkoop, E., Faber, A. W. and Van Loey, N. E. E. (2007). Non-pharmacological nursing interventions for procedural pain relief in adults with burns: A systematic literature review. *Burns*, 33(7), 811–27.

Flor, H., Miltner, W. and Birbaumer, N. (1992). Psychophysiological recording methods. In D.C. Turk and R. Melzack (Eds.), *Handbook of Pain Assessment*, pp. 169–90. New York, London: The Guilford Press.

Friederich, M., Trippe, R. H., Ozcan, M., Weiss, T., Hecht, H. and Miltner, W. H. R. (2001). Laser-evoked potentials to noxious stimulation during hypnotic analgesia and distraction of attention suggest different brain mechanisms of pain control. *Psychophysiology*, 38(5), 768–76.

Ginestet, C. (2006). Hypnosis: Theory, research and applications. *Psychologist*, 19(12), 745.

Halliday, A. M. and Mason, A. A. (1964). Cortical evoked potentials during hypnotic anaesthesia. *Electroencephalography and Clinical Neurophysiology*, 16, 312–14.

Hammond, D. C. (2010). Hypnosis in the treatment of anxiety- and stress-related disorders. *Expert Review of Neurotherapeutics*, 10(2), 263–73.

Hauser, W. (2003). Hypnosis in gastroenterology. *Zeitschrift für Gastroenterologie*, 41(5), 405–12.

Hilgard, E. R. (1973). A neodissociation interpretation of pain reduction in hypnosis. *Psychological Review*, 80(5), 396–411.

Hilgard, E. R. (1974). Toward a neodissociation theory – multiple cognitive controls in human functioning. *Perspectives in Biology and Medicine*, 17(3), 301–16.

Hilgard, E. R. (1994). Neodissociation theory. In S. J. Lynn and J. W. Rhue (Eds.), *Dissociation: Clinical and theoretical perspectives*, pp. 32–51. New York: The Guilford Press.

Hilgard, E. R. and Hilgard, J. R. (1983). Hypnosis in the relief of pain, 2nd edn. Los Altos, CA: Kaufmann.

Hinterberger, T., Wilhelm, B., Mellinger, J., Kotchoubey, B. and Birbaumer, N. (2005). A device for the detection of cognitive brain functions in completely paralyzed or unresponsive patients. *IEEE Transactions on Biomedical Engineering*, 52(2), 211–20.

Jensen, M. P. (2009). Hypnosis for chronic pain management: A new hope. *Pain*, 146(3), 235–7.

Johnson, R., Miltner, W. and Braun, C. (1991). Auditory and somatosensory event-related potentials: I. Effects of attention. *Journal of Psychophysiology*, 5(1), 11–25.

Jones, L., Othman, M., Dowswell, T., Alfirevic, Z., Gates, S., Newburn, M. and Neilson, J. P. (2012). Pain management for women in labour: an overview of systematic reviews. *Cochrane Database of Systematic Reviews*, 3.

Kihlstrom, J. (2012). www.psychologicalscience.org/index.php/publications/observer/2011/september-11/identity-shift.html#comment-5336.

King, B., Nash, M., Spiegel, D. and Jobson, K. (2001). Hypnosis as an intervention in pain management: A brief review. *International Journal of Psychiatry in Clinical Practice*, 5(2), 97–101.

Kotchoubey, B., Lang, S., Bostanov, V. and Birbaumer, N. (2002). Is there a mind? Electrophysiology of unconscious patients. *News in Physiological Sciences*, 17, 38–42.

Kristensen, P., Weisaeth, L. and Heir, T. (2012). Bereavement and mental health after sudden and violent losses: A review. *Psychiatry–Interpersonal and Biological Processes*, 75(1), 76–97.

Kuebler, A. and Kotchoubey, B. (2007). Brain–computer interfaces in the continuum of consciousness. *Current Opinion in Neurology*, 20(6), 643–9.

Michaux, D. (2008). A history of hypnotic analgesia. *Douleur et Analgesie*, 21(1), 15–19.

Miltner, W. H. R., Braun, C. and Revenstorf, D. (1992). Nociception ist nicht gleich Schmerz. Eine Studie über schmerzreizkorrelierte hirnelektrische Potentiale unter Hypnose (Nociception does not equal pain. A study on pain-related brain electrical potentials during hypnosis). *Hypnose und Kognition*, 10, 22–34.

Miltner, W. H. R., Johnson, R., Braun, C. and Larbig, W. (1989). Somatosensory event-related potentials to painful and non-painful stimuli – effects of attention. *Pain*, 38(3), 303–12.

Miltner, W. H. R. and Weiss, T. (2007). Cortical mechanisms of hypnotic pain control. In G. A. Jamieson (Ed.), *Hypnosis and Conscious States. The cognitive neuroscience perspective*, pp. 51–66. Oxford: Oxford University Press.

Montgomery, G. H., DuHamel, K. N. and Redd, W. H. (2000). A meta-analysis of hypnotically induced analgesia: How effective is hypnosis? *International Journal of Clinical and Experimental Hypnosis*, 48, 138–53.

Morina, N. (2011). Rumination and avoidance as predictors of prolonged grief, depression, and posttraumatic stress in female widowed survivors of war. *Journal of Nervous and Mental Disease*, 199(12), 921–7.

Morina, N., Rudari, V., Bleichhardt, G. and Prigerson, H. G. (2010). Prolonged grief disorder, depression, and posttraumatic stress disorder among bereaved Kosovar civilian war survivors: a preliminary investigation. *International Journal of Social Psychiatry*, 56(3), 288–97.

O'Connor, M.-F. (2012). Physiological mechanisms and neurobiology of complicated grief. In M. Stroebe, H. Schut and J. van den Bout (Eds.), *Complicated Grief. Scientific foundations for health care professionals*, pp. 204–18. London: Routledge.

Patterson, D. R. and Jensen, M. P. (2003). Hypnosis and clinical pain. *Psychological Bulletin*, 129(4), 495–521.

Peter, B. (1998). Möglichkeiten und Grenzen der Hypnose in der Schmerzbehandlung (Chances and limits of hypnosis in the control of pain). *Der Schmerz*, 3, 179–86.

Porter, L. S. and Keefe, F. J. (2011). Psychosocial Issues in Cancer Pain. *Current Pain and Headache Reports*, 15(4), 263–70.

Revenstorf, D. (1993). *Klinische Hypnose*, 2nd revised edn (Clinical hypnosis). Berlin: Springer Verlag.

Revenstorf, D. and Peter, B. (Eds.) (2008). *Hypnose in der Psychotherapie, Psychosomatik und Medizin: Manual für die Praxis*, 2nd revised edn (Hypnosis in psychotherapy, psychosomatic and medicine: Manual for practical applications). Berlin: Springer Verlag.

Rynearson, E. K., Schut, H. and van den Bout, H. (2012). Complicated grief after violent death: Identification and intervention. In M. Stroebe, H. Schut and J. van den Bout (Eds.), *Complicated Grief. Scientific foundations for health care professionals*, pp. 278–92. London: Routledge.

Schuler, G., Braun, C., Miltner, W. and Revenstorf, D. (1996). Evozierte Potentiale unter hypnotischer Analgesie und Ablenkung bei Schmerz (Evoked potentials during hypnotic analgesia and distraction from pain). *Hypnose und Kognition*, 13(1+2), 79–98.

Serebro, L., Kleinhauz, M., Levi, N. and Eli, I. (1988). Hypnosis, an approach to treatment in dentistry. *Journal of Dental Research*, 67(4), 713.

Shear, K. M., Jackson, C. T., Essock, S. M., Donahue, S. A. and Felton, C. J. (2006). Screening for complicated grief among Project Liberty service recipients 18 month after September 11, 2001. *Psychiatric Services*, 57(9), 1291–1297.

Shear, M. K., McLaughlin, K. A., Ghesquiere, A., Gruber, M. J., Sampson, N. A. and Kessler, R. C. (2011). Complicated grief associated with hurricane Katrina. *Depression and Anxiety*, 28(8), 648–57.

Spanos, N. P. (1982). Hypnotic behavior – a cognitive, social psychological perspective. *Research Communications in Psychology Psychiatry and Behavior*, 7(2), 199–213.

Stroebe, M., Schut, H. and van den Bout, J. (Eds.) (2012). *Complicated Grief. Scientific foundations for health care professionals*. London: Routledge.

Toblin, R. L., Riviere, L. A., Thomas, J. L., Adler, A. B., Kok, B. C. and Hoge, C. W. (2012). Grief and physical health outcomes in US soldiers returning from combat. *Journal of Affective Disorders*, 136(3), 469–75.

Trippe, R. H., Weiss, T. and Miltner, W. H. R. (2004). Hypnotically induced analgesia – mechanisms. *Anasthesiologie und Intensivmedizin*, 45(11), 642–7.

Wagstaff, G. F. (1995). What is hypnosis? Paper presented at the British-Association Meeting, Newcastle, England, 13 September.

Wobst, A. H. K. (2007). Hypnosis and surgery: Past, present, and future. *Anesthesia and Analgesia*, 104(5), 1199–208.

Wood, C. and Bioy, A. (2008). Hypnosis and pain in children. *Journal of Pain and Symptom Management*, 35(4), 437–46.

Commentary on 'Implications of emerging areas for psychology education and training'

Andreas Beelmann

Considering and discussing psychology education and training (PET) is necessary in order to establish a unified concept of a scientific discipline that enables students to apply the most recent scientific standards to their professional work as psychologists. Therefore I would like to thank the editors of this book for giving me the opportunity to comment on two of the contributions to this discussion of PET, although I have to admit in advance that I am neither an expert in neuroscience/biological psychology (NS/BP) nor in gerontopsychology (GP). However, I have several comments, some where I largely agree with the authors and some where I feel points or issues need further reflection.

I would like to start with some important points that both authors have in common. First, both convincingly demonstrate that NS/HB and GP really are emerging fields within psychology; one stems from basic research, largely influenced by technical progress within the last few decades; the other from the applied perspective and arising from changes in the age distribution of the population in many countries throughout the world. Both contributions show that these fields should be in some way integrated in PET.

Second, I appreciate that both chapters emphasize the importance of practical experiences in PET, although again for different reasons. Fernández-Ballesteros illustrates the need for practice principally with respect to applied work fields and for skills in assessment, counseling, or psychotherapy. Wolfgang Miltner argues more from the research perspective, i.e. for enhanced experimental, technical and assessment skills. As an applied researcher in intervention and evaluation I absolutely support these requirements for practical education and training, not only for applied fields outside the universities but also for those working in psychological research. Practical experience is essential for students because it keeps psychological theories and knowledge alive.

Third, both texts make it clear that we should be open to change when talking about PET. Naturally, this includes changes from scientific progress (e.g. in research methods, psychological knowledge) and advanced opportunities to study human behavior, cognitions and emotions. It also includes recent developments in assessment, evaluation, and intervention techniques to work within practical fields of psychology. In addition, thinking about education and training should comprise constant attention to changes within our societies and the need for psychological expertise emerging from these changes. We are living in a rapidly changing world and nobody knows how the world will be in 10, 20 or 50 years time. Curricula need to be flexible and sensitive to societal changes to ensure high scientific standards and practically relevant education and training in psychology.

Notwithstanding these aspects, I would like to mention some points for further discussion. Fernández-Ballesteros proposes that GP should not be viewed as a special field of clinical psychology because it cannot be reduced to human problems or the negative side of ageing. I agree with this perspective but would like to suggest conceptualizing GP as part of developmental psychology (or more broadly within developmental science). Fernández-Ballesteros correctly mentions the roots of GP in lifespan psychology, but I would like to add the roots in developmental psychopathology and developmental intervention. The main reason for conceptualizing GP within a broader psychological field is the shared principles in development (including deviant development), assessment, and intervention. To establish another subfield of investigation and education/training creates a risk of losing these principles for PET. GP justifies a right to its own identity mainly because of the increasing percentage of older people within our society, and not because psychological processes, assessment and intervention issues are different from other psychological subdisciplines. Therefore, for future curricula I would like to recommend inserting GP as part of applied developmental psychology or developmental science (including developmental psychopathology and developmental intervention).

A second point is that ageing will be a highly relevant field primarily for well-developed countries compared to developing countries because of the different age distribution of their population. Therefore, I am not sure that GP should be the first topic when developing countries create a psychology curriculum. They would perhaps be better to focus more on the development of young children and youth, because they are the primary group that will be responsible for changes and further development in these countries. However, even though I recommend a more general framework of developmental science, research and education on youth would also have positive effects on questions of ageing and older populations.

With regard to the question of implementing NS/BP into PET, this depends to some extent on the question of what should be viewed as a psychological subject. One can of course conceptualize human behavior, cognition, and emotion at several analytical levels: as chemical, neurocognitive, behavioral or societal processes. As Miltner has pointed out, knowledge and theories of human behavior and especially clinical problems can clearly profit from NS/BP. At the same time, however, psychological theories can profit from investigations at diverse levels of human behavior, as well as from research on the societal level. For example, to the best of my knowledge, all clinical problems have some social or societal risk factor and are only fully understandable and treatable in light of social norms and their social context. Would this be a reason for putting sociology into PET? Or, just to take another example, all neurological, physiological and biological processes could also be described as chemical processes. Is this the reason for putting chemistry into PET? Therefore, the basic question is this: What is the main subject of psychology and what is our unit of analysis? Again, there is no doubt that knowledge gained from diverse scientific fields is necessary to understand human behavior, human cognition, learning, emotion etc. and that basic knowledge in all these fields is therefore important for psychologists, whether they are applied practitioners or researchers. In my opinion, this does not require the implementation of all these disciplines into PET. However, aside from the question of implementation into PET, neuroscientists and other basic researchers have to make it clear exactly what their results mean for human behavior and human cognition, emotions and action. For further understanding of these objectives and psychological progresses, it is not only necessary to go into depth, but also to illustrate the meaning of basic results for higher levels of analyses and explanations, i.e., at behavioral and social levels.

Part V

Bridging scientific universality and cultural specificity in PET

6 Psychology education and training

A perspective from the United States of America

Oscar Barbarin

Introduction

What is psychology as a science and as a professional practice? Who determines who can appropriately be called a psychologist? What constitutes adequate training for psychological research and practice? Do shifts in psychological science and practice require the adaptation of current approaches to psychology education and training? These questions go to the heart of the identity and scope of psychology today.

In the US, a doctoral degree has become the minimum educational standard for assuming independence in the role of psychologist, with a few notable exceptions such as school psychology. To understand the development of a psychologist in the US it is necessary to consider undergraduate preparation, graduate training, post-doctoral specialization and how these fit into the larger picture of training for psychological scientists and practitioners. The pathway to a career in psychological research or practice consists of a four-year bachelor-level degree followed by five to seven years of training at graduate level and a one-year supervised post-doctoral fellowship.

In the US university faculties, psychological associations (state and national), state psychology licensing boards and state legislatures all play a role in defining the field of psychology (see Figure 6.1). Of these stakeholders, it is university faculty, psychological associations and state licensing boards who are most influential in shaping the goals, structure, and content of psychology training. Beyond these, there are many other stakeholders who have an interest and a role in defining psychology as a science and as a practice. These stakeholders overlap in membership and are mutually influential. Figure 6.1 depicts the key stakeholders and their relationships to one another, to psychological training, and to use of the title psychologist.

Through their research and training functions, universities and other bodies of higher education shape the contours of psychology as a discipline and influence the nature of psychological practice. National scientific and professional associations also have a strong influence on psychology through their ability to convene meetings, reach national consensus, and promulgate guidelines, as well as through the publication of journals, which can shape the content of the field as a science and practice. National associations draft model legislation for adoption

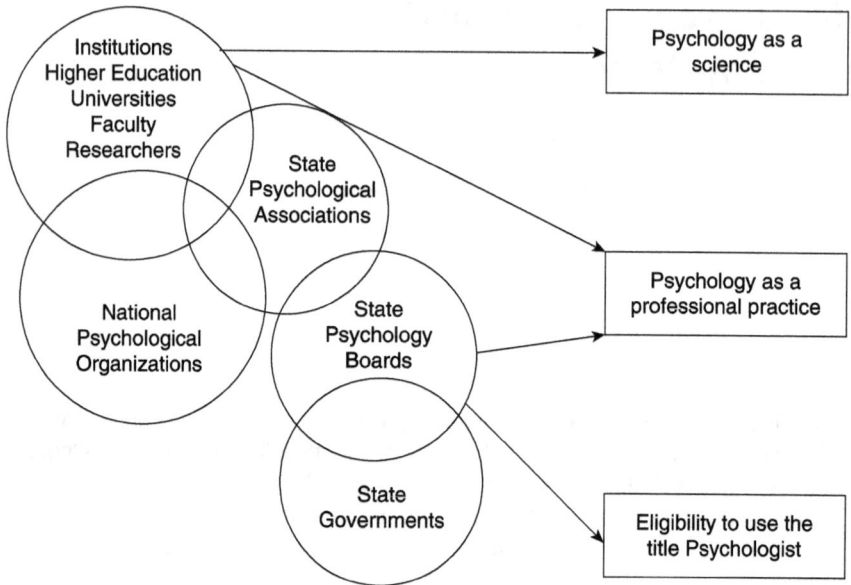

Figure 6.1 Key forces constituents in defining psychology.

by state legislatures. State psychological associations operate at the local level but usually coordinate with and look to national organizations for expertise and support. These associations are the advocacy arms of psychology who work with state legislatures to enact laws regulating the practice of psychology. State psychology boards are created as a part of state government to oversee the practice of psychology. They accept applications from persons wishing to register as psychologists, review credentials, examine candidate knowledge and competencies, set rules and issue opinions, and sanction individuals concerning legal and ethical violations. As already noted, these stakeholders are interdependent and have overlapping membership. In this way, university faculties often take leadership roles in national and state professional associations; and state associations coordinate their efforts with national organizations, who in turn work with the state legislature on laws governing psychology. The state boards of examiners are sometimes elected by psychologists, sometimes appointed by the state governor based on recommendations from the state association. Psychologists who are active in the state association often serve on the psychology examination boards. State governments, through their power to legislate and regulate, have the ultimate authority over who can be called a psychologist. However, their authority is limited to defining psychology and the scope of practice within their state boundaries.

Following this summary of key stakeholder involvement in defining and regulating psychology, the chapter continues with a discussion of the goals and outcome for the training of individuals who aspire to become psychologists.

It then moves to a discussion of the role of faculties in undergraduate, doctoral and post-doctoral training. Next it describes the contributions of psychological associations. The role and contributions of state psychology licensing boards (e.g. Boards of Examiners of Psychology) who regulate use of the title 'psychologist' will be addressed in a separate chapter and therefore will not be covered here. The chapter concludes with a consideration of emergent trends shaping psychology as a field and affecting training in psychology.

Graduate training goals and outcomes

The recent emphasis in America on evidence-based practice has given rise to a major push to develop a consensus about the principal goals and the expected outcomes for persons who will become psychologists. This has occurred mostly in the realm of programs designed to train psychologists who will deliver services, although it may carry over to and have implications for the training of psychological scientists. For example, Kaslow *et al.* (2009) identified the competencies that should be the outcome of professional training in psychology. This represents a movement away from relying on evaluating the extent to which students meet the objectives of courses in a curriculum. Two categories of professional competencies were identified: foundational and functional. Foundational competencies include:

- Professionalism – i.e. integrity, deportment, accountability, concern for the welfare of others and professional identity.
- Reflective practice – self-critical thoughtful analysis of one's practice, self-assessment, self-care.
- Scientific knowledge and methods – understanding the structure, use and limits of science; knowledge of the scientific basis of practice.
- Relationships, capacity for meaningful interpersonal relationships, skills in expressing and responding to emotions in self and others.
- Individual and cultural diversity – appreciation of how self and others are shaped by the International Classification of Diseases (ICD) and context.
- Ethical and legal standards and policy – understanding of and compliance with ethical legal and professional standards, ethical decision-making and behavior.
- Interdisciplinary systems – knowledge of the shared and unique contributions of diverse disciplines to psychology and its practice; ability to function in multi- and interdisciplinary settings, respectful and productive relationships with other disciplines.

Functional competencies include:

- Assessment – measurement theory and psychometrics; evaluation methods, diagnosis, conceptualization of cases; ability to communicate findings to professional and lay audiences.

- Intervention – intervention planning and implementation skills, evaluate progress.
- Consultation – understand the role of consultant, address referral question, communicate findings.
- Research/evaluation – employ a methodical scientific approach to generating knowledge, use of scientific approaches in intervention.
- Supervision – understand role, expectations, processes and procedures; effective in developing skills.
- Teaching – knowledge of content, pedagogical skills in delivering content.
- Administration – management, administration, leadership.
- Advocacy – empower and motivate system change.

The change represented in enumerating these competencies is that both programs and students can be judged on the extent to which these competencies can be demonstrated by program graduates. These outcomes can be measured. Increasingly, professional programs are being asked to provide data that demonstrate that their students acquire and display these skills by the time they graduate from the program.

University faculties as arbiters/gatekeepers for undergraduate and graduate training

Because most of the training of psychologists occurs within accredited colleges and universities, disciplinary faculties have an important influence over the goals and the content of psychological training. Faculties establish curricular guidelines and set the coursework and other requirements for the completion of degrees in psychology at undergraduate and graduate levels.

Undergraduate training: laying generic foundation program goals

Undergraduate education in psychology is intended to familiarize students with multiple areas of psychology as a science, with courses providing a base of knowledge about the neural, genetic, development, social and environmental basis of human behavior; familiarizing the student with scientific methodology; and exposing students to the application of psychology for public good. Undergraduate education in psychology also complements a broad liberal arts education that prepares students to think critically, write lucidly and communicate effectively. For example, undergraduate training in the University of Michigan's Department of Psychology is designed so that students learn the following:

- how behavior is motivated
- how people perceive, learn, and think
- how individuals differ from one another
- how personality develops from infancy to maturity and is expressed by behavior

- how interpersonal factors affect human relationships in the home, on the job, and in the community.

Among undergraduate college students, psychology is a popular subject. It is an attractive major subject because it is a gateway to many different types of careers in the corporate world and in human services. More often than not, it is among the top three areas of study chosen by students at major universities.

Admission process

Students are admitted to study at university level after completing 12 years of schooling. They are admitted without having to designate the major area of study they intend to pursue and generally have up to two years before having to make that decision, although most students do this early in their second year. Students declare a major and, as long as they meet a minimal grade point average and complete the introduction to psychology, admission to undergraduate study in psychology is a mere formality.

Length of training

At the undergraduate level, students are considered full time if they enroll for 12 credit hours in a semester. Each credit hour involves one hour of lecture per week and three hours of study and preparation outside of lectures, used for reading, projects and assigned tasks and preparation for examinations. A semester is about 15 weeks long. Bachelor degrees in most American universities require about 120 credit hours, which is usually accomplished by taking fifteen credit hours in each of eight semesters across four years. Some students complete this requirement in a shorter time by taking on heavier credit hour loads (up to 21 credit hours per semester) or by enrolling in summer courses. Recently, there has also been a trend toward taking five years to complete the Bachelors as students try to fit in courses to complete a double majors or multiple minor concentrations, or spend time studying outside of the country.

Organization, structure and content

Psychology training at undergraduate level is built on a foundation of liberal arts, mathematics, science and focus on psychological theory and research methods. The undergraduate program consists of a broad set of liberal arts, science and math courses not specific to the major that are required of all students enrolled in the university, course requirements of a major in a discipline or area of concentration, an optional minor concentration with fewer required courses than a major and finally electives to help the student reach the total number of credit hours needed to attain the Bachelors degree. General education requirements are intended to provide a broad-based liberal arts background with additional exposure to science and mathematics. The major or concentration in psychology usually includes a general survey course that introduces the student to the important ideas within contemporary psychology, covering topics such as heredity and behavior, principles of learning, physiological substrates of behavior, perception, social interaction, and mental health. In addition, there are required courses in univariate statistics, research design and experimental laboratory procedures (minimum two courses) that introduce students to psychology as a science. Beyond these courses are entry-level specialized courses in development, cognition, neuroscience, social/personality or clinical psychology. In the third and fourth year of undergraduate training, students can often pursue their own interests by taking advanced courses built on the entry-level specialized courses. The specialized courses often track the research interests of the department faculty and are built around the substantive strengths of the department. Many programs impose an additional writing requirement for graduation that may be met by a defended thesis for those in the department's honors-level program or an integrated capstone paper by those who were not admitted to honors. Although undergraduate programs share a common structure, there is surprising variation in the number of credit hours required to complete majors (mode = 30 hours). As part of colleges or universities they build psychology training on a foundation of liberal arts, mathematics, science and focus on psychological theory and research methods.

A review of undergraduate education in psychology was undertaken and its findings summarized in a report entitled *Undergraduate psychology major learning goals and outcomes* (APA, 2007). The report reaffirms that psychology is a basic science, built on a foundation of the liberal arts with the aim of contributing to human welfare. In addition to a widely accepted conception of the field, the report gives new emphasis to ethical practices, use of technology, effective communication skills; respect for cultural diversity; effective coping and self-improvement. The report is worth noting because it identifies measurable indicators that a psychology program can use to evaluate a department's effectiveness.

Graduate training in psychology: preparation for entry-level work program goals

In the US, graduate training in psychology is almost synonymous with doctoral-level education. This is in contrast to the approach to graduate training taken in most other parts of the world where the Masters level tends to be treated as the entry level for psychological practice. For example, in Europe, graduate training typically refers to programs leading to a Master of Science (MSc) degree, which individuals may qualify for after having completed a post-baccalaureate research honors degree. After earning an MSc, individuals may engage in professional practice, go on to additional graduate training, or take a position as a research associate and pursue a doctoral degree in this role. Establishing doctoral training as the floor for psychology practice is set in model licensure laws often developed in consultation with psychological associations. An exception to the doctoral rule is school psychology in which Masters level individuals can be certified by State Departments of Education to use the title school psychologist.

In the US, doctoral training is offered in a variety of specialties or subdisciplines of psychology including, among others, biopsychology, clinical, cognitive neuroscience, community, counseling, cultural, developmental, educational, environmental, experimental, forensic, health, measurement, medical, organizational, rehabilitation, school, social/personality, and statistics. Some of these programs focus on training students for careers in basic research; others are intended to provide professional training, which sets students on the path to offering psychological consultation and services. For a *research-focused* training program, the main goal is to prepare psychological scientists who can employ state-of-the-art methods and implement programs of research that advance knowledge in the field. In contrast, *practice-focused* or professional programs prepare practitioners to become competent in psychological assessment, treatment planning, service delivery and evaluation of treatment outcomes. Research training is valued in professional training programs to the extent that it improves service delivery through rigorous evaluation of clinical practice. It is assumed and hoped that students graduating from programs based on the scientist-practitioner model would conduct clinically relevant research related to professional practice. Time will tell how well the scientist-practitioner model is one that leads to advances in clinical research.

Admission process

Although some universities offer masters programs, the doctoral degree is considered the final degree. As a consequence, admission to graduate training is usually synonymous with admission to study for the doctoral degree. Unlike admission to undergraduate training, admission to doctoral training in psychology is not perfunctory or easily accessible to all who desire it. Admission to graduate training is very competitive and done by application to graduate schools in universities or professional schools. Students typically apply to multiple schools to improve their odds of admission to a program. Program faculty consider applicants' undergraduate training with special attention to how well they performed in psychology and statistics courses. Most programs only accept students who have majored in psychology, although some will consider applicants with no psychology background if they have relevant accomplishments or superior academic performance in other disciplines. A high scholastic average, such as A-, or a grade point average (GPA) of 3.5 or better, is essential for admission to many programs. Because of the variability of undergraduate training institutions, most admission committees require that students take and do well on the Graduate Record Examination (GRE). Each program sets its own standards for admission. Information on the average GRE scores and GPA's of admitted students are published in a variety of guides to psychology graduate programs. Performing well in undergraduate courses and on standardized tests is a necessary but not a sufficient condition for admission to most doctoral training programs in psychology. An evaluation of students' personal backgrounds and their interpersonal skills is also a part of the review process. In addition, students must write well and their given interests must match the program's emphases and strengths. This is most often assessed by personal essays in which students describe themselves and indicate why they wish to pursue graduate education in psychology. Some programs, particularly clinical psychology training programs, require an in-person interview as part of the admission process. In the written statement and personal interviews, admission committees look not only for quality and clarity of communication but also for indications that the student has a sense of direction, is interested in research, has an insight into their own psychological functioning and – for clinical programs – has had experience as an effective helper (e.g., as indicated by volunteering in hospital, on help hotlines, or as peer counselors) or paraprofessional experience (e.g. resident assistance in college dormitories, camp counselors). Even when students do well on the GRE and earn mostly excellent marks in their courses, admission to many graduate programs, especially professional programs such as clinical psychology, is so highly competitive that students with very strong backgrounds and high academic achievement are turned away. With limited openings at the most selective programs, there can be over 200 applicants for every student admitted. The situation is less dire for those seeking admission to programs focused exclusively on research training, where the ratio of those seeking admission to those admitted may be as small as 1:4.

Length of training

Research doctoral programs often estimate that it will take four years beyond the bachelors to complete two to three years of course work, an apprenticeship in a lab, an empirical masters, comprehensive examinations, proposal and thesis defense. For applied and clinical students, practica add to the time along with the required year for the pre-doctoral internship. In many cases, five years easily becomes six years. For some who dawdle, it can take much, much, longer.

Organization, structure and content

The organization of doctoral-level training is somewhat less uniform than undergraduate training. Most graduate training programs require a period of residency (full-time study on campus), two to three years of formal coursework (about 60 credit hours), comprehensive examinations, formal admission to doctoral candidacy, independent research activity, and a defended doctoral thesis. For clinical and counseling programs, semester-long practica and a year-long internship are required before the degree is awarded. There is discussion about requiring two years pre-doctoral internship but eliminating the post-doctoral year of training. In practica and internships, students provide services under the supervision of a licensed psychologist. The work on practica is not remunerated financially, i.e. there is no salary. Students pay school fees but some schools offer scholarships, teaching assistantships or research assistantships, which cover school fees plus a stipend for living expenses. Internships are full time but do not require tuition payments. In most internships, students are given a stipend to cover living expenses.

Many graduate training programs rely on a combination of required courses and a research apprenticeship, with the addition of supervised practical experience in the case of a professional program. At the center of training for research intensive specialties in psychology is on-the-job experience in conducting research. In these programs, primacy is given to direct sustained involvement in an active research laboratory as a way of learning methods, theory and problem-solving. For a professional program, the training clinic often takes on the role of the research lab as a place to get directly supervised experience in applying psychological principles to the assessment of and intervention with individuals, groups, families, organizations and communities. In the case of both research and professional programs, the apprenticeship model of providing a graded series of increasingly demanding tasks complements didactic courses, workshops and highly participatory seminars.

With respect to content, most doctoral training programs require courses that integrate psychological theory and research, statistics, and research methods, as well as practice or intervention courses in applied programs, such as clinical, counseling or school psychology. Although the structure of doctoral-level training tends to be very similar across universities, the exact courses to be taken, and their content, are heavily influenced by the research interests, theoretical inclinations and strengths of a department's faculty. As we will note later, licensing boards have specific requirements as to the content areas that must be included for a program of study to be considered psychological for the purposes of licensing and certification.

Post-doctoral training: program goals toward specialization and independence

The principal aim of post-doctoral training is to build on pre-doctoral training, especially the internship, which sets out to deepen the skills of the trainee through intensive hands-on experience. Post-doctoral training is often very specialized. For example, it may focus on the use of a novel technique, such as neuroimaging with specialized population such as children with ADHD or autism. Typically, the aim of post-doctoral training is to raise the skill level of the trainee in a specific content area to the extent that prepares the trainee to be competitive for academic or clinical/professional positions in that field.

Admission process

Post-doctoral study is offered on a program basis, for example in a hospital or research laboratory. Multiple students may apply, but only a small number are selected for the program. Alternatively, a post-doctoral experience can arise in situations where a doctoral-level psychologist has funds to support a post-doc and will recruit applicants through formal advertisement or via word of mouth from colleagues. The criteria for selection vary greatly but they are determined by the supervising person responsible for hiring the post-doc.

Length of training

Training takes place after the doctoral degree is awarded. It requires full time participation, i.e. 40–50 hours a week and is most often one year in duration, although it is not uncommon for trainees to spend up to three years in supervised post-doctoral training.

Organization, structure and content

Post-doctoral training is even less structured and uniform with regard to organization, structure, and content than doctoral training. The one-on-one mentoring relationship between the supervisor and the post-doctoral fellow is the centerpiece of the training. Within the supervisory relationship, information of a technical nature is conveyed, but professional issues are also covered. In addition, post-doctoral experiences may include training seminars on advanced research issues, opportunities to teach and lecture, and to attend professional conferences. In post-doctoral research experiences, the post-doc may work on a single project, implement a specific paradigm or master a specific research technique, run subjects, analyze data, and write papers in preparation for seeking appointment as a faculty member, employment in industry, or as a researcher in research lab. In a good clinical training program, the post-doctoral fellow may be involved in a range of experiences that include assessment, intervention, consultation, evaluation, analyzing data and publishing papers.

Role of psychological associations and their accrediting bodies

Psychological associations, such as the American Psychological Association (APA) and the Association for Psychological Science (APS) have a deep and pervasive influence in defining psychology, what it means to be a psychologist, and in setting standards for the training of psychologists. Psychological associations influence both substantive discourse and training through several means: journals and scientific meetings, their ability to convene and shape consensus, to promulgate guidelines and standards and in their capacity to offer or deny accreditation to a training program. Through their psychological journals and the peer review process that underpins them, and via scientific meetings, psychological associations provide channels for the flow of scientific ideas among psychologists and map the ever-changing contours and boundaries of the field. In this sense, psychology as a discipline is what the associations publish in their journals, and what they talk about in their meetings. These associations also shape the field through their power to convene and legitimize groups to work on scientific and professional issues, and to promulgate consensus reports. Examples include the many different conferences on psychology education, such as the Boulder and Vail conferences on psychology training.

Over time, the Boulder Conference has had an especially profound and lasting effect in shaping doctoral-level clinical psychology training. In 1949, the conference proposed the scientist-practitioner model that is the most widely accepted approach to professional training (e.g. clinical, counseling, school) in the United States. Programs following this model take on an identity as both a science that probes fundamental questions about human behavior, thinking and emotions, and as a profession seeking to apply that knowledge for improving human welfare. The foundation of this dual identity was established early in its development as a discipline but codified with great clarity in 1945 by the Boulder Conference on Psychology Education, where the term scientist-practitioner became a permanent fixture in the lexicon of psychology training.

In addition to questions of training, task forces have been formed to address professional ethics and cultural competence in research and clinical practice. These task forces deliberate and generate a set of guidelines, which as the word suggests are aspirational and lack the force of regulations that might involve sanctions for failure to comply. Professional associations also utilize their convening authority to sponsor conferences that articulate general training principles and propose training models, such as the scientist practitioner and scholar practitioner model after which most applied doctoral programs are patterned. The professional associations promote these models by identifying and promulgating specific core competencies, recognizing sub-specialties, prescribing minimal standards of practice and utilizing their accrediting powers to approve doctoral and internship training.

The APA has a special relationship to the training of professional psychologists in the US because it oversees the government-recognized accrediting body for clinical, counseling, and school psychology training programs and internships. It establishes the criteria for meeting standards and receiving program accreditation (APA, 2002). This is important because to obtain a license to practice psychology requires attendance at an accredited program. The accreditation process is overseen by the Commission on Accreditation within the Office of Program Consultation and Accreditation in the APA Education Directorate. Programs apply for accreditation and if fully approved are reviewed periodically, usually every five to seven years. Evaluation begins with a self-study by the program that describes the program's philosophy and goals and summarizes data collected by the program to demonstrate the attainment of its goals. The guidelines for receiving accreditation are usually aligned with requirement specified by licensing boards. Therefore it is not surprising that accreditation guidelines are reflected in the description of the typical psychology doctoral program outlined earlier. This includes exposure of trainees to psychology as a science, its history and methods and applications. The program of study must also include training in the affective, biological, cognitive, and social aspects of behavior, psychological measurement and statistics. With respect to psychology as a practice, students should be exposed to issues of individual differences and development, psychopathology, and ethics. Training in psychological intervention techniques should begin with training in psychological assessment and formulation of presenting problems followed by training in evidence-based practice. In light of the cultural and ethnic differences in the US, training must be provided to increase cultural competence in both assessment and intervention. Training programs cannot rely on lectures alone to promote skill development; they must also provide supervised professional experiences in settings committed to training and offer a range of experiences. These guidelines, along with standards for faculty, are used to judge the adequacy of the program for accreditation. Given the importance of accreditation for students' access to advanced training in internships and post-doctoral fellowships, and later to professional employment, these guidelines exert a powerful influence over the shape and content of programs, even though they lack the force of law. If a program successfully navigates the accreditation process, it is reviewed about every five years for renewal of accreditation.

Evaluations of research-focused training programs in psychology are less routinized and scripted than those for professional training programs. Nevertheless, like accreditation reviews, reviews of departments and their graduate programs begin with a self-study that is largely focused on process issues and productivity. The self-study often describes the program in terms of the selectivity of its students, their time to graduation, students' scholarly productivity, faculty teaching and service loads, scholarly productivity and the department's status in the field. The reviews are conducted by prominent scholars from other universities who prepare an evaluative report that describes the strengths and weaknesses of the department and its programs. The report often describes steps that might be taken to address any issues raised and can recommend directions the department or program may take for it future development.

Evaluation of student competence is embedded in the program requirements. In addition to evaluating performance in individual courses on research and theory, students are required to show mastery of psychological theory and research through examinations that comprehensively assess knowledge across multiple domains and theories. These take the form of one- to two-day written examinations, 'take home' examinations, or extensive essays reviewing theory and research literature in a specific area. In addition to evaluating student performance, evaluations are done at the program level. These may occur at the behest of the graduate school dean, who undertakes a review of graduate programs for the departments in their university. Alternatively, these evaluations may occur within the context of a review of a department's academic programs initiated by the provost, the chief academic officer of the university.

Emergent trends affecting the definition of psychology and psychology training

Conceptions of psychology as encoded in state law and regulations are stable and remarkably consistent across the states, as are requirements related to professional standing. Nevertheless, psychology is a dynamic field with many changes in its content, training and practice. These changes are driven by a number of developments including the ascendance of professional schools of psychology outside of universities, increasing specialization, advertence to the role of culture, genomic research, biopsychology and neuroscience, an emphasis on evidence-based practice, and a focus on specifying competencies and measuring the outcomes of training programs.

The rise of professional schools of psychology outside of universities

Almost from the time of its adoption, concerns have been raised about the adequacy of the scientist-practitioner model for preparing professionals who provide psychological services. These concerns centered around skepticism about how realistic it was to train students to be consummate clinicians and rigorous researchers at the same time. Some felt that clinical training was short-changed because teaching faculty built their careers and valued achievement in research over clinical skills. As a consequence, students coming out of typical PhD programs did not evidence sufficient clinical acumen and experience to function independently. In response to these concerns, proposals were made for new models of training that would provide more in-depth professional experience. These models were given diverse names, such as practitioner-scholar, scholar-practitioner, local clinical scientist, practitioner, and practitioner-scientist etc. In 1973, the Vail Conference on Levels and Patterns of Professional Training in Psychology endorsed the awarding of a Psy D or Doctor of Psychology degree to signal the focus on practice. In the beginning, these professional programs were initiated in traditional Departments of Psychology in universities such as the University of Illinois and Adelphi University (Peterson, 1968). The National Council of Schools and Programs of Professional Psychology (NCSPP), an association of professional training programs, identified six core competency areas: relationship, assessment, intervention, research and evaluation, consultation and education, and management and supervision. A seventh competency, diversity, was added in 2002. Ethics and advocacy are identified as core values that cut across and apply to all of the core competencies.

   Programs emphasizing professional practice often require fewer courses on psychology theory and research but offer more courses on psychological assessment and intervention, and perhaps a wider selection of specialized therapy courses. In addition, students devote more of their instructional time to practica in which students conduct psychological assessment and provide a range of clinical services. For example the typical scientist practitioner model PhD program students spend eight to ten hours per week in supervised practica and receive one hour of individual supervision by a licensed psychologist; in scholar practitioner model programs student might be expected to devote twenty to twenty-four hours per week to psychological assessment and intervention services. This means that much more instructional time is spent outside of the classroom in affiliated professional settings where students offer services under supervision. The theory is that students learn by doing.

Since the 1960s there has been a significant growth in professional programs, mostly in independent and sometimes for-profit professional schools of psychology. The growth has been such that more than half of all doctoral students in US-based clinical psychology programs are working toward the PsyD in professional programs based on the scholar practitioner model. Although these programs arose out of a desire to provide more extensive training in professional skills, their growth has given rise to concerns that many psychologists may be trained who lack sufficient grounding in science and the methods that contributed so much to its flourishing as a field over the past 50 years.

Trends in psychological training and practice

There has also been a growing tendency toward specialization at the doctoral level. For example, instead of generic programs in clinical or counseling psychology, we have programs that focus on a sub area, such as child clinical, health, neuropsychology, experimental psychopathology, developmental psychopathology, school, family and community clinical. Some of these programs have arisen in response to rapid scientific development in the life sciences, especially genomic and neuroscience research. An interesting development in the specialization of psychologists is the aspiration to gain hospital privileges and the legal right to prescribe psychotropic medication. Several states have included prescription privileges as part of the practice of psychologists for those willing and able to complete the equivalent of a masters degree in psycho-pharmacology. Boards of Examiners of psychology in several states have been empowered to provide a 'Certificate of prescriptive authority' which, in the State of Louisiana for example, means a certificate issued by a state licensing board which grants to the licensee the authority to prescribe and distribute drugs.

In a related trend, there is increased interest in the expansion of the role of psychologists in primary health care. Psychologists are already involved as consultants to help physicians and their patients deal with the psychological sequelae of illness and its treatment. However, psychological practitioners are looking to provide direct and adjunctive services in primary health care settings where a substantial number of complaints that bring patients to the doctor's office or hospital to seek medical care are psychosocial in nature.

At the opposite end of the continuum, the role of culture and the social environment in psychological research and practice has given rise to sensitivity to diversity, and to the inclusion of notions of cultural competence as an expected training outcome. The driving force behind this move is the principle that psychologists should practice only within the scope of their competencies. In a diverse society, knowledge of client populations is imperative, and an aspect of professional competence is working with ethnically and culturally diverse populations whose world views and perspectives need to be understood if we are to deliver relevant and effective services. To this end, the APA established a Joint

Task Force to help articulate guidelines for training programs that promote development of cultural competence. This was also motivated by a desire to lead psychology beyond a position of ethnocentrism and monoculturalism to a recognition and appreciation of the diversity of social and cultural groups that make up the population. The group proposed guidelines on multicultural education, training, research, practice, and organizational change for psychologists. These guidelines, the ideas for which were actually shaped over a twenty-two-year period, push the field of psychology to consider its commitment to cultural awareness, and the role of culture and ethnicity in knowledge of self and others, education, research, practice, organizational change and policy development. This represented a significant step forward in the direction of intercultural sensitivity and respect for diversity. In 2002 these guidelines were formally approved as Association policy by the Council Representatives, the governing body of the APA. These six principles are intended not to be prescriptive or proscriptive but to serve as a guide for training programs and for the practice of psychology. They are as follows:

1   Psychologists are encouraged to recognize that, as cultural beings, they may hold attitudes and beliefs that can detrimentally influence their perceptions of and interactions with individuals who are ethnically and racially different from themselves.
2   Psychologists are encouraged to recognize the importance of multicultural sensitivity/responsiveness, knowledge, and understanding about ethnically and racially different individuals.
3   As educators, psychologists are encouraged to employ the constructs of multiculturalism and diversity in psychological education.
4   Culturally sensitive psychological researchers are encouraged to recognize the importance of conducting culture-centered and ethical psychological research among persons from ethnic, linguistic, and racial minority backgrounds.
5   Psychologists should strive to apply culturally appropriate skills in clinical and other applied psychological practices.
6   Psychologists are encouraged to use organizational change processes to support culturally informed organizational (policy) development and practices.

Similar guidelines have been developed and promulgated with respect to services to gay, lesbian, and bisexual clients (APA, 2000).

The push to develop cultural competence is part of a larger effort to increase the consistency and quality in the preparation of individual psychologists to deliver effective services. Another aspect of this effort is the push toward greater and greater reliance on clinical practices for which there is convincing evidence of their efficacy. For example government-sponsored research has established that a combination of pharmacotherapy and cognitive behavior therapy is an effective approach for the treatment of depression. For ADHD it is a combination of stimulant medication and behavior management. Associated with this approach are specific treatment protocols and interventions in which the therapeutic procedures and the theory underlying the practices are spelled out in sufficient detail that they can be replicated across multiple settings with fidelity to the approaches on which evidence for efficacy was based. These are sometimes referred to as manualized treatments. Individual and group programs have been developed for conduct disorders, emotional dysregulation and posttraumatic stress disorder (PTSD) in young children (PATHS, Second Step, Coping Power, and Cognitive Behavioral Intervention for Trauma in Schools [CBITS]). Doctoral-level trainees are expected to learn about these intervention programs as an integral part of their clinical training.

Conclusion

The purpose of this chapter was to provide information about the scope and nature of psychology in the US, the forces which govern its development, and about emerging trends that are likely to shape its future. It sought to provide sufficient details about training and standards that would contribute to understanding similarities and differences in psychology across the globe as an essential first step toward discovering ways to arrive at a global consensus defining psychology and its training needs. The chapter has presented details about the definition and training of psychology in the US. It suggests that answers to the questions of what psychology is and how psychologists should be prepared are complex. Moreover, even within the US, there is no single definition of psychology that has garnered the imprimatur of the national government. On the surface, this might make for an inefficient system with dizzying inconsistencies from state to state. What could potentially be a disastrous situation with diverse jurisdictions creating unique and conflicting regulations of psychology has turned out to be remarkably ordered and consistent thanks in no small part to collaboration among the different stakeholders, as depicted in Figure 6.1. A close working relationship founded on recognition of interdependence among institutions of higher education, national and state associations provides an incentive for all parties to collaborate in advancing psychology as a scientific discipline and a professional practice.

Moreover, this lack of government-sanctioned definition has advantages. It is actually a good thing, because it means that we have an open system and not one set in stone by the government. It also has the advantage that psychologists have the autonomy to define the field for themselves, which makes it possible to adapt more quickly to emerging trends in the science and practice. Moreover this freedom makes it possible for psychologists in different governments to come together and to generate definitions of psychology that represent a consensus across multiple nations. This may contribute to the goal of IUpsyS to facilitate cross national mobility and cooperation among psychologists around the world.

References

APA (American Psychological Association). (2000). Professional practice guidelines for psychotherapy with lesbian, gay and bisexual clients. *American Psychologist*, 55, 1440–51.

APA (American Psychological Association). (2002). *Guidelines and Principles for Accreditation*. Washington, DC: Author.

APA (American Psychological Association). (2007). *APA Guidelines for the Undergraduate Psychology Major*. Washington, DC: Author. Available at www.apa.org/ed/resources. html26

Kaslow, N., Grus, C., Campbell, L., Fouad, N., Hatcher, R., and Rodolfa, E. (2009). Competency assessment toolkit for professional psychology. *Training and Education in Professional Psychology*, 3 (4 Supplement), 827–45.

Peterson, D. R. (1968). The doctor of psychology program at the University of Illinois. *American Psychologist*, 23, 511–16.

7 Bridging scientific universality and cultural specificity in psychology education and training

A Chinese perspective

Kwang-Kuo Hwang

As a result of globalization, human beings have more and more opportunities to interact with people from different cultures. However, despite apparent similarities in urban ways of life, differences related to religion and language also persist in today's world, and may hinder social discourse. In order to prepare people to have a meaningful dialogue with others from different cultures, researchers in the field of psychology have developed various intercultural training programs that can be used both in academic courses and professional training for intercultural understanding and tolerance.

This chapter contains four parts: the first reviews several models on the basic processes of intercultural learning with a common concern for the importance of culture theories. The second indicates the neglect of cultural issues in the theories of mainstream psychology. The third discusses the inappropriateness of using individualism and collectivism as theoretical frameworks for intercultural learning. In the fourth and final part, I will present my approach of multiple philosophical paradigms for constructing culture-inclusive theories to bridge scientific universality and cultural specificity in psychology.

Culture theory and intercultural learning models

In his model of intercultural expertise development, Bhawuk (1995, 1998) differentiates four types of people with different levels of cross-cultural competence. A person at the level of unconscious incompetence is a *layperson* who has no knowledge of another culture. This person tends to misinterpret others' behavior by referencing it in terms of their own cultural framework; they are usually not aware that this is happening. When social interactions do not have the expected results, the layperson does not understand why, and therefore cannot make real progress in intercultural relations.

People with extended intercultural experience, or those who have gone through a formal intercultural training program that discusses differences between two cultures, may develop some degree of intercultural expertise and are labeled *novices*. When a *novice* becomes aware that they have failed to behave appropriately in an intercultural situation – that their *conscious incompetence* has failed them in making correct attributions – they can usually find out about the relevant cultural differences, either through direct contact with persons in the respective culture or through experience with non-theory-based training programs.

By going through a theory-based intercultural training program, a level of *conscious competence* can be achieved that enables an individual to organize their understanding of cultural differences more meaningfully around a theory and thereby become an *expert*. By definition, an expert understands covert principles and theories behind overt behaviors; in this way, they can explain intercultural issues to others with understanding.

According to Bhawuk (1995, 1998), the final level of competence is that of an *advanced expert*. Here, one has to undertake behavioral training to practice different behaviors, leading to a level of *unconscious competence*. Once this is achieved, the individual has not only the relevant theoretical knowledge, but also the level of practice needed to perform the relevant tasks automatically.

Model for expertise development

Bhawuk's (1998) model of intercultural expertise development highlights the importance of culture theory, whereby it posits that intercultural training based on culture theory will make a person an expert, whereas training that is not theory-based will only result in novices. The importance of culture theory can also be seen in Anderson's (2000) model of cognitive stages for describing how people develop expertise.

Specifically, Anderson's model identifies three steps of skill learning for an individual to develop expertise. In the first cognitive stage, knowledge is *declarative*, the names and definitions of concepts and key entities are committed to memory. A person has to make an effort to be aware of the entire process of recalling knowledge and applying what they have learned in a situation. In the second *associative* stage, people have to convert their declarative knowledge of a domain into a more efficient procedural representation. Based on what they have learned in the first cognitive stage, they begin to detect mistakes in performing a skillful task, eliminate some of their mistakes and remember the elements of the procedure and their sequence, with practice. As they get to the associative stage, learners follow a procedure that they know leads to a successful result; this is referred to as *procedualization*.

In the third *autonomous* stage, the skill is developed, through practice, to become increasingly habitual and automatic. Finally, people know the task so well that they can perform it very quickly with few or no errors. Now they are sophisticated users of knowledge in a particular domain who can use broad principles to categorize and solve problems of that culture.

The neglect of culture in scientific psychology

Anderson's (2000) model for expertise development can be applied to different domains of knowledge. When it is applied to the domain of psychology education and training, a crucial question for serious consideration is: do we have sound culture theories in the domain of psychology?

A brief review of the history of mainstream psychology may provide a fair answer to this question. When Wundt established his first laboratory at Leipzig in 1879, he conducted experiments on consciousness using the scientific methods of so-called *physiological psychology* (Wundt, 1874/1904). In recognizing the difficulty of linking science to culture, he studied cultural issues of *Völkerpsychologie* by historical methods (Wundt, 1916). Cultural psychologist Cole (1996) indicated the problematic situation left by Wundt:

> In recent years interest has grown in Wundt's 'second psychology,' the one to which he assigned the task of understanding how culture enters into psychological processes . . . My basic thesis is that the scientific issues Wundt identified were not adequately dealt with by the scientific paradigm that subsequently dominated psychology and other behavioral-social sciences . . . cultural-inclusive psychology has been . . . an elusive goal.
>
> (Cole, 1996: 7–8)

In the early days of behaviorism, some Western psychologists tried to elude cultural issues by excluding content of consciousness from the domain of psychological study and advocating a positivistic approach of science. For example, at the beginning of his famous article, J. B. Watson (1913) claimed that:

> Psychology as the behaviorist views it is a purely objective experimental branch of natural science. Its theoretical goal is the prediction and control of behavior. Introspection forms no essential part of its methods, nor is the scientific value of its data dependent upon the readiness with which they lend themselves to interpretation in terms of consciousness. The behaviorist, in his efforts to get a unitary scheme of animal response, recognizes no dividing line between man and brute. The behavior of man, with all of its refinement and complexity, forms only a part of the behaviorist's total scheme of investigation.
>
> (1913: 158)

Culture has no position at all in the behaviorist's total scheme of investigation. When the trend of mainstream psychology has switched from behaviorism to cognitive psychology, most Western psychologists still eluded cultural issues and assumed that theories of Western psychology (WP) are universal and can be applied worldwide.

WEIRD psychology

It is a widely recognized fact that most theories of WP have been constructed on the basis of some particular groups from cultures of individualism. For instance, Henrich *et al*. (2010 a, b) reported that 96 percent of the samples of psychological research published in the world's top journals from 2003 to 2007 were drawn from Western, Educated, Industrialized, Rich, and Democratic (WEIRD) societies, which account for just 12 percent of the world's population. For their study, they reviewed a comparative database from the behavioral sciences, and found that the WEIRD research subjects are particularly unusual compared with the rest of the species across diverse domains, including visual perception, fairness, cooperation, spatial reasoning, moral reasoning, reasoning styles, self-concepts and related motivations, and the heritability of IQ. They thus concluded that there is no obvious a priori ground for claiming that such a particular psychological phenomenon is universal based on the sampling of such a single subpopulation.

In order to put theories of human behavior and psychology on a firmer empirical footing, they suggested that granting agencies should prioritize cross-disciplinary and cross-cultural research; researchers must strive to evaluate how findings of their research apply to other populations; reviewers and editors of academic journals should give researchers credit for comparing diverse and inconvenient subjects and push them to support any generalizations with evidence.

Nevertheless, it seems to me that suggestions of this kind advocate for an approach of studying the psychology of non-WEIRD populations in the theoretical contexts of mainstream psychology, which represents a perspective of cross-cultural psychology, but not cultural psychology or indigenous psychology (Shweder, 2000). Therefore, I strongly oppose this approach and advocate for the construction of culture-inclusive theories of psychology. Why?

Criticism on researches of individualism and collectivism

The most popular 'culture theory' that has been widely used for cross-cultural comparison is the research paradigm of individualism and collectivism. Even in his review article on intercultural training for the global workplace, Bhawuk (2009) used it as a cultural-theoretical framework for presenting findings of previous research on related topics. Nevertheless, is individualism and collectivism a sound culture theory for psychology education and training?

Hofstede (1980), a well-known Dutch organizational psychologist, was the first to conduct research on individualism-collectivism. When he was a director in the department of human resource management at IBM, Hofstede constructed a scale of 32 items to measure work goals or values. He administered this scale to equivalent, stratified samples of IBM staff in 40 countries, calculated means of the endorsement on 32 work values for samples from each country, and created a correlation matrix amongst the 32 average nation-values. Four factors were thus obtained as a result of factor analysis: individualism, power distance, masculinity, and uncertainty avoidance. Factor scores of the 40 countries were marked to show their positions on the map of space constituted by any two of these four dimensions respectively.

His empirical mapping of the world's 40 major countries on these four cultural dimensions attracted great attention from the psychology community. Inspired by this work, in the following decades many psychologists began to conduct research on related topics. Indeed, a tremendous amount of research has been done on the dimension of individualism-collectivism. For example, an intensive review by Oyserman *et al.* (2002) showed that psychologists had constructed at least 27 distinct scales for measuring individualism-collectivism (IND-COL) tendencies, and completed numerous empirical studies on related topics in the last two decades.

A positivist approach

Most researchers engaging in this topic generally considered collectivism as the opposite of individualism. They assumed that the social structure of Western societies shaped by Protestantism and the process of civic emancipation contributed to such psychological traits of individualism as individual freedom, right of choice, self-realization and so on (Triandis, 1995). In this way, countries or ethnic groups that inherited a Protestant tradition should demonstrate more individualistic characteristics than the traditional cultures of non-Western countries. Therefore, individualism is more prevalent in Western industrialized countries than in other countries, especially in contrast to the more traditional societies of developing countries. The individualistic tendencies of European Americans in the United States should be higher than other minority groups, and their tendencies for collectivism should be lower than that of other minority groups (Oyserman *et al.*, 2002).

Researchers in this field mostly followed a research orientation of positivism. They adopted the method of trait approach in personality psychology, conceptualized individualism or collectivism as a kind of psychological syndrome, and constructed various scales to measure the traits and to test their hypotheses. This approach represents research typical of Western psychology, which has been deliberately constructed on the presumption of individuality, reductionism, experiment-based empiricism, scientism, quantification/measurement, materialism, and objectivity so as to obtain homothetic laws (Marsella, 2009). Some researchers even attempted to formulate theories in support of this stance once they had accumulated a certain degree of empirical data.

However, from the perspective of post-positivism, a theory is constructed by scientists through their creative imagination for explaining observed facts (Hempel, 1966), rather than induced from data accumulated via empirical research. In order to illustrate his philosophy of evolutionary epistemology, Popper (1972) proposed the metaphor of a bucket and a searchlight to explain the difference between these two approaches: the accumulation of empirical data might be viewed as pouring water into a bucket. It is impossible for any theory to emerge from it, even if the bucket is filling up with water of empirical facts. He argued that a theory is something like a searchlight that has been constructed by a scientist with his creative imagination. Once constructed, the searchlight might cast light on the future.

When researchers attempt to induce theory from findings of empirical studies on individualism-collectivism, they may encounter many difficulties as do other positivists. For example, Triandis (1994), the first psychologist who attempted to produce such a theory, and other psychologists, conceptualized individualism and collectivism as two independent dimensions that can exist simultaneously to varying degrees within an individual in different cultural contexts. In contrast, Hofstede (1980), who adopted an ecological factor analysis method for his study at a cultural level, conceptualized individualism (IND) and collectivism (COL) as two opposite poles of one dimension.

Attributes of antithetical other

In order to emphasize the difference between the individual and cultural level, Triandis (1994) proposed a set of contrasts between idiocentrics and allocentrics as a way to indicate the concept of individualism-collectivism at the individual level. Triandis attempted to define these two sets of personality dispositions with various attributes. However, in his attempt to define these two sets of concepts at the theoretical level, several obvious weaknesses of the positivist approach were revealed.

First, when Triandis (1994) attempted to define allocentrics with a group of attributes, he often used the antithetical attributes of the idiocentrics to define the personality disposition. This method of theoretical construction, however, inevitably invites the question is this the correct way to describe behavior in so-called collectivist cultures? Put another way, is it right that psychologists studying individualism-collectivism have taken European-American psychological characteristics as a frame of reference for constructing their images of other cultural groups? European-Americans are situated at one end of the dimension, with their cultural and psychological characteristics as coordinates of reference for understanding other ethnic groups around the world. These other ethnic groups are situated at different locations along the dimension, suggesting that their cultural identities are so vague that their own psychological characteristics can be understood only if they are described in contrast to Americans.

For this reason, Fiske (2002) criticized previous individualism-collectivism researchers and indicated that individualism is the sum of cultural characteristics by which Americans define themselves, while collectivism is formalized to show characteristics of the antithetical other in accordance with the American ideological understanding that '[w]e are not that kind of person' (Fiske 2002: 84).

This trait approach represents a kind of Orientalism in psychology (Said, 1978). The traits of individualism in Western culture are simple, clear, and well known to most researchers, but the traits of non-Western cultures are complicated, ambiguous, and not well-defined to most Western educated social scientists. For example, the trait approach for developing the individualism-collectivism scale – as adopted by Triandis (1994) to describe idiocentrics and allocentrics – used behavioral sampling to select representative items with which to construct a scale. Many psychologists have suggested that this approach attempts to use a 'catch-all' way to present various forms of cultural differences (Bond, 2002; Hofstede, 1994; Hui and Yee, 1994; Kagitçibasi, 1997; Rohner, 1984; Triandis, 1994), and an examination of various scales in terms of their components does show that their contents vary substantially. If this is the case, what are the adequate attributes for representing the personality dispositions of individualism-collectivism?

For instance, Triandis' (1994) article, 'Theoretical and methodological approaches to the study of collectivism and individualism', was included in a book entitled *Individualism and collectivism: Theory, method, and applications* (Kim *et al.*, 1994). This book also contained an article by Ho and Chiu (1994) entitled 'Component ideas of individualism, collectivism and social organization: an application in the study of Chinese culture', which also used the antithetical proposition of individualism to define collectivism in Confucian society. They re-integrated eighteen components of individualism-collectivism into five categories; namely, values, autonomy/conformity, responsibility, achievement, and self-reliance–interdependence. However, a careful comparison of their attributes or components of individualism-collectivism with that listed by Triandis (1994) reveals many discrepancies between these two lists; some refer to the same domains, but nevertheless define them in different ways.

Two irrelevant constructs

Earley and Gibson (1998: 291) pointed out that there are no parallels in the content measured by individualism and collectivism, and speaking rather bluntly, with regard to the highly varied operational definitions of individualism and collectivism, regardless of their underlying constructs, deemed these scales to measure irrelevant constructs. Oyserman *et al.* (2002: 28), who carried out a content analysis of the 27 individualism-collectivism scales most widely used in cross-cultural studies, showed individualism to comprise seven components: independence, individual goal-striving, competition, uniqueness, self-privacy, self-knowledge, and direct communication; while collectivism embodies eight components: relatedness, group-belonging, duty, harmony, seeking advice from others, contextualization, hierarchy, and preference for group work. An examination of various scales in terms of these components demonstrated that their contents vary substantially. The lack of parallels between components of individualism and collectivism suggests that it is not feasible to compare them directly.

A yet to be developed approach of collectivism

An analysis by Oyserman *et al.* (2002) provided concrete evidence to indicate that early understandings of individualism and collectivism by psychologists represent two types of different behavioral categories. They indicated that there is considerable heterogeneity among conceptual definitions of collectivism and contents of scales for measuring it. The cultural difference in this respect may reflect its multifaceted nature in the way of connections between an individual and others. Following an intensive review of previous literature, they pointed out that

American and Western psychology are infused with an understanding of human nature on the basis of individualism, raising the question of our ability to separate our current way of understanding human nature based on individualism from a yet to be developed approach of collectivism.

(Oysermen *et al.*, 2002: 44–5)

After a similar review and the re-analysis of data in previous literature, Schimmack *et al.* (2005) indicated that the conceptual definition of individualism is clear, that instruments for measuring it are significant, and that it is a valid and important dimension for measuring cultural differences. However, the definitions of collectivism are ambiguous and varied, and the validity of instruments for measuring it is undetermined. Therefore, they suggested that it is necessary for cross-cultural psychologists to re-evaluate the meaning of collectivism.

In summary for this section: conducting psychological research in terms of paradigms of Western mainstream psychology, such as individualism and collectivism, may only provide us with fragmentary knowledge of empirical findings rather than any theory with which to understand a given culture in an unbiased way.

As a final support of this argument, I would like to use the example of a review of *The Oxford Handbook of Chinese Psychology*, edited by Michael Bond and published in 2010. This book, the third in a series on Chinese psychology edited by Bond, contains 41 chapters by 87 authors who had intensively reviewed previous works on a variety of topics related to Chinese psychology. In his careful review of this book, however, Lee (2011) noted that 'There is a general lack of theory in the whole handbook' and that

> very few chapters offer indigenous theories of Chinese psychology (e. g. the chapter of Hwang and Han). Most of them stay at the level of confirming/disconfirming western findings, referring to well-known cultural dimensions such as collectivism, power distance to explain the variation found, despite the openly stated effort to push for indigenous research. Moreover most of the studies cited in the book simply dichotomized their findings as Chinese vs. Western, failing to capture the much more refined complexity of the world.

(Lee, 2011: 271–2)

Bridging scientific universality and cultural specificity in psychology

Based on the learning-how-to-learn model proposed by Hughes-Weiner (1986), Bhawak (2009) suggested that if we engage in reflective observation in an intercultural setting we can learn about cultural differences, especially if the other cultural practices are drastically different from our own, and some emic aspects of the host culture often emerge. If we go beyond reflective observation and develop abstract conceptualization, we may acquire theoretical insights and develop an understanding of etics or universals and understand emics as cultural representations of those etics. This may help us realize that our own cultural practices are not universal but emic reflections of some etics. I agree with this suggestion, but it seems to me that psychologists, particularly non-Western psychologists, are obligated to construct culture-inclusive theories to bridge scientific universality and cultural specificity in psychology (Hwang, 2013).

In order to construct such a culture-inclusive theory, special attention should be paid to an important principle proposed by cultural psychologists for explaining their fundamental view of human nature: one mind, many mentalities; universalism without uniformity (Shweder *et al.*, 1998: 871). Mind means the totality of actual and potential conceptual contents of human cognitive processes, which is determined by biological factors (Shweder, 2000: 210). Mentality denotes a cognized and activated subset of mind that had been cultivated and owned by a particular individual or group so that it can be taken as the subject of research by cultural psychologists. This principle indicates that the psychological functioning or mechanisms of the human mind are the same all over the world, but that people may evolve various mentalities in different social and cultural environments.

Deep structure of mind

Some cultural psychologists advocated a similar epistemological goal for indigenous psychology. For instance, Greenfield (2000) delivered the following statement in her keynote speech at the third Conference of Asian Social Psychology in Taipei in August 1999:

> The incorporation of culture into mainstream psychology will *not* come from simply presenting data on group differences, no matter how exciting or dramatic these differences may be. My most important theoretical mission is to introduce the idea of a *deep structure of culture.* As in language, deep structure of culture generates behaviors and interpretations of human behavior in an infinite array of domains and situations. I believe that the concepts behind individualism and collectivism, independence and interdependence, a relational vs. an individual orientation and so on are all indexing a common deep structure.
>
> (Greenfield, 2000: 229)

In other words, what psychologists should do is to assume that the deep structures of the human mind, as well as its psychological functioning, do not vary across different cultural populations, but that people living in different societies may develop various mentalities in response to diverse cultural contexts (Berry *et al.*, 1992; Poortinga, 1997). The goal of universal psychology or global psychology, which can be attained, is to construct a series of formal theories that can reflect both the universal deep structure of the human mind and the specific mentalities of people in a given culture. This will allow us to understand the manifestations of people's mentality within their cultures in terms of a larger common framework.

Foundations of Chinese psychology

Recently, I published a book entitled *Foundation of Chinese psychology: Confucian social relations* (Hwang, 2012), which represents my effort in striving to attain this epistemological goal. Based on the philosophy of post-positivism, the book emphasizes that the epistemological goal of indigenous psychology is to constitute a scientific micro world by a series of theoretical models, which may represent the universal mind of all human beings as well as the specific mentalities of people in a particular culture. With such a premise, I explained how I constructed the theoretical model of *face and favor*, and used it as a framework to analyze the inner structure of Confucianism. I reviewed previous researches on Chinese moral thinking and moral judgment, and discussed the features of Confucian ethics from various perspectives. I then constructed a series of culture-inclusive theories to integrate findings of previous empirical researches on social exchange, face dynamism, achievement motivation, organizational behavior, and conflict resolution in Confucian society.

Face and favor model

From the perspective of philosophy of science, such a series of theoretical models constitute the scientific research programme of Confucian Relationalism (Lakatos, 1978), having the theoretical model of *face and favor* as its core (Hwang, 1987). In this model, the dyad involved in social interaction was defined as petitioner and resource allocator. When the resource allocator is asked to allocate a social resource to benefit the petitioner, the resource allocator will first consider: 'What is the *guanxi* (relationship) between us?'

In Figure 7.1, within the box denoting the psychological processes of the resource allocator, the shaded rectangle represents various personal ties. It is first divided into two parts by a diagonal. The shaded part stands for the affective component of relationships, while the unshaded part represents the instrumental component.

The same rectangle denoting *guanxi* (interpersonal relationships) is also divided into three parts (expressive ties, mixed ties, and instrumental ties) by a solid line and a dotted line. These parts are proportional to the expressive component. The solid line separating expressive ties within the family and mixed ties outside the family indicates a relatively impenetrable psychological boundary between family members and people outside the family. Different distributive justice or exchange rules are applicable to these two types of relationships during social interactions. In expressive ties, the need rule for social exchange should be adhered to and people should try their best to satisfy the other party with all available resources. In mixed ties, following the *renqing* rule, when individuals want to acquire a particular resource from someone with whom they have instrumental ties, they tend to follow the equity rule and use instrumental rationality.

In Chapter 4 of my book, I elaborate on the meaning of the *renqing* rule in Chinese society and argue that if it is conceptualized as a special case of

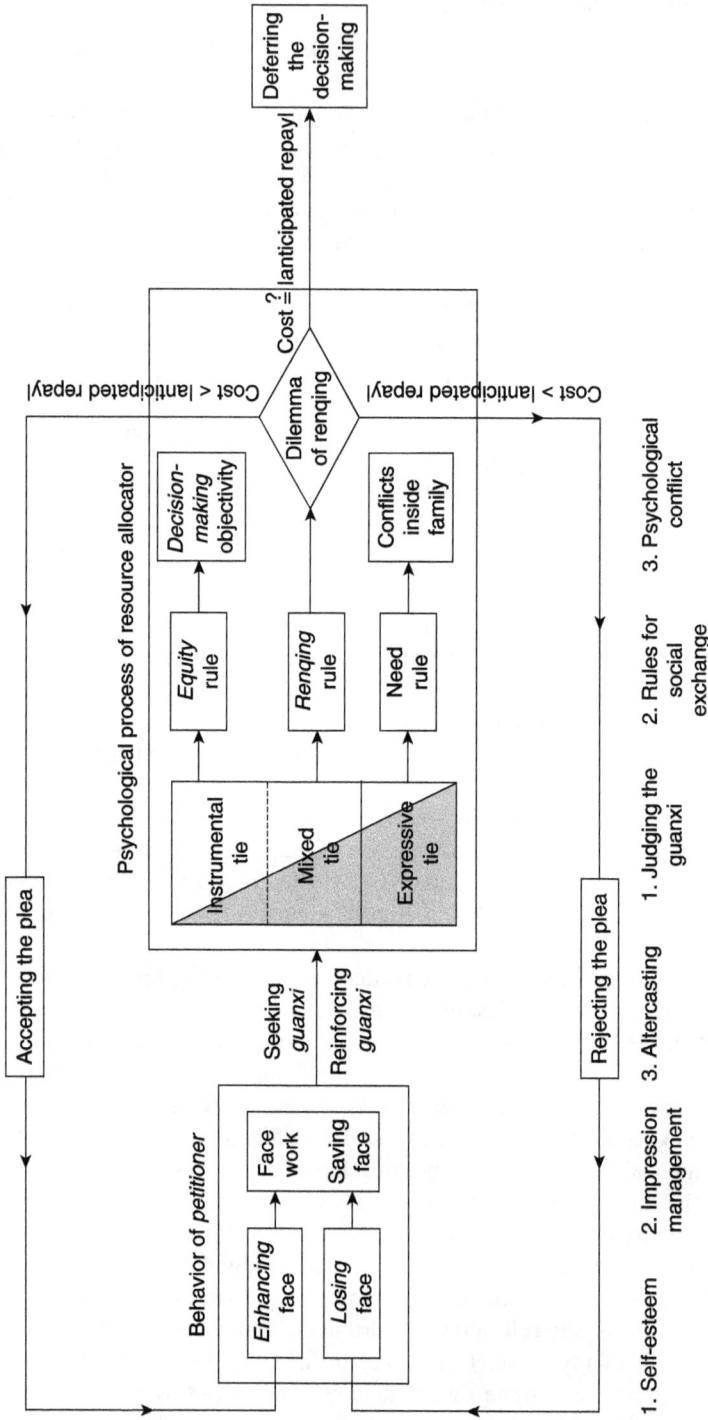

Figure 7.1 A theoretical model of face and favor in Chinese society (adapted from Hwang 1987: 948).

equality rule, which emphasizes that once an individual has received favor from another, they are obligated to reciprocate in the future, then the *face and favor model* can be viewed as a universal model. Is there any evidence to support my argument?

Elementary forms of social behavior

This question can be answered by Fiske's works on the deep structure of social relationships. In his book, *Structures of social life,* and following an intensive review of sociology, anthropology and psychology literature, Fiske (1991) proposes four relational models:

1   Communal sharing. This is a relationship of equivalence in which people are merged to achieve particular goals so that boundaries among individual selves are indistinct. They attend to membership of common identity, but not individuality. Their major concerns are superordinate goals beyond individuals, membership, and the boundary of a group (between inside and outside). The insiders of a group share a feeling of solidarity, unity, and belonging. They strongly identify with the collective and think of themselves as identical 'we' in some significant aspects, but not as individual 'I'.

2   Authority ranking. This is an unequal relationship with transitive asymmetry. If the particular hierarchy includes three or more people, people in this relationship see each other as different in social importance or status. They can be ordered in a linear ranking, which may not be transitive across other ranking systems. Their ranking is associated with the extent of oneself, and the high-ranking people control more persons, things, and resources; they are regarded as possessing more knowledge and capacity of mastery over events. People in successively higher ranks dominate greater numbers of subordinates; their authority confers certain privilege of making choice and preference. Attention paid to them is asymmetric, with authority figures more salient than subordinates. Inferiors tend to show deference and loyalty to their superiors, whereas leaders are obligated to provide protection and support to their followers.

3   Equality matching. This is an egalitarian relationship among distinct and individual peers; each of them has equal social presence including shares, contributions, and influence. The one-to-one equality matching may be manifested in turn-taking, in which everyone in the relationship takes the same action in temporal sequence. It may imply in-kind reciprocity, people exchange resources reciprocally. The meaning of 'sameness' depends on how people conceive their actions and the entities involved, rather than their objective differences. People in this relationship are supposed to be distinct and with equivalent rights, duties, and actions, so they are interchangeable. It entails matched contributions of the same kind and quantity. As distributive justice, it takes the form of even distribution in equal parts; all people receive an identical share. In case of conflict or assignation, this relationship requires

an-eye-for-an-eye retaliatory vengeance: if someone takes something out, they have to compensate in equal measure, so that the exchange relationship is balanced.

4   Market pricing. This exchange relationship is mediated by the price determined in a market system. People evaluate others' actions, services, and products according to the exchange rate for other commodities. The rates are indicated by price. Money is the most important medium in market pricing, and people can decide whether to trade with each other or not on the basis of this universal metric. They may consider potential substitutes, complements, and the temporal conditions in the market, bargain with others for self-interests, and then decide whether to buy a certain commodity or not. Ideally, any honest and capable person can participate in this exchange relationship as long as they have items for sale or they have money.

In *Structures of social life*, Fiske (1991) argues that these four relational models are fundamental for the social life of human beings. In addition to the reciprocal exchange, distributive justice, and contribution just described, he also includes the domains of work, meaning of things, orientation to land, social influence, constitution of groups, social identity and the relational self, motivation, moral judgment and ideology, moral interpretation of misfortune, aggression and conflict, etc. This implies that these structures are derived from the same set of psychological schemata, or the universal deep structure of mind.

Conclusion

Comparing Fiske's four elementary forms of social behaviors with my *face and favor model*, it can be seen that Fiske's *communal sharing, equality matching* and *market pricing* types of social behavior correspond to the three kinds of interpersonal relationships in the *face and favor model*; namely, *expressive tie, mixed tie* and *instrumental tie*. In consideration of the power distance implied in the relationship between a petitioner and resource allocator, it can be conceptualized as *authority ranking* in terms of Fiske's (1991) theory. In terms of constructive realism (Wallner, 1994), this means the terminology of the *face and favor model* can be stratified into Fiske's theory of relational models.

   From the perspective of anthropological psychology, Fiske (1991) pointed out that the four elementary forms of social behavior represent the universal mind for dealing with interpersonal relationships which can be found in every culture around the world. From this point of view, the emphasis on individualism in Western civilization has over-exaggerated the relationship of market pricing or instrumental ties, while ignoring other kinds of interpersonal relationships. This is undoubtedly a bias. From the perspective of structuralism, any theoretical model constructed on a biased presumption will inevitably suffer from crises of infinite regress. In contrast, any psychological theory that has been constructed on the presumption of universal mind will be more robust in withstanding the examination of empirical research.

Comparing my approach with that of individualism-collectivism in terms of critical realism (Bhaskar, 1975: 174), the trait approach of individualism-collectivism represents a tradition of empiricism and reductionism in the field of personality psychology without seeking the deep structures or mechanisms underlying empirical facts about social behavior. As I have argued in this chapter, the meaning of collectivism is ambiguous and yet to be fully developed. It is ontologically empty and has nothing to do with either scientific universality or cultural specificity. Researchers using this approach try to locate people from different cultures along some pan-cultural dimensions; findings might be applied in preliminary psychology education and training for *novice* or *expert* (Bhawuk, 1998). Nevertheless, from the perspective of a scientific revolution (Kuhn, 1969), such an approach is destined to be enriched or replaced by genuine culture-inclusive theories of psychology.

On the contrary, my approach highlights the importance of the culture system. My *face and favor* model (1987) represents a mechanism of interpersonal interaction which contains four elementary forms of social behavior that are supposed to be ontologically real and universal for people all over the world. When I used the *face and favor* model as a framework to analyze the inner structure of Confucianism in Chapter 5 of my book, *Foundations of Chinese psychology* (Hwang, 2012), I outlined a culture-specific theory of Confucian ethics for ordinary people. Thus my approach enables us to bridge scientific universality and cultural specificity in constructing theories that can be used either to derive hypotheses for empirical research or to advance psychology education and training for *advanced experts* (Bhawuk, 1998).

I understand that my approach seems more complex and harder to follow than the more expedient approach of cultural reductionism, such as the research paradigm of individualism and collectivism, but I feel it is a better way to construct culture-inclusive theories for theory-based intercultural training programs. I encourage indigenous psychologists of non-Western psychologists to think about it and apply it to establish their indigenous psychologies, as I have done in establishing Chinese psychology. By doing so, we may have a genuine culture-grounded global psychology in the future.

References

Anderson, J. R. (2000). *Cognitive psychology and its implications*, 5th edn. New York: Worth Publishing.

Berry, J. W., Poortinga, Y. H., Segall, M. H. and Dasen, P. R. (1992). *Cross-cultural psychology: Research and applications*. Cambridge: Cambridge University Press.

Bhaskar, R. A. (1975). *A Realist Theory of Science*. London: Verso.

Bhawuk, D. P. S. (2009). Intercultural training for the global workplace: Review, synthesis and theoretical explorations. In S. Rabi Bhagat and R. Steers (Eds.), *Handbook of culture, organization, and work*, pp.462–88. Cambridge: Cambridge University Press.

Bhawuk, D. P. S. (1995). *The role of culture theory in cross-cultural training: A comparative evaluation of culture-specific, culture general, and theory-based assimilators*. Unpublished doctoral dissertation, University of Illinois at Urbana-Champaign.

Bhawuk, D. P. S. (1998). The role of culture theory in cross-cultural training: A multimethod study of culture-specific, culture-general, and culture theory-based assimilators. *Journal of Cross-Cultural Psychology*, 29 (5), 630–55.

Bond, M. H. (2002). Reclaiming the individual from Hofstede's ecological analysis – a 20-year odyssey: Comment on Oyserman *et al.* (2002). *Psychological Bulletin*, 128, 73–7.

Bond, M. H. (2010). *The Oxford handbook of Chinese psychology*. New York, NY: Oxford University Press.

Cole, M. (1996). *Culture in mind*. Cambridge, MA: Harvard University Press.

Earley, P. C. and Gibson, C. B. (1998). Taking stock in our progress on indiviualism-collectivism: 100 years of solidarity and community. *Journal of Management*, 24, 265–304.

Fiske, A. P. (1991). *Structures of social life: The four elementary forms of human relations*. New York: The Free Press.

Fiske, A. P. (2002). Using individualism and collectivism to compare cultures – A critique of the validity and measurement of the constructs: Comment on Oyserman *et al.* (2002). *Psychological Bulletin*, 128(1), 78–88.

Greenfield, S. A. (2000). *The private life of the brain*. London: Penguin Books.

Hempel, C. (1966). *Philosophy of natural sciences*. Englewood Cliffs, NJ: Prentice-Hall.

Henrich, J., Heine, S. J. and Norenzayan, A. (2010a). The weirdest people in the world? *Behavioral and Brain Sciences*, 33(2–3), 61–83.

Henrich, J., Heine, S. J. and Norenzayan, A. (2010b). Beyond WEIRD: Towards a broad-based behavioral science. *Behavioral and Brain Sciences*, 33(2–3), 111–35.

Ho, D. Y. F. and Chiu, C. Y. (1994). Component ideas of individualism, collectivism, and social organization: An application in the study of Chinese culture. In U. Kim, H. C. Triandis, C. Kagitçibasi, S.-C. Choi and G. Yoon (Eds.), *Individualism and collectivism. Theory, method, and applications*, pp. 137–56. Thousand Oaks, CA: Sage.

Hofstede, G. (1980). *Culture consequence: International differences in work-related values*. London and Beverly Hills, CA: Sage.

Hofstede, G. (1994). *Values survey module 1994 manual*. Masstricht, The Netherlands: University of Limburg.

Hughes-Weiner, G. (1986). The 'learning how to learn' approach to cross-cultural orientation. *International Journal of Intercultural Relations*, 10, 485–505.

Hui, C. H. and Yee, C. (1994). The shortened individualism–collectivism scale: Its relationship to demographic and work-related variables. *Journal of Research in Personality*, 28, 409–24.

Hwang, K. K. (1987). Face and favor: The Chinese power game. *American Journal of Sociology*, 92(4), 944–74.

Hwang, K. K. (2012). *Foundations of Chinese psychology: Confucian social relations*. New York: Springer.

Hwang, K. K. (2013). Linking science to culture: challenge to psychologists. *Social Epistemology*, 27(1), 105–22.

Kagitçibasi, C. (1997). Individualism and collectivism. In J. W. Berry, H. Segall and C. Kagitçibasi (Eds.), *Handbook of cross-cultural psychology*, vol. 3, pp. 1–49. Needham Heights, MA: Allyn and Bacon.

Kim, U., Triandis, H. C., Kagitçibasi, C., Choi, S-C. and Yoon, G. (1994). Introduction. In U. Kim, H. C. Triandis, C. Kagitçibasi, S-C. Choi and G. Yoon (Eds.), *Individualism and collectivism. Theory, method, and applications*, pp. 1–16. Thousand Oaks, CA: Sage.

Kuhn, T. S. (1969). *The structure of scientific revolutions*. Chicago, IL: University of Chicago Press.

Lakatos, I. (1978). *Popper on Demarcation and Induction. The Methodology of Scientific Research Programmes*. Cambridge: Cambridge University Press.

Lee, Y. T. (2011). Book review (Review of the book *The Oxford Handbook of Chinese Psychology*). *International Journal of Cross Cultural Management*, 11(2), 269–72.

Marsella, A. J. (2009). Diversity in a global era: The context and consequences of differences. *Counseling Psychology Quarterly*, 22, 119–35.

Osyerman, D., Coon, H. M. and Kemmelmeier, M. (2002). Rethinking individualism and collectivism: Evaluation of theoretical assumptions and meta-analyses. *Psychological Bulletin*, 128(1), 3–72.

Poortinga, Y. H. (1997). Towards convergence. In J. W. Berry, Y. H. Poortinga, J. Pandey, P. R. Dasen, T. S. Saraswathi, M. H. Segall and C. Kagitçibasi (Eds.), *Handbook of cross-cultural psychology*, 2nd edn, vol. 1, pp. 347–87. Boston, MA: Allyn and Bacon.

Popper, K. (1972). *Objective knowledge: An evolutionary approach*. Oxford: Oxford University Press.

Rohner, R. P. (1984). Toward a conception of culture for cross-cultural psychology. *Journal of Cross-Cultural Psychology*, 15, 111–38.

Said, E. (1978). *Orientalism: Western representations of the Orient*. London: Routledge and Kegan Paul.

Schimmack, U., Oishi, S. and Diener, E. (2005). Individualism: A valid and important dimension of cultural differences. *Personality and Social Psychology Review*, 9, 17–31.

Shweder, R. A. (2000). The psychology of practice and the practice of the three psychologies. *Asian Journal of Social Psychology*, 3, 207–22.

Shweder, R. A., Goodnow, J., Hatano, G., LeVine, R., Markus, H. and Miller, P. (1998). The cultural psychology of development: One mind, many mentalities. In W. Damon (Ed.), *Handbook of child psychology: Theoretical models of human development*, vol. I, pp. 865–937. New York: Wiley.

Triandis, H. C. (1994). Theoretical and methodological approaches to the study of collectivism and individualism. In U. Kim, H. C. Triandis, C. Kagitçibasi, S.-C. Choi and G. Yoon (Eds.), *Individualism and collectivism. Theory, method, and applications*, pp. 41–51. Thousand Oaks, CA: Sage.

Triandis, H. C. (1995). *Individualism and collectivism*. Boulder, CO: Westview Press.

Wallner, F. (1994). *Constructive realism: Aspects of a new epistemological movement*. Wien: W. Braumuller.

Watson, J. B. (1913). Psychology as the behaviorist views it. *Psychological Review*, 20, 158–77.

Wundt, W. (1916). Völkerpsychologie und Entwicklungspsychologie (Ethnic psychology and developmental psychology). *Psychologische Studien*, 10, 189–238.

Wundt, W. M. (1874/1904). *Principles of physiological psychology* (E. B. Titchner, Trans.). Cambridge, MA: Harvard University Press.

8 Bridging scientific universality and cultural specificity in PET

An African voice

A. Bame Nsamenang

This chapter advocates for a psychology education and training that is more comprehensive and inclusive than its current Westernized status, but that is in tandem aptly differentiated to serve human diversity in the huge variety of cultures and ecologies of human life across the globe. A noteworthy point often not invoked but that is perhaps the kernel of universalism versus localism thinking is the differing history and experience with scientific psychology as an export community (Danziger, 2006) from the minority to the majority world (Kağitçibaşi, 1996). Psychology education and training (PET) in all cultures and contexts should strive to ensure the discipline's status and credibility as a science and profession. In fact, first and foremost psychology should be about rigorous science to understand all cultural specificities, and as far as possible, develop scientific universals from such specificities. As such, PET should entail the acquisition of knowledge and skills that enable all aspects of science generation, science dissemination and scientifically based or inspired social policies.

These are requirements for psychology as a science in its entirety, and of course PET should serve this overarching goal, albeit in the face of limitations and non-deliberate human errors that research contexts and low resource-bases tend to impose. Indeed, the fulcrum for PET curricula should be the scientific method and the position that 'all cultures can contribute scientific knowledge of universal value' (UNESCO, 1999). Such a curricular thrust would be consistent with a principle in the UN *Convention on the Rights of the Child* (UNICEF, 2003) that enshrines every child's right to a cultural identity and respect of everyone's cultural background. That is, PET must acknowledge, respect, and sensitize psychology students and researchers to the cultures of human development and livelihoods (Nsamenang, 2004, 2009) in general, and in particular the cultural embededness or specificity of every psychological precept and research participant. The search for scientific universals within cultural specificities should be driven by the canons of scientific rigor.

This chapter is organized in five parts. A critical scrutiny of issues that I consider central to the dichotomy between *scientific universality* and *cultural specificity* and why this scientific distinction persists follows this introduction. In so doing, I discursively highlight selected key issues I think stifle bridging the gulf between scientific universalism and local specificity. The third part broadly critiques the dichotomies that underlie the introduction and sustenance of psychology in non-Western societies. Next, I articulate one view of how to endeavor to bridge this scientific chasm. The defining concept of this integrative approach and holistic framework is the scientific method, which should equally become the leitmotif of PET curricula that every psychology student and researcher should master and apply with the cultural and contextual sensitivity that psychology exemplifies. In so positioning the scientific method, I seek to chart how to foster and factor inclusivity and originality into psychological theorizing and research methods, particularly in the less 'psychologized' communities of the majority world, like those of Africa. I also endeavor to illumine how the most scientifically valid research findings or psychological principles derived from one culture, and it does not matter which, may not be so valid and applicable in other cultural contexts and ecologies. Finally, part five concludes the chapter.

As a chapter in a book on education and training, my discourse is deliberately evocative and challenging. I am aware that some deep-seated shortcomings in the field are rights-based issues and theoretical and methodological narratives that impede rather than foster objective search for scientific universality in all cultural specificities.

Conceptual and theoretical issues: either scientific universality or cultural specificity?

In a nutshell and broadly, this chapter hops from critical examination of some of the key issues that stifle the development of an inclusive psychology into an attempt to instigate an integrative conceptual framework for PET that does not pit *scientific universality* against *cultural specificity*, one that positions them in a continuum of scientific endpoints with an indistinct in-between. So far, the field has narrowly focused on or highlighted only the scientific universality versus cultural specificity endpoints, thereby ignoring the obscure in-between the two concepts and the human conditions they engender and evoke. That is, the chapter represents an effort to communicate a position to bridge the dichotomy between scientific universality and cultural specificity. After all, there is a priori no scientific universalism; thus far, the posited scientific universality is crafted social reality from some cultural specificity. In addition, both scientific universality and cultural specificity potentially symbolize the human condition of all cultures and races, requiring only rigorous science to 'discover' and map out. I consider the scientific method to be the handiest universally valid tool applicable to the psychological knowledge embedded in cultural specificities. For example, what is the difference between nudity at summer beaches and that at carnivals and some ethnic rituals, or the developmental impact of such life transitions as naming or marital observances and college graduation ceremonies on the personality of their participants? Although culture has long been recognized as having a significant impact on human development and its variations (Nsamenang, 2008; Harkness and Super, 2008), many child and adolescent psychiatrists and mental health clinicians assume a universal nonvariance to normal development, with the risk of identifying variations as pathologic (Pumariega and Joshi, 2010).

Human life universally begins when the ovum and sperm fuse to form a zygote, but how this momentous biological event of human conception and its ontogenesis is interpreted and handled is intensely imbued with culturally specific significance (Nsamenang, 2011). Some cultural signification has been posited as scientifically universal. Every human newborn is a biological organism that is progressively enculturated or socialized into a 'committed' agent of a specific culture (Nsamenang, 2012). In a fundamental sense, the human being is an organic compound, a natural 'reality' to which culture begins to directly write its text or to imprint its knowledge systems and values from the moment of conception or soon thereafter. For instance, the pregnant woman's nutrition, emotional state and conformity to taboos or other *normative social influences* (Deutsch and Gerard, 1955) influences the baby's health status and this varies across cultures, depending on these and other culturally determined factors.

At any developmental point, every human being has a health status which is the outcome of the interaction of biological, ecological and culture-bound psychological, socioeconomic and spiritual influences. Their behavior or action may, wittingly or unwittingly, improve, sustain, terminate or worsen it. Inherent in this health–illness nexus are beliefs, attitudes, values, interests, emotions, strivings, and practices that derive strongly from culture. The enduring role of culture is to transform the human 'animal' into a specific psychic outlook and cultural identity; culture humanizes the human animal. The cultural 'transformation' includes socialization into a cultural theory of the universe which fleshes out the health–illness continuum. Thus the existential human, who may be healthy or ill, is a 'cultivated' or raised reality. The cultivation or construction of a healthy or ill status does not occur in a cultural void or in a universal civilization. Wholesome or tangled development takes place in an individual's developmental or living environment, defined by a physical and social setting, belief systems and customary traditions and the psychology of the individual's people (see Super and Harkness, 1986), if not that of the dominant culture. Thus health or illness behavior is a manifestation of the interplay of genotype, human biochemistry, and psychic forces contingent on the cultural meaningfulness of that behavior in a specific ecological context at a given point in time. When human action or behavior becomes meaningless within a given social or cultural context and beyond a certain culturally perceived threshold of tolerance and acceptability, abnormal health status or illness tends to be imputed.

From a global perspective, the cultural symbolism of human conception, like all other aspects of human existence, has produced differing knowledge systems, values, and behavioral patterns, which should be subject matter for scientific psychology. No matter where in our common world people live, they share certain traits or behavioral tendencies that are common or universal to human nature and that, in turn, are hued by the specific eco-cultures in which they evolve. Examples of human traits with universal but varying character include

1 using a verbal or sign language,
2 using age and gender to classify people (e.g., woman, man, minor, teenager, senior citizen),
3 classifying people on the basis of marital status or kinship ties (e.g., son, daughter, wife, mother, uncle, cousin),
4 having a system for bringing up and educating children,
5 having a gendered division of labor (e.g., children's versus adult roles, and men's work versus women's work),
6 having rules to regulate sexual behavior,
7 distinguishing between good and bad or tolerable and intolerable behavior,
8 having a concept of privacy,
9 making jokes and playing games,
10 having art and being artistic,
11 having some sort of body ornamentation,
12 having some sort of leadership roles to keep societal peace and order and for implementation of community decisions.

The foregoing examples foreshadow elasticity or divergent communality in human nature, such that determining which set of human attributes or values are normative becomes a fraught matter that scientific psychology has yet to undertake rather than claim on thin data. This is an onerous task for a PET project of inclusivity.

UNESCO (1999) has rightly pointed out that in addition to shared universal human attributes and behavioral tendencies, societies the world over, most of them like those in Africa with timeless cultural traditions, have over millennia nurtured and refined culturally specific systems of knowledge and practices, relating to such diverse fields as astronomy, meteorology, geology, ecology, botany, agriculture, physiology, psychology and health, which represent enormous human wealth. Not only do they harbor information as yet unknown to modern science but derided by it, particularly psychology; they are also expressions of other ways of living in the world, other relationships between society and nature, and other approaches to the acquisition and construction of knowledge. Wright (1984, p. xiv) has advised that 'We must begin to look for alternatives to the traditional views, not so that those views may be necessarily replaced, but so that we may come to wider, fuller understanding' of humanity. If we learn that some views are useless, we have learned important lessons.

One objective of this chapter is to introduce one way of thinking about how PET could endeavor to evolve a framework that would foster conservation and cultivation of the world's fragile and diverse heritages that are increasingly threatened by globalizing homogenization and the growing dominance of a single view of the natural world, as promoted by science (UNESCO, 1999). Pence and Nsamenang (2008) observe that the forces of homogenization that concern us are largely invisible, as the assumptions and understandings of the minority World, especially those of the US and the UK, have become the normal and natural ways to see and understand, for instance, child development, regardless of context or culture. Which is why local perspectives, activities, and practices pertaining to human psychosocial functioning, which have collectively been stigmatized cultural specificities or indigenous knowledges, are all too often considered to be deviant or deficient by comparison and, like local languages, are submerged in their wake. To question these Anglo-American best practices, understandings and governing narratives is akin to questioning 'Motherhood' – an apt analogy as 'Motherhood' with a capital M is itself one of the powerful constructs that has emerged from the West to become a lens to view, and a standard used to assess, other societies, mothers and families around the world (Pence and Nsamenang, 2008). Through such lenses, differences have become deficiencies, or in the thrust of this chapter, cultural specificities that are juxtaposed against scientific universalities.

All states of human 'being' mirror not only human biology in general and genetic potentiality in particular, but also daily routines like food habits and fads and the realities in which those states are meaningfully actualized in a given culture. They also involve concerns about an individual's future (spiritual) life. Many are those unaware that the human afterlife (Wilkinson, 1992) is longer than the physical one (MacLachlan, 2000), but scientific psychology and biomedicine trivialize or dismiss behaviors and practices relating to the afterlife. Concerns or considerations of what would happen to the individual at the termination of their existential life are universal; of which religious beliefs and practices are only part of the lived range. For example, some people are apprehensive about how their corpses and property would be handled after they die, and others leave wills that instruct or plead with loved ones who survive them not to forget them in their death (Nsamenang, 2005). Subjective life, religious behavior and transcendent experience or expectations deserve incorporation into explanatory developmental trajectories, health behavior models and healing regimens, because 'psychological science has verified the existence of the unconscious as exemplified in the phenomenon of implicit memory and blind sight' (Barlow and Durand, 1995, p. xix). Psychic forces are integral to African ethnomedical practice, particularly ethnopsychiatry. Whereas the foundational philosophy of Western biomedicine is Cartesian dualism, the seminal principle of African ethnomedicine is holism, exemplified by spiritualism that channels personal and societal factors into a *web of causation* (Brannen, 2005), including imbalances in social relationships and transgressive behavior (Hewson, 1998). Africa's ethnomedicine is people-focused and context-bound; it connects practitioner–patient–context into a therapeutic nexus, which deserves keen research and psychotherapeutic or developmental attention. By contrast, Western biomedicine and psychological thinking focuses primarily on the sovereign individual as a prime causative agent for their healthy or abnormal development!

It is in the backdrop of the foregoing that scholarly efforts to bridge the simple-minded 'realities' of scientific universality and cultural specificity run into convoluted polemics, particularly when the origins and history of 'science' are under scrutiny and in particular if we invoke continuing commodification and exchange of the 'other' to yield political stability (Haraway, 1989). Nigh (2010) has followed Barzun's (1964) logic to question chemistry, an otherwise 'objective' field of scientific study, but its theories promote equilibrium as a dynamic, ultimately stable condition where both forward and reverse reactions occur at an equal rate with no observable net change. The language and basic concepts of chemistry, like those of scientific psychology and other scientific disciplines, conveniently map onto various grids of Western hegemonic systems (Nigh, 2010). For instance, psychological science bypasses 95 percent of the world's population that lives in the majority (non-Western) world while 'American psychology' produces 'research findings that implicitly apply to the entire human population, the entire species' (Arnett, 2008, p. 602)! How would PET stop or at least curtail this state of the field?

Through the lens of scientific 'objectivity' chemistry, and more so psychology, offers a scientifically prescribed notion of a politically positive 'universal equilibrium'. In conditions where dynamic equilibrium is synonymous with stability, chemical discourse, like psychological universals, simply reinforces and thereby (self) justifies a cyclical investment in an inherently unequal 'equilibrium'. That is, PET has thus far focused on the lopsided scientificity of Western scientific psychology, which is the psychology of affluent, educated, largely white European and American middle-classes (Lamb, 1992). Furthermore, social institutions that benevolently advance psychology education and knowledge production juxtapose the disembodied scientific rhetoric of chemical reaction with the embodiment and objectification of politically advantageous categories of people (Nigh, 2010). As such, the frameworks of chemistry and psychology are among the systems that purport the concept of 'universal equal' – universal value – and thus respond directly to a social hierarchy built to maintain and reinforce particular notions of universality as juxtaposed against particular types of cultural specificity. That is, chemical jargon, like psychological lingo, operates in ways that are consistent with the construction of scientific authority that maintains structures of domination and oppression. In this sense, science (from Latin *scientia*, meaning 'knowledge'), especially the science of psychology, that should be a systematic enterprise that builds and organizes knowledge in the form of testable explanations and predictions about human behavior in all parts of the universe (Heilbron, 2003), has instead become an asymmetrical focus of research attention on the behavior of one portion of Western humans for comparison with the rest of humanity. PET should pay serious attention to transcending this point in an era when skeptics suspect the value of the so-called 'reliable knowledge' about almost every sphere of human life.

Is there any fundamental difference in research orientation in Western and non-Western societies?

Psychological research in non-Western contexts

A reality of the discipline that continues to sustain universalism versus specificity thinking is the fact that scientific psychology in general and programmatic psychological research in particular is an export commodity (Danziger, 2006) out of the West into Africa and other majority world contexts. It first arrived in service-based applied fields of education, health care, social work, etc. and later as cross-cultural psychology (Nsamenang, 2000). For Ho and Wu (2001), cross-cultural psychology is the scientific study of human behavior and mental process, including both their variability and invariance, under diverse cultural conditions. Aligned to its import value, a key scientific focus of cross-cultural research has from the outset included a search for universals in behavior and mental processes; a search that has mostly focused on gauging whether and how Western behavioral scripts or developmentally appropriate norms exist in non-Western cultures. The search has seldom been the reverse, implying that the scientific search for behavioral universals and the ways in which behaviors are shaped and influenced by social and cultural forces (Berry *et al.*, 1992) has rarely been undertaken with non-Western lenses. One expectation is that PET programmes would contain strategies and resources to systematically chart non-Western lenses and to incorporate non-Western voices and visions.

Another set of dichotomous perspectives – *emic* and *etic* approaches – heighten scientific universalism versus cultural or local specificity and were first introduced into social science and behavioural research by anthropologists to distinguish two sources of data about human conditions or behaviors (Headland *et al.*, 1990; Jahoda, 1977). An emic account in cross-cultural research is a description of behavior or a belief in terms meaningful (consciously or unconsciously) to the 'native' actor; that is, an emic account comes from a person indigenous to or 'native' to the culture. Whereas an emic perspective is an indigenous account, an etic report is an outsider's account in terms that have impulsively or tacitly been assumed to be more scientific and accurate than an emic one. That is, an etic perspective has been claimed to be 'culturally neutral'. As such, some writers use 'etic' to refer to objective accounts and 'emic' to refer to opinionated or subjective views, respectively, interpreted as accurate versus inaccurate accounts. Curiously, even a cursory review of the extant literature would reveal that those who have provided the printed perspectives in both mainstream and cross-cultural psychology are Western scholars whose accounts across noticeable global diversity have instinctually been taken to be normative. Thus, a critique of the emic–etic research lens reveals cross-cultural psychology as a lopsided, Westernized discipline. However, it is hardly ever voiced that the Western psychological databases that have supplied scientific universality or the referential benchmarks for determining which cultural specificity becomes psychological knowledge are devoid of etic accounts; they have been accumulated exclusively by Western scholars and researchers. As such, the psychological literature exemplifies emic Western perspectives that have been used to compare the rest of humanity and contains negligible critical or etic perspectives from non-Western scholars.

In the throes of the foregoing, a muted but derisive theory in emic–etic psychological research is that owners of non-Western cultures are incapable of objectively studying their own behaviors or psychological phenomena. This outlandish position suggests that non-Western psychologists or researchers are incapable of applying the scientific method in their contexts. PET should desist from such derision and set out to train psychologists and psychological researchers everywhere in resourceful and skilled application of the scientific method, the hallmark of science.

PET as one approach to bridge scientific universality and cultural specificity

The discussion so far may be summarized as the view that scientific universality and cultural specificity derive substantially from ideologies and cognitive systems about positing knowledge and truth claims. In brief, this rift can be attributed to ethnocentric intellectualism that has fixatedly been numb to human variety. The gap exists because human knowledge has been dichotomized, as Enlightenment intellectualism evolved and is being perpetuated in unreserved disregard and scorn of pre- and coexisting systems. In scientific psychology, it is now glorified in linguistic, epistemic and other superiority hegemonies. The *universality* of *science* in its broadest sense should be about developing a truly global *scientific* psychology community on the basis of scientific fairness, equity, non-partiality, and much more. This condition requires PET to develop a framework that equips psychology students of all cultures and countries with the requisite knowledge and skills to handle and practice psychology as a science and profession and in doing so to evolve community-sensitive outreach products and services. This is a tall order but not an impossible goal!

There is, therefore, a need to endeavor in PET to evolve mindsets and conceptual systems that can forge close linkages between scientific knowledge and older coexistent knowledge, as this is expected to bring important advantages to and unify both forms of human knowledge. It seems to have been forgotten that indigenous or local knowledge and cultural specificities are ubiquitous universals. Scientific psychology in essence, as the study of human behavior and mental processes, requiring integrative conceptual systems, stands to enhance the unity of universal knowledge trends and the insistent specificities of local knowledge, which is all about human nature and human psychological functioning. Cartesian and holistic conceptual systems about this knowledge coexist and underpin polemics of universalism and localism or the so-called globalization and localization of psychological realities across the globe. Whereas Western psychological reality anchors on Cartesian thinking and sovereign individualism, a holistic and non-Cartesian African cosmology, for example, interconnects the sacred and the secular worlds, blending them into a conceptually inseparable complexus. The integrative concepts of biological embedding (Hertzman, 1999), contextual interactionism (Nsamenang, 2012) and bisociation (Koestler, 1976) reinforce this bridging theoretical stance. The five theoretic strands (see Nsamenang, 2012) that can frame and guide integrative bridging of universalism versus specificism thinking are briefly sketched below.

* *Biological embedding*: children do not live and develop in a universal civilization; they develop in a specific place. Human development is context-sensitive and culture-bound.

- *Contextual interactionism*: children do not merely exist, they are active agents who are responsive, interactive and curious about their own developmental experiences and learning in the contexts in which they find themselves. Even very young children generate their own actions and thoughts.
- *Ontogenetic holism*: every child has their own developmental story that can be framed within an African holistic theory of the universe. The sum total of all science-based disciplinary evidences brought together cannot represent or capture the child as a unique, context-bound entity. The foundations of human development are laid in the family long before a child is born, so the pre-birth period and environment is crucial.
- *Biosociation*: there are a huge variety of scientific and lay views on the best interests of children, as well as the dichotomous positioning on developmental influences. Biosociation can integrate all the perspectives. Why and how is the same child 'seen' in their situation differently? The conflict is not with the 'embedded' child but with the different 'lenses' with which scientists, laypersons or universalist and localist scholars 'see' and analyze the 'embedded' child.
- *Developmental learning*: children everywhere are curious actors and learners from conception. They learn in the processes of development and much of their useful and developmentally impactful learning is self-generated and peer-based, i.e., much of it occurs in peer groups. Thus far, psychology has focused only on a narrow range of such developmental learning, rooted in the history of experiments on animal learning.

A central strand of majority world theories of the universe is holistic and theocentric in nature, exemplified by the African, which reveal 'the interplay of social, religious, and political roles, working together to ensure the well-being of the people' (Bongmba, 2001, p. 7). The field has regrettably been overwhelmed by bifurcated or dichotomous mindsets – Cartesian versus holistic thinking. For instance, discourse on health and illness behavior which reflects thinking in mainsteam psychology, tends to invoke the body–mind dualism or the assumption that the 'mind' and the 'body' are two separate entities. Such thinking ignores the contextual situativity of the human being and psychological phenomena, that is, the psychosocial individual is nested within multiple layers of a developmental context, characterized by factors that summarize into differing life circumstances and levels of quality of life. The ecological systems theory (e.g., Bronfenbrenner, 1979; Vygotsky, 1978) informs us that the state of the human mind and the state of the body reflect each other (Asuni, Schoenberg, and Swift, 1994), but what does this portend for psychology in a cultural context?

   That all cultures can contribute scientific knowledge of universal value is a scientific position yet to be fully accepted and acted on in the psychological community. That psychological functioning is a universal feature of humanity is also yet to be meaningfully factored into PET programs, research agendas and policy development. The acceptance of and education into these two realities of human nature would rouse integrative or inclusivity thinking in the philosophical foundations, conceptual systems and theoretical and methodological frameworks on which to anchor scientific psychology. The challenge is for PET to transcend psychology's narrow base with the objective of evolving a science of psychology for humanity in its huge diversity. As such, the emphasis in PET ought to shift from excessive focus on psychology's Eurocentric roots and flourishing American research enterprise to the acquisition of scientific and technological knowledge and skills that would be required to participate meaningfully and competently in generating psychological knowledge and products of the future. However, attention only to the rapid advances in scientific and technological knowledge per se cannot alone ensure coping with the enormous variation in the human condition, nor would it adequately address the changing needs of populations at various levels. In order to gain from both knowledge systems, PET must complement the established formal education with non-formal or indigenous channels (UNESCO, 1999). PET should have the scientific method and sensitivity to the ecological and cultural context as the centerpiece of its curriculum and practice of psychology.

PET should use the current state of Euro-American scientific psychology not as the last word in psychological theorizing and methodological rigor but as an entrée route into other psychologies. In so doing, it should simultaneously and gradually introduce local epistemes, theoretical and methodological ideas and policy strategies to outgrow and extend it into a science of human beings that is at once global and at the same time nuanced to the species in context. Developers, implementers and students within every PET program must work from the reminder that the movement for indigenous psychologies 'arose as a reaction to the mainstream version of psychology' that did not and still largely does not 'reflect the social, political, and cultural character of peoples around the world' (Allwood and Berry, 2006, p. 243). In this direction, fair, inclusive science of psychology obliges us to craft PET and strategize for resources to permit innovative theorizing, development of contextualized epistemes, and creative context-responsive methodologies that permit contributions from across the globe to extend and enrich the frontiers of the discipline. Thus, contributions of non-Western precepts such as social ontogeny (Nsamenang, 1992), a developmental theory that differs from the individualistic accounts by Freud, Erikson and Piaget (Serpell, 1994) and child-to-child sociability (Pence and Nsamenang, 2008) could introduce alternative thinking and action into the field.

Psychology students must learn and act from the ethical position that cultural identity is a right of every human being which their research should not ridicule or undermine. They should also be taught that psychological knowledge exists in all cultural contexts and that rigorous application of the scientific method by any well-trained but context-sensitive scholar can objectively outsource it. PET may use grand narratives for didactic purposes but prime theory development within mindsets of the nonexistence of 'an absolute mind, not subject to the environmental setting in which it lives . . . the existence of a mind absolutely independent of the conditions of life is unthinkable' (Boas, 1911, p. 133). Contextual thinking would enable students to learn and act from the premise that the 'content of thought, in its concreteness, [reflects] environmental factors' (Weisz, 1978, p. 1). Furthermore, they must become resourceful by learning that 'when professional social researchers set out to investigate the human situation, a way of thinking about and describing their work travels with them' (Agar, 1986, p. 11). Not only do they discover that most of their familiar concepts, taxonomic labels, and conceptual systems have become partly inapplicable, they equally find it difficult, sometimes impossible, to employ the technology they know so well to make sense of phenomena they encounter in unfamiliar contexts (Nsamenang, 1992). The treacherous nature or pecularity of contextual variables may prevent replication or application of the findings of an otherwise excellent study carried out in a different context.

PET should ascertain that all human beings have the right to participate in scientific psychology. Equity in entering and pursuing a career in science is one of the social and ethical requirements of human development; there should be no discrimination in science against any sector or individual (UNESCO, 1999). The increasing participation or involvement of all regions of the world and sectors of society in the scientific enterprise entails a systemic revision of science; it is clear that the gate-keeping and normative mechanisms of psychology would inevitably change. In particular, any kind of central monitoring or gate-keeping in psychological science, whether political, ethico-scientific or economic, needs to sensitively and respectfully take into account the increasingly diverse actors entering into the community of psychological science. Who determines what 'is' and 'is not' psychological knowledge is a fraught matter.

Two inventive frameworks – a discovery disposition and a learning posture (Agar, 1996) – to the application of the scientific method are the fairest approach to access and outsource the psychological knowledge of all cultures. In other words, the handiest tool for psychological research is the scientific method that PET should ensure is mastered and applied by psychology students worldwide. Of course, science is not a body of any specific knowledge per se, but the orderly and systematic process of applying the scientific method to data sources, no matter how diverse. The challenge is for PET to provide for how the scientific method would be rigorously applied to access hitherto underrepresented sources of psychological knowledge across the globe. Another fraught matter is the interpretation of research findings from cultural specificity vis-à-vis the databases from which *scientific universality* has been constructed. In so doing, it must be realized that the processes underlying present global problems and challenges need the concurrence of all scientific disciplines. As such, it is imperative to figure out how to attain a proper balance in their support: hence the need to break traditional barriers between the natural and the social sciences and to adopt interdisciplinarity as an integrative strategy.

In the majority world, research resources and infrastructure are conspicuous by their dearth. There is much the minority world and the International Union of Psychological Science (IUPsyS) can do to support the majority world in its quest to develop the science of psychology, for funds and influence reside in the West in disproportionate quantities (Pence and Nsamenang, 2008). However, those powers and funds should not be used to 'show the way' (the legacy of social Darwinism, colonization), but to support the majority world's efforts to study its own psychology and to seek its own way forward into scientific psychology. It will find that way through psychologists who understand and appreciate multiple worlds, through young scholars who frame their own contextually sensitive research questions, and through leaders who are not intimidated by scientific universality but are courageous and proficient to research their cultural specificities and disseminate findings into psychology's databases. PET must develop the science and profession of psychology to serve humanity everywhere.

Conclusion

The intention of this chapter is to prompt not only inclusive ways of thinking about psychosocial functioning but more so to instigate integrative, generative research that can be undertaken from a rigorous learning posture (Agar, 1986) within an interdisciplinary framework. PET should transcend the seemingly out-dated but deeply entrenched conventional scientific ethos of a single discipline that has so far failed to speak to a vibrant multicultural world in need of investigative discovery. Accordingly, PET curricula must incorporate how to extend and enrich the governing narratives to suitably apply to all of humanity, including immigrant populations in considerable difficulty across the globe. PET must act within the framework that sociocultural environments are not static either in the minority or majority worlds and, therefore, must be treated dynamically in psychological research (Greenfield, 2009).

Modern science does not construct the only form of knowledge. However, as a more privileged form it must forge mutual links with other forms of knowledge, either to benefit from them or to enhance them. Nevertheless, scientific psychology is expected to fulfill its intrinsic mission, which is the generation of human knowledge and understanding that benefits from the creativity of scientists around the world. The main challenge for PET is to equip psychology students with this vision. In doing so, cognizance that the majority world, especially Africa, has not received the commensurate psychological research attention the minority world has received and continues to obtain is needed. If science must be at the service of humanity as a whole, then psychology must contribute to improving the quality of life for every member of present and future generations.

References

Agar, M.H. (1986). *Speaking of Ethnography*. Newbury Park, CA: Sage.

Allwood, C.M. and Berry, J.W. (2006). Origins and development of indigenous psychologies: an international analysis. *International Journal of Psychology*, 41, 243–68.

Arnett, J.J. (2008). The neglected 95%: Why American psychology needs to become less American. *American Psychologist, 63 (7)*, 602–14.

Asuni, T., Schoenberg, F.S. and Swift, C. (1994). *Mental Health and Disease in Africa*. Ibadan, Nigeria: Spectrum Books Ltd.

Barlow, D.H. and Durand, V.M. (1995). *Abnormal Psychology: An Integrative Approach.* Pacific Grove, CA: Books/Cole.

Berry, J.W., Poortinga, Y.H., Segall, M.H. and Dasen, P.R. (1992). *Cross-cultural Psychology: Research and Applications.* Cambridge: Cambridge University Press.

Brannen, G.E. (2005). *Tikari Traditions of Cameroon Grassfields: Explanatory Models of Illness.* Bamenda, Cameroon: Anoh's Printing Service.

Barzun, J. (1964). *Science: The Glorious Entertainment.* New York: Harper and Row.

Boas, F. (1911). *The Mind of the Primitive Man.* New York: Macmillan.

Bongmba, E.K. (2001). *African Witchcraft and Otherness: A Philosophical and Theological Critique of Intersubjective Relations.* New York: New York University Press.

Bronfenbrenner, U. (1979). *The Ecology of Human Development.* Cambridge: Cambridge University Press.

Danziger, K. (2006). Comment: Special issue on indigenous psychologies. *International Journal of Psychology,* 41 (4), 259–75.

Deutsch, M. and Gerard, H.B. (1955). A study of normative and international social influences on individual judgment. *Journal of Abnormal and Social Psychology,* 51, 629–36.

Greenfield, P.M. (2009). Linking social change and developmental change: shifting pathways of human development. *Developmental Psychology,* 45, 401–18.

Haraway, D.J. (1988). Situated knowledges: The science question in feminism and the privilege of partial perspective. *Feminist Studies* 14 (3), 575–99.

Harkness, S. and Super, C.M. (2008). Globalization and its discontents: challenges to developmental theory and practice in Africa. *International Journal of Psychology,* 43(2), 107–13.

Headland, T., Pike, K.L and Harris, M. (eds). (1990). *Emics and Etics: The Insider/Outsider Debate. Frontiers of Anthropology,* vol. 7. London: Sage.

Heilbron, J.L. (Editor-in-chief) (2003) *The Oxford Companion to the History of Modern Science* New York: Oxford University Press.

Hertzman, C. (1999). The biological embedding of early experience and its effects on health in adulthood. *Annals of New York Academy of Sciences,* 896, 85–95.

Hewson, M.G. (1998). Traditional healers in Southern Africa. *Annals of Internal Medicine,* 15, 1029–34.

Ho, D.Y.F. and Wu, M. (2001). Introduction to cross-cultural psychology. In L.L. Adler and U.P. Gielen (eds), *Cross-cultural Topics in Psychology,* pp. 3–13. Westport, CT: Praeger.

Jahoda, G. (1977). In pursuit of the emic-etic distinction: can we ever capture it? In Y.H. Poortinga (ed.), *Basic Problems in Cross-Cultural Psychology,* pp. 55–63. Amsterdam: Swets & Zeitlinger.

MacLachlan, M. (2000). Cultivating pluralism in health psychology. *Journal of Health Psychology,* 5 (3), 373–82.

Nsamenang, A. B. (1992). *Human Development in Cultural Context: A Third World Perspective.* Newbury Park, CA: Sage.

Nsamenang, A.B. (2000). Critical psychology: a Sub-Saharan African voice from Cameroon. In Tod Sloan (Ed.), *Voices for Critical Psychology,* pp. 91–102. London: Macmillan.

Nsamenang, A.B. (2004) *Cultures of Human Development and Education: challenges to growing up African.* New York: Nova.

Nsamenang, A.B. (2005). Educational development and knowledge flow: local and global forces in human development in Africa. *Higher Education Policy,* 18, 275–88.

Nsamenang, A.B. (2008) Culture and human development. *International Journal of Psychology*, 43(2), 73–7.

Nsamenang, A.B. (2009). Conceptualizing developmental assessment within Africa's cultural settings. In E.L.Grigorenko (Ed.), *Multicultural Psychoeducational Assessment*, pp. 95–131. New York: Springer.

Nsamenang, A.B. (2011). L'émigration clandestine des jeunes camerounais en Europe (Illegal youth emigration into Europe from Cameroon). In C. Bolzman, T.-O. Gakuba and I. Guissé (Eds), *Migrations des jeunes d'Afrique subsaharienne: Quels defis pour l'avenir?* (Migration of Sub-Sharan African Youth: What future consequences?), pp. 139–61. Paris: L'Harmattan.

Nsamenang, A.B. (2012). On researching the agency of Africa's young citizens: challenges and prospects for identity development. In D.S. Slaughter-Defoe (Ed.), *Racial Stereotyping and Child Development*, pp. 90–104. Basel: Karger.

Nigh, A. (2010). Universal equilibrium: sociopolitical aspects of the rhetoric of chemistry. *Feminism, Science & Values*, June 25–28. Available at http://ir.lib.uwo.ca/iaph/June25/Presentations/20/, accessed 23 May 2012.

Pence, A.R. and Nsamenang, A.B. (2008). *Respecting Diversity in an Age of Globalization: A Case for ECD in Sub-Saharan Africa.* The Hague: BvLF.

Pumariega, A.J. and Joshi, S.V. (2010). Culture and development. *Child and Adolescent Psychiatric Clinics of North America*, 19(4), 661–80.

Serpell, R. (1994). An African social ontogeny: Review of A. Bame Nsamenang (1992): *Human development in cultural context. Cross-Cultural Psychology Bulletin*, 28(1), 17–21.

Super, C.M. and Harkness, S. (1986). The developmental niche: A conceptualization at the interface of child and culture. *International Journal of Behavioral Development*, 9, 545–69.

UNESCO. (1999). *UNESCO World Conference on Science Declaration on Science and the Use of Scientific Knowledge.* Retrieved on 4/24/2003, from www.unesco.org

UNICEF. (2003). *Convention on the Rights of the Child.* Available from www.unicef.org/crc/crc.htm.

Vygotsky, L. (1978). *Mind in Society: The Development of Higher Psychological Processes.* Cambridge: Cambridge University Press.

Weisz, J. R. (1978). Transcontextual validity in development research. *Child Development*, 49, 1–12.

Wilkinson, R. (1992) Income distribution and life expectancy. *British Medical Journal*, 304, 165–68.

Wright, R.A. (1984). Preface. In R.A. Wright (Ed.). *African Philosophy*. Lanham, MD: University Press of America.

Commentary on 'Bridging scientific universality and cultural specificity in PET'

Pascal Huguet

One important lesson from the three chapters written by Barbarin, Hwang, and Nsamenang is that Psychology Education and Training (PET) should pay special attention to cultural diversity. As noted by Barbarin in his wonderful presentation of PET in the United States of America, our American colleagues are motivated by a desire to lead psychology beyond a position of ethnocentrism and monoculturalism to a recognition and appreciation of the diversity of social and cultural groups that make up the population. The specific guidelines that were shaped in the past two decades on multicultural education, training, research, practice, organizational change and policy development indeed represent a significant step forward towards greater intercultural sensitivity and respect for diversity. For example, psychologists are now explicitly encouraged to recognize that, as cultural beings, they may hold attitudes and beliefs that can detrimentally influence their perceptions of and interactions with individuals from other cultures. This principle, and others in the same vein, should indeed be encouraged.

However, as clearly pointed out by Hwang and Nsamenang, the recognition of cultural diversity in the context of mainstream psychology does not guarantee to go beyond ethnocentrism and monoculturalism. This is a major point. Hwang illustrates this point with reference to Western paradigms, like individualism and collectivism, which from his point of view attempt to understand non-Western cultures from the perspective of West-centrism. Likewise, according to Nsamenang, special efforts should be made to develop a framework that would foster the conservation and cultivation of the world's fragile and diverse heritages, which are increasingly threatened by the growing dominance of a single view.

Both Hwang and Nsamenang lead to the general idea that the dominant viewpoint (Western psychology) is limited in scope without being conscious of its own limitations, so that the science could be correct (within its framework) and yet not be true because it has failed to really take into account larger contexts, such as human behavior in its global diversity. It is perfectly true that PET has thus far focused on Western scientific psychology, which is the psychology of affluent, educated, largely white European and American middle-classes. An a priori requirement for PET is, therefore, to cultivate the notion that all cultures can contribute to scientific knowledge of universal value; in Hwang's own words: 'One mind, many mentalities, universalism without uniformity'; a basic principle according to many cultural psychologists.

With this principle in mind, Hwang suggests that the goal of universal psychology or global psychology is to construct a series of formal theories that can reflect both the universal, deep structure of the human mind and the specific mentalities of people in a given culture. It follows in both chapters – Hwang and Nsamenang – that a psychology of cultural diversity is needed, which ensures that the role of the cultural context is addressed properly, that is, *not simply by using Western psychology as a frame of reference*, and across many (if not all) areas of psychological inquiry. Thus, not only should individuals be viewed as products of different environments, but also individual functioning should be understood within the context of particular cultural traditions and norms. This is an important message, and I completely agree with Hwang and Nsamenang that it should be developed in PET. This is a fascinating challenge for IUPSyS, which has already promoted multiple initiatives toward considering cultural diversity.

At least two points can be made here, however. First of all, the notion of 'diversity' should not be restricted to that of 'cultural diversity'. Diversity is a fundamental principle of living, a golden rule of biological organisms across cultures. There is nothing more universal than diversity, another reason – perhaps the most fundamental – not to consider *cultural* diversity as an obstacle to scientific universality. We all agree that everywhere on the planet, humans create emergent organizations beyond the individual – structures that range from dyads, families, and groups to cities and civilizations, whose own values and norms evolve continuously over time and space. Diversity, however, also exists at much lower levels, both within and between populations, from the physicochemical and genetic level to the neurophysiological and behavioral levels. The observation of biological differences within and between populations does not call into question the legitimacy of the biological sciences. On the contrary, these differences are useful and even essential to our understanding of universal biological phenomena. Likewise, the observation of cultural differences should not be used to call into question the legitimacy of the psychological sciences. *Cultural* diversity is not 'something special' that should be taken into account to adjust the use and application of the supposedly 'universal knowledge'. It should be considered as an integral part of that knowledge, a view that is actually essential to the development of psychology education and training (as also noted in the three chapters).

Second, although I agree with Hwang and Nsamenang on many points, I also believe that their chapters may sometimes give the impression that cultural forces make a major difference for everything, whatever the 'object of study'. However, the importance attached to the issue of cultural diversity depends heavily on the type of behavior we are talking about. Whereas this issue may be insignificant for our understanding of, let's say, some basic properties of the visual or auditory systems and related psychophysical phenomena, its importance increases dramatically regarding our understanding of people's mentalities and conducts, and the efficacy of our psychological interventions. Put differently, whereas psychological knowledge about elementary phenomena may be valid across cultures, its external validity regarding more integrated behaviors such as social conducts may be reduced. This does not necessarily mean that cultural differences prevent any generalization about psychological knowledge of social behavior.

Let me take simple examples: the most elementary social influences in humans and other social animals concern the effects, positive and negative, caused by the simple physical presence of a conspecific. After more than a century of research, there is good reason to believe that these effects are valid across cultures. Likewise, in most cultures people engage in basic social categorization processes resulting in many psychological simplifications of their social world, with various consequences at the cognitive (assimilative and contrastive biases), affective and behavioral levels (in-group favoritism, social stereotypes, discrimination of out-group members). The content of the social categories involved may radically change from one culture to another, but the social categorization processes per se are universal.

There is something surprising in not making these basic distinctions in a debate on the universality of psychological knowledge. These distinctions are vital in clarifying the debate over cultural diversity and universality of psychological knowledge, and also to make practice, education, and training more efficient.

Part VI

Balancing basic and applied research with national needs in PET

9 Optimizing the relationship between basic and applied research for psychology education and training

Lawrence Aber

Introduction

There is a serious disjunction between many large-scale 'social' (sociocultural, political–economic and environmental) phenomena that affect human psychological well-being (e.g. wars, human migration, social inequality, economic shocks, national disasters, epidemics) and the psychology education and training (PET) that universities and other such institutions currently provide. This disjunction raises questions about the kind of curricula and experiences that university training could and should provide in order to close this disjunction. What kind of PET should universities provide in the early twenty-first century in specific countries and across countries and regions of the globe? In order to answer (and ultimately reframe) these questions, I argue that PET needs to be adapted to (a) optimize the relationships between basic and applied science, and (b) improve the power and utility of psychological science to understand and address the large-scale social phenomena that affect psychological development and well-being both within and across countries.

Psychological science in a period of rapid change

The last several decades have witnessed very rapid development of psychology as a basic science. Some domains of inquiry, for instance brain- and neuroscience, pursue psychology as a natural science. Technological advances in, for instance, brain imaging and in genotyping, have led to greater depth and increasing precision of our knowledge in psychology. But because such technical advances remain quite expensive, this depth and precision may be accompanied by a growing inequality across countries of the world in their contributions to basic psychological science (Arnett, 2008).

Other domains of inquiry – for instance social, developmental, organizational, clinical, counseling and educational psychology – pursue psychology more as a social-behavioral science. These domains are developing increasingly deep and precise knowledge of the etiology of a broad range of psychological problems (e.g. prejudice/discrimination, aggression/conduct disorder, depression, anxiety, learning disorders, academic underachievement, and a myriad of problems in self-regulation, from eating disorders to substance abuse). But because research on the etiology and epidemiology of psychological problems is also expensive, there are considerable inequalities across countries/regions of the world in psychology as a basic social and behavioral science. And of course, there are many domains of inquiry which draw heavily on psychology as both a natural and a social science, like studies of the complex interplay of biology and experience in human psychological development and functioning.

The last several decades have also witnessed the very rapid evolution of psychology as an applied science. Both the natural science and the social science approaches to psychology have influenced psychology as an applied science. Psychology as an applied science has relied heavily on the role of experimentation in identifying, testing and scaling psychological interventions. Most 'clinical'-type interventions target individuals as the 'unit of change' and thus the 'unit of analysis', but increasingly, larger groups of individuals and their 'settings' (e.g. classrooms, schools, peer groups, etc.) are the targets of change and analysis (Boruch *et al.*, 2004; Tseng and Seidman, 2007). Examples include efforts to prevent aggression, conduct disorder and other problems via social-emotional learning interventions in schools (e.g. Aber *et al.*, 2011; Durlak *et al.*, 2011; Weare, 2010; Sherman, 2011); improve early child development both in the U.S. (Love *et al.*, 2005; Olds *et al.*, 2007) and in low- and middle-income countries throughout the world (Alderman, 2011; Engle *et al.*, 2011). While large-scale intervention trials are also very expensive (like brain imaging and genotyping technologies), they appear to be a bit more evenly dispersed both within and across countries, probably because many national governments and international organizations (e.g. the World Bank, WHO, etc.) have keen interest in learning more about effective interventions in low-income countries (and low-income regions of middle- and high-income countries).

As rapidly as psychology is evolving as both a basic and applied science, the world is evolving even faster. The world population recently reached seven billion people: about a billion in high-income countries like the U.S. and most E.U. countries; but nearly five billion in middle-income countries and the 'bottom billion' in low-income countries (Population Reference Bureau, 2012). While there has always been great diversity in human and social experiences across the world, the global North and West never fully confronted this reality. That has changed due to a growing sense of global interdependence. Most high-income countries have experienced the 'demographic transition' in which children are being born at or below 'replacement rate' (2.0 children per woman of childbearing age). But some countries, especially in sub-Saharan Africa and South Asia, are and will continue to experience a dramatic 'youth bulge' for the next 20–40 years (Doyle and Prewitt, 2012). So the majority of rich countries are aging and the majority of very poor countries are youth-bulging. Thus, low-income countries will contribute disproportionately to global population growth at least through 2050 when the world's population is expected to exceed nine billion (United States Census Bureau, 2012; United Nations Population Fund, 2012). These and other demographic dynamics have very significant impact on variation in the nature of and influences on psychological development and well-being across the countries of the world. In addition to great diversity in population dynamics and national wealth, the countries of the world vary greatly in other dimensions of social, cultural and political development and rights and in public policies (Heymann, 2013).

In short, we all live in a world of rapid changes and increasing diversity that influence many dimensions of psychological development and well-being. What are the implications of such changes and diversity for PET? As I will argue below, I believe that we need to understand variation in large-scale social dimensions of human life and in their associations with psychological development and well-being across *time* and *space* (via social demography and epidemiology).

Finally, in addition to the rapid changes in psychological science and in the world population, there are changes occurring in the organizational, institutional and funding systems that enable and support psychological science and the use of psychological science to address problems of human well-being. Important trends include: increases in the number of democracies in the world, changes in the proportion of gross national income (GNI) that countries invest in the health, education and social sectors; the articulation and enforcement of 'universal rights' like those in the International Convention on the Rights of the Child; public, measurable commitments from most countries in the world to address the most important problems of human development (e.g. the Millennium Development Goals); and changes in public policies that are associated with changes in psychological development and well-being (although often in complex and sometimes in counter-intuitive ways).

It is against this background of rapid evolution and change in psychological science, in world populations and in the organizational/institutional/funding systems that support psychological science and psychological well-being that we must reconsider the nature and course of PET for the twenty-first century. In the remainder of this chapter, I'll make two more arguments about the implications of these changes for how to think about university-based PET.

1   Psychology is both a basic and an applied science, both a natural and a social science. Rather than fall prey to one form of subdisciplinary hegemony or another, rather than view psychology's dualities as a weakness, we can and should see these dualities as a source of creative provocation and strength. I will illustrate this through several examples of mutually beneficial transactions across the basic/applied and natural/social science dualities. My examples will focus primarily on the opportunities to rigorously test basic scientific theoretical propositions via well-designed experimental evaluations of 'psychological' interventions.

2   The world's human population is enormously diverse and rapidly changing. Consequently, PET in the early twenty-first century would benefit from inclusion of basic literacy in three non-psychological disciplines:ethics, epidemiology and comparative policy analysis[1]. These are perspectives

needed to help society (and the field of psychological science) to manage 'informed choices' in shaping and adapting PET to national and global needs.

Optimizing the relation between basic and applied psychological science

My analysis and recommendations for PET are based on the assumptions that (i) psychology is both a basic and applied science; and (ii) psychological science draws heavily from theory and methods of the natural and social sciences. I believe that psychology is enriched by its dual nature (Table 9.1). Both facets of psychological science increase its potential to better understand and more effectively address large-scale social phenomena and their influence on psychological development and well-being. But there are some in our field who turn the dual nature of psychology into a binary system of positive/negative (good/bad, us/them).

A similar system of binary thinking is at work underneath the dualism of psychology as a natural *versus* a social science. These systems of thinking seem wrong to me on logical/analytic grounds, and deeply unuseful on practical grounds. If we are to adapt PET for a twenty-first century diverse, rapidly changing, global society, we should overcome these false dichotomies and seek to optimize the relationship between psychology as a basic and applied science. Undoubtedly, there are many ways to optimize. I'll explore one critically important way in this chapter as an exemplar.

In many areas of psychology, basic theoretical propositions about causal processes can be tested most effectively (and ethically) via rigorous, experimental theory-based evaluations of psychological interventions. Below, I outline three of many potential examples of basic theoretical propositions, relevant to varying degrees to most countries of the world, which are beginning to be most effectively tested via rigorous program or policy evaluations.

First, does poverty (economic shock? economic distress?) have a causal influence on the mental, emotional and behavioral health of children, youth and/ or adults? If so, by what mechanisms?

At least since the 1950s, psychology has examined the question of poverty (and poverty-related cofactors) on human and animal psychological development and well-being. In animal models for example, macaque monkeys (or other species) can be assigned to experimental conditions that resemble 'human poverty'

Table 9.1 Psychological science and its dual nature

Basic science		Applied science	
Positive	*Negative*	*Positive*	*Negative*
• Rigorous	• Artificial	• Useful	• Undisciplined/soft
• Deep	• Narrow	• Broad/integrative	• Unfocused

(insufficient resources to meet basic needs) and other confounding conditions (e.g. the predictability/unpredictability of resource availability). Classic experiments in this mode by Rosenblum and Paully (1984) clearly demonstrate the unique damaging effects of unpredictability on macaque mothers' quality of child-rearing and subsequently on juvenile macaque behavioral development. Subsequent research has demonstrated how insufficient and unpredictable resources affect multiple neurotransmitter systems (Stevens *et al.*, 2009).

Fortunately, ethics prohibits psychological scientists from randomly assigning humans to poverty. And while interesting and valued quasi-experimental work on the impact of poverty and negative economic shocks on human psychological functioning is possible, the most influential causal evidence comes from studies which randomly assign parents and/or their children to specific antipoverty programs and policies (for a recent review, see Yoshikawa *et al.*, 2012). From numerous studies over the last two decades, evidence is accruing that significant increases in income of poor families with children (read significant reductions in poverty) have positive effects on both parents' and children's psychological and behavioral development and well-being. And now that evidence is mounting that poverty reduction can prevent or reduce mental-, emotional and behavioral health problems, new questions arise and can best be tested via social experiments: on which specific outcomes? for which subgroups? by which mechanisms? and under what conditions? These questions in turn require expert collaboration between applied scientists and basic scientists. Two examples of expert collaboration on mediators of poverty effects on psychological well-being:

1 Executive function as a causal mediator.

- Until basic scientists articulated a theory of the nature and development of 'executive function' (EF), e.g. working memory, flexibility of attention; behavioral control (Blair, 2010), and valid, reliable measures of Executive Function (Blair *et al.*, 2005), EF could not be seen by applied scientist as a *potential measurable mediator* of the impact of poverty and of antipoverty interventions on human psychological and behavioral development.
- Until applied scientists began to use theory and measurement of EF in rigorous program evaluations (e.g. of preschool interventions like Tools of the Mind (Barnett *et al.*, 2008) and of modifications of Head Start (Raver *et al.*, 2011)), basic scientists did not have ways to estimate changes in the plasticity of EF over the course of development.

2 Family investment vs. family stress.

- Similarly, until basic scientists articulated family investment (Foster, 2002; Haveman and Wolfe, 1994; Mayer, 1997) and family stress (Conger and Elder, 1994; Conger *et al.*, 2002) theories of the influence of poverty on children's psychological development, and until they developed valid, reliable measures of parental time and financial investments in their children and parental stress (Gershoff *et al.*, 2007), family investment and family stress were not viable targets for antipoverty programs and policies.

- And until applied scientists began to design evaluations of how antipoverty interventions impacted parent investments and stress, basic scientists could not test the causal relations among poverty, parenting behavior and child outcomes (Morris *et al.*, 2005; Morris and Gennetian, 2003).

Second, does exposure to violence have a causal influence on psychological development and well-being? And if so, by what mechanisms?

Throughout the world, children, youth and adults are exposed to many forms of violence, ranging from experiencing child abuse, witnessing/experiencing domestic violence, school bullying, gang violence, community violence and war (UNICEF, 2005). Once again, much like poverty, it is scientifically quite challenging to understand the effects of violence on psychological development and well-being. We do not conduct studies which randomly assign humans to exposure to violence, and even very good quasi-experimental studies of violence are replete with threats to internal validity like third-variable confounds and selection bias. But what we can do is rigorous experimental studies on the prevention of violence or on the mental health treatment of people exposed to violence. And we can use these intervention studies to test theories of causal mediation of how exposure to violence affects psychological development and well-being.

- Until basic scientists articulated a social information processing theory of the development of aggression and antisocial behavior, and until they developed specific measures of deviant social information processing (like hostile attribution bias), hostile attribution bias could not be seen by applied scientists as a potential causal mechanism of the impact of preventive interventions on human psychological and behavioral development (Dodge *et al.*, 1990; Dodge, 2006) and hence a target for intervention.
- Until applied scientists began to use theory and measurement of hostile attribution bias in rigorous program evaluations (of school-based preventive interventions) for aggressive behavior problems like the 4Rs program (Aber *et al.*, 2011) or Fast Track (Conduct Problems Prevention Research Group, 2010), basic scientists did not have ways to test the causal influence of social information processing on the development of behavior problems.

Third, do functional polymorphisms in particular genes moderate the influence of social environments on particular aspects of psychological development and well-being?

There has been a strong shift in psychological science away from 'main effects' and simple deterministic views of the influence of nature and nurture on psychological development to more 'interactionist' and probabilistic views.

Evidence is mounting that allele variation is associated with human variation both in response to poverty/socioeconomic deprivation (Kim-Cohen *et al.*, 2004) and in response to violence (Caspi *et al.*, 2002). However, the first wave of such research has not been able to rule out that genetic variation affects selection into poor and violent environments, and so such research has only demonstrated 'passive GxE interactions'. Basic science wishes to test 'active GxE interactions'. Once again, applied intervention science can help answer basic science questions.

Gene x intervention interaction

*   Until the human genome was mapped and until basic scientists began to test the association between particular alleles (gene variants) and variation in human response to risks/adversities/threats (Caspi *et al.*, 2002; Moffit *et al.*, 2005), applied scientists could not formulate and test theories of genetic moderation of intervention impact.
*   Until applied scientists began to collect genetic data that allowed them to measure particular genotypes associated with variability in response to environmental risks, basic scientists could not test causal models of genetic moderation. These are possible where the environment (E) of an intervention is randomly assigned to humans with and without specified risk alleles. See Belsky and Pluess (2009); Velderman *et al.* (2006) and Brody *et al.* (2009) for examples of gene x intervention studies.)

These three examples of research which optimize the relation between basic and applied science primarily cite work from the global North and West. But increasingly, randomized trials of preventive interventions addressing issues of poverty and violence and their effects on child, youth and parent psychological development and well-being are being conducted in low- and middle-income countries as well (e.g. see Engle *et al.*, 2011, for a recent review). Thus, both the needs and the opportunities to optimize the relation between basic and applied psychological science are global in scope and relevance. Intensive PET in this perspective is, in my opinion, of paramount importance at this point in the development of our fields.

Making informed choices in shaping and adapting PET to national and global needs

Many in our field hope to improve the power and utility of psychological science to understand and address large-scale social phenomena (wars, economic shocks, etc.) of special importance to particular countries and regions of the world and the impact of these social phenomena on psychological development and well-being. In order to do so, I believe that PET in the early twenty-first century should include basic literacy in epidemiology, ethics and comparative program and policy analyses.

Epidemiology

Because psychological science is a more 'micro' discipline (focused relatively more on psychological phenomena at the intra-individual or inter-individual levels) and less a 'macro' discipline (focused relatively more on places, groups, populations, cultures, societies) much of its work can and does proceed without much attention to large-scale social phenomena. The lack of attention to social phenomena like economic crises and epidemics is limiting to the development of psychological science in at least two important ways.

First, at least since Bronfenbrenner (1979) proposed his bioecological theory of human development (including psychological development), it has been clear that development occurs in contexts. These include not only the micro-contexts traditionally studied by psychology (e.g. parents-families-teachers-peers-classrooms) but also meso-contexts (e.g. parents' workplaces, friends' parents) and macro-contexts (e.g. neighborhoods, policy regimes, etc.). Consequently, understanding the spatial distribution and temporal stability and change in meso- and macro-contexts that affect psychological development and well-being are increasingly important to PET.

Second, society has a desire for psychological science to address those problems in psychological development and well-being that are the fastest growing, most prevalent and/or more serious. The spatial and temporal distribution of psychological problems is a concern for the field of epidemiology (e.g. Kessler *et al.*, 2005). And spatial and temporal variation in population exposure to wars, disasters and economic crises is likely associated with spatial and temporal variation in psychological well-being. These associations are also the foci of population studies and epidemiological and demographic analysis. PET should prepare future psychological scientists to use epidemiology to identify fast-growing, high prevalence, serious problems in psychological development and well-being, and to understand whether and how large-scale social phenomena are driving some of these patterns. Only such competencies will enable psychological scientists to identify and address issues of special regional, national and/or local concern.

Ethics

Of course, even with the best epidemiologic data and analyses, there will be more social problems and more constraints on psychological development and well-being than psychological science can address. A related issue is that there are a very large number of elements to quality of life and basic human needs. This is what Sabina Alkire (2002) means when she says human development is 'multidimensional'. That there are numerous problems to address, numerous positive features of development to promote, leads to the requirement to choose among many valuable dimensions those finite number that can be addressed at any one time in any one place by any finite group of individuals.

Choosing what to focus on in basic, and applied psychological science is a philosophical exercise, not just an empirical one. It requires that psychological

Table 9.2 Action implications of major schools of moral thought (adapted from Alkire and Chen, 2004)

- Humanitarianism: acting virtuously toward those in need.
- Utilitarianism: maximizing aggregate subjective happiness.
- Equity: achieving a fairer distribution of human capabilities.
- Rights: fulfilling our obligations so others are dignified.

---

scientists (and practitioners) think critically about the assumptions – the concepts and categories – that underlie programs of psychological science and systems of psychological interventions. Alkire and Chen (2004) make the same argument in deciding what to focus upon in understanding and alleviating health problems more broadly. They urge us to evaluate our choices rationally. And they draw on Amartya Sen (2002: 4) to guide them. 'Rationality', writes Sen, 'is interpreted here broadly, as the discipline of subjecting one's choices – of actions as well as of objectives, values and priorities – to reasoned scrutiny.' In short, which social phenomena and psychological problems should we focus our scientific research and practical interventions upon? How should we decide upon our priorities? Alkire and Chen (2004) argue that scientific and practical choices should be guided by ethical vision and moral philosophy (Table 9.2).

Decisions about which social or psychological programs or policies to design and implement could be and are made on relatively more humanitarian or utilitarian grounds. Or they could be mounted in pursuit of equity or rights. Whether explicitly or implicitly considered, such values strongly affect what psychological science chooses to focus upon and what it chooses to do about it. PET adequate to the challenges of a rapidly changing, increasingly diverse world requires preparation in the sort of ethics and reasoned scrutiny championed by Alkire and Sen among many others.

Comparative program and policy analysis

In this chapter, I've argued that a good way to optimize the relationship between basic and applied psychological science is to test theoretical propositions on causal processes via randomized trials of psychological interventions. I've also argued that in the face of rapid change and growing diversity of human populations and their social contexts, it is valuable to educate emerging psychological scientists in epidemiology/demography. Together these two issues raise a final critical issue for twenty-first century PET: understanding variation in the efficacy and effectiveness of psychological interventions across communities, countries and regions of the world. The intervention literature is replete with examples of interventions that work in some contexts or for some subpopulations, but not in other contexts or with other subpopulations (e.g. Bloom *et al.*, 2003; Olds *et al.*, 2007). Similarly, some interventions work in initial efficacy trials but then appear not to work in subsequent effectiveness trials or scalability trials. There is a growing research agenda on the program, community and policy factors that may moderate the impact of an intervention on psychological (and other) outcomes (Granger, 2010, 2011). As certain types of interventions developed in one country or region are increasingly being replicated and/or adapted and implemented in other countries or regions, the need for comparative program and policy analysis grows (e.g., see Knerr *et al*, (2013) for a discussion of the 'transportability' of parenting interventions across countries). Without the skill set to understand (at a minimum) and conduct (ideally) rigorously comparative analyses, psychological science will not be prepared to adapt its basic and applied research to the unique conditions and needs of particular countries. Intervention work in areas as diverse as parenting, early childhood education, school-based social emotional learning interventions and conditional cash transfer antipoverty initiatives appear to suggest both cross-site/common and specific-site/unique processes and outcomes. We are in the very earliest stages of developing the theory and methodology for comparative program and policy analysis, but PET for the twenty-first century would do well to prepare the next generation of psychological scientists to make progress on this critically important task.

Conclusion

If I am right about some of the challenges facing psychological science in a period of rapid change, and if I am right about some of the strategies to meet these challenges (by optimizing the relation between basic and applied research and by preparing young psychological scientists in ethics, epidemiology and comparative program and policy analysis), it still begs the question about *how* to do the PET in universities. The obvious place to start is via masters and doctoral-level course work. For example, I have designed courses that (a) explicitly consider how to optimize the relation between basic and applied psychological science, and (b) integrate some ethics, epidemiology and comparative policy analyses into the courses. Of course, exactly how to do this should be country- and context-specific. In the course 'Risk and Resilience: Science for Practice', both the basic science of GxE interactions (in conduct disorder, depression and reading problems) and the emerging of GxI interventions (to reduce risk for the same disorder) are introduced. In the 'Child Development and Social Policy in a Global Society' course, students are directed to websites on the spatial distribution of indicators of human development and child well-being; and students read Alkire (2002) and Alkire and Chen (2004) and learn to submit their choices for research on action foci to reasoned scrutiny. Finally, in both courses, literatures on cross-national variation in risks and in intervention impacts are included. (Full syllabi of these courses are available from me on request at LA39@nyu.edu.)

PET adequate to the challenges of the twenty-first century will need to go way beyond course work to changes in both research training and practice training that address the same underlying issues. PET that helps meet national and international needs will prepare young psychologists to: reject certain dualisms; optimize the relationship between basic and applied psychological science; learn the ethic of subjecting our choices in research and action to reasoned scrutiny; understand the variation of social and psychological problems across time and space; and enable rigorous comparative analysis of what works, what doesn't and why across the diverse contexts of the contemporary world in which psychological science is practiced.

Note

1 These disciplines are not economics, sociology, anthropology, biology, chemistry, and genetics. Work at the intersections of psychology and these disciplines is already happening.

References

Aber, L., Brown, J.L, and Jones, S.M., Berg, J. and Torrente, C. (2011). School-based Strategies to Prevent Violence, Trauma and Psychopathology: The Challenges of Going to Scale. *Development and Psychopathology, 23*, 411–21.

Alderman, H.H. (2011). *No Small Matter: The Impact of Poverty, Shocks, and Human Capital Investments in Early Childhood Development.* Washington, DC: World Bank Publications.

Alkire, S. (2002). Dimensions of Human Development. *World Development, 30*(2), 181–205.

Alkire, S. and Chen, L. (2004). Global Health and Moral Values. *The Lancet, 364*, 1069–74.

Arnett, J.J. (2008). The Neglected 95%: Why American Psychology Needs to Become Less American. *American Psychologist, 63*, 602–14.

Barnett, W.S., Jung, K., Yarosz, D.J., Thomas, J., Hornbeck, A., Stechuk, R. and Burns, S. (2008). Educational Effects of the Tools of the Mind Curriculum: A Randomized Trial. *Early Childhood Research Quarterly, 23*, 299–313.

Belsky, J. and Pluess, M. (2009). Beyond Diathesis Stress: Differential Susceptibility to Environmental Influences. *Psychological Bulletin, 135*(5), 885–908.

Blair, C., (2010). Stress and the Development of Self-Regulation in Context. *Child Development Perspectives, 4*(3), 181–8.

Blair, C., Zelazo, P.D. and Greenberg, M.T. (2005). The Measurement of Executive Function in Early Childhood. *Development Neuropsychology, 28*(2), 561–71.

Bloom, H.S., Hill, C.J. and Riccio, J.A. (2003). Linking Program Implementation and Effectiveness: Lessons from a Pooled Sample of Welfare-to Work Experiments. *Journal of Policy Analysis and Management, 22*(4), 551–75.

Boruch, R., May, H, Turner, H., Lavenberg, J., Petrosino, A., De Moya, D., Grimshaw, J. and Foley, E. (2004). Estimating the Effects of Interventions that are Deployed in Many Places. *American Behavioral Scientist, 47*(5), 608–32.

Brody, G.H., Beach, S.R.H., Philibert, R.A., Chen, Y. and McBride Murry, V. (2009). Prevention Effects Moderate the Association of 5-HTTLPR and Youth Risk Behavior Initiation: Gene × Environment Hypotheses Tested via a Randomized Prevention Design. *Child Development, 80*(3), 645–61.

Bronfenbrenner, U. (1979). *The Ecology of Human Development: Experiments by Nature and Design.* Cambridge, MA: Harvard University Press.

Caspi, A., McClay, J., Moffitt, T.E., Mill, J., Martin J., Craig, I.W., Taylor, A. and Poulton, R. (2002). Role of Genotype in the Cycle of Violence in Maltreated Children. *Science Magazine, 297*(5582), 851–4.

Conduct Problems Prevention Research Group (2010). The Effects of a Multi-year Universal Social-emotional Learning Program: The Role of Student and School Characteristics. *Journal of Consulting and Clinical Psychology, 78*(2), 156–68.

Conger, R. and Elder, G.H. (1994). *Families in Troubled Times: Adapting to Change in Rural America*. New York, NY: A. de Gruyter.

Conger, R. D., Ebert-Wallace, L., Sun, Y., Simons, R. L., McLoyd, V. C. and Brody, G. H. (2002). Economic Pressure in African American families: A Replication and Extension of the Family Stress Model. *Developmental Psychology, 38,* 179–93.

Dodge, K.A., Bates, J.E. and Pettit, G.S. (1990). Mechanisms in the Cycle of Violence. *Science Magazine, 250,* 1678–83.

Dodge, K.A. (2006). Translational Science in Action: Hostile Attributional Style and the Development of Aggressive Behavior Problems. *Development and Psychopathology, 18*(3), 791–814.

Doyle, M.W. and Prewitt, K. (2012). *21st Century Youth in the Developing World: Research Report*. Global Colloquium of University Presidents, Columbia University, April 2–3, 2012.

Durlak, J.A., Weissberg, R.P., Dymnicki, A.B., Taylor, R.D. and Schellinger, K.B. (2011). The Impact of Enhancing Student's Social and Emotional Learning: A Meta-analysis of School-Based Universal Interventions. *Child Development, 82*(1), 405–32.

Engle, P.L., Fernald, L.C.H., Alderman, H., Behrman, J., O'Gara, C., Yousafzai, A., Cabral de Mello, M., Hidrobo, M., Ulkuer, N., Ertem, I., Iltus, S. and and the Global Child Development Steering Group (2011). Strategies for Reducing Inequalities and Improving Developmental Outcomes for Young Children in Low-income and Middle-income Countries. *The Lancet, 378*(9799), 1339–53.

Foster, M.E. (2002). How Economists think about Family Resources and Child Development. *Child Development, 73*(6), 1904–14.

Gershoff, E. T., Aber, J. L., Raver, C. C. and Lennon, M. C. (2007). Income is not Enough: Incorporating Material Hardship into Models of Income Associations with Parenting and Child Development. *Child Development, 78*(1), 70–95.

Granger, R. G. (2010). Learning from Scale-up Initiatives. *Education Week,* November 1726–7.

Granger, R.G. (2011). The Big Why: A Learning Agenda for the Scale-up Movement. *Pathways,* Winter, 28–32.

Haveman, R.L. and Wolfe, B.H. (1994). *Succeeding Generations; On the Effects on Investments in Children*. New York, NY: Russell Sage.

Heymann, S.J. (2013). *Children's Chances: How Countries can Move from Surviving to Thriving*. Cambridge, MA: Harvard University Press.

Kessler, R.C., Berglund, P., Femler, O., Jin, R., Merikangas, K.R. and Walters, E.E. (2005). Lifetime Prevalence and Age-of-onset Distributions of DSM-IV Disorders in the National Comorbidity Survey Replication. *Archives of General Psychiatry, 62*(6), 593–602.

Kim-Cohen, J., Moffitt, T.E., Caspi, A. and Taylor, A. (2004). Genetic and Environmental Processes in Young Children's Resilience and Vulnerability to Socioeconomic Deprivation. *Child Development, 75*(3), 651–68.

Knerr, W., Gardner, F. and Cluver, L. (2012). Improving Positive Parenting Skills and Reducing Harsh and Abusive Parenting in Low- and Middle-income Countries: a Systematic Review. *Prevention Science,* 14 (4), 352–63.

Love, J.M., Kisker, E.E., Ross, C., Raikes, H., Constantine, J., Boller, K., Brooks-Gunn, J., Chazan-Cohen, R., Tarullo, L.B., Brady-Smith, C., Fuligni, A.S., Schochet, P.Z., Paulsell, D. and Vogel, C. (2005). The Effectiveness of Early Head Start for 3-year-old Children and their Parents: Lessons for Policy and Programs. *Developmental Psychology, 41,* 885–901.

Mayer, S.E. (1997). *What Money Can't Buy: Family Income and Children's Life Changes*. Cambridge, MA: Harvard University Press.

Moffitt, T.E., Caspi, A. and Rutter, M. (2005). Strategy for Investigating Interactions Between Measured Genes and Measured Environments. *Archives of General Psychiatry, 62*, 473–81.

Morris, P.A. and Gennetian, L.A. (2003). Identifying the Effects of Income on Children's Development Using Experimental Data. *Journal of Marriage and Family, 65*, 716–29.

Morris, P., Duncan, G.J. and Clark-Kauffman, E. (2005). Child Well-Being in an Era of Welfare Reform: The Sensitivity of Transitions in Development of Policy Change. *Developmental Psychology, 41*(6), 919–32.

Olds, D.L., Sadler, L. and Kitzman, H. (2007). Programs for Parents of Infants and Toddlers: Recent Evidence from Randomized Trials. *Journal of Child Psychology and Psychiatry, 48*(3/4), 355–91.

Population Reference Bureau (2012). *Population and Economic Development 2012 Data Sheet*. Washington, DC: PRB.

Raver, C.C., Jones, S.J., Li-Grining, C., Zhai, F., Bub, K. and Pressler, E. (2011). CSRP's Impact on Low-income Preschoolers' Preacademic Skills: Self-regulation as a Mediating Mechanism. *Child Development, 82*(1), 362–78.

Rosenblum, L. A. and Paully, G.S. (1984). The Effects of Varying Environmental Demands on Maternal and Infant Behavior. *Child Development, 55*, 305–14.

Sen, A. (2002). *Rationality and Freedom*. Cambridge, MA: Harvard University Press.

Sherman, R.F. (2011). Social and Emotional Learning Action Network White Paper. Clinton Global Initiative Social and Emotional Learning Network. http://novofoundation. org/wp-content/uploads/2011/09/CGI-SEL-Action-Network-White-Paper.pdf

Stevens, H.E., Leckman, J.F., Coplan, J.D. and Suomi, S.J. (2009). Risk and Resilience: Early Manipulation of Macaque Social Experience and Persistent Behavioral and Neurophysiological Outcomes. *Journal of American Academy of Child and Adolescent Psychiatry, 48*(2), 114–27.

Tseng, V. and Seidman, E. (2007). A Systems Framework for Understanding Social Settings. *American Journal of Community Psychology, 39*, 217–28.

United National International Children's Emergency Fund (2005). *The State of the World's Children 2006 – Excluded and Invisible*. New York, NY: UNICEF Publications.

United Nations Development Program. (2011). *Millennium Development Goals Report 2011*. New York, NY: UNDP. Available at www.undp.org/content/undp/en/home/mdgoverview.html

United Nations Population Fund (2012). *Linking Population, Poverty and Development*. New York, NY: UNFPA. Available at www.unfpa.org/pds/trends.htm

United States Census Bureau (2012). *The 2012 Statistical Abstract*. Washington, DC: U.S. Census Bureau. Available at www.census.gov/compendia/statab

Velderman, M.K., Bakermans-Kranenburg, M.J., Juffer, F. and van IJzendoorn, M.H. (2006). Effects of Attachment-Based Interventions on Maternal Sensitivity and Infant Attachment: Differential Susceptibility of Highly Reactive Infants. *Journal of Family Psychology, 20*(2), 266–74.

Weare, K. (2010). Mental Health and Social and Emotional Learning: Evidence, Principles, Tensions, Balances. *Advances in School Mental Health Promotion, 3*(1), 5–15.

Yoshikawa, H., Aber, J.L. and Beardslee, W.R. (2012). The Effects of Poverty on Children's Mental, Emotional and Behavioral Health: Implications for Prevention. *American Psychologist, 67*(4), 272–84.

10 Basic and applied research in psychology education and training

South Africa as a case study

Cheryl de la Rey

Introduction

The development of psychology as a discipline and profession in South Africa has been intricately related to the country's history of race and racism. Various publications have reflected on the question of how a discipline ostensibly intended for the promotion of human well-being responded to the injustices that pervaded South African society for most of the twentieth century (Duncan et al., 2001). After the public acknowledgement of the complicity of psychology with apartheid at the 1994 national psychology conference which saw the demise of the previous white professional society and the launch of a new non-racial organization, the Psychological Society of South Africa, any claim to being a neutral science was shattered irreversibly.

From the late 1980s into the early 1990s, as opposition to apartheid reached greater levels of intensity, a small group of South African psychologists earnestly debated the question of how psychology could become more relevant to the local socio-political context. Due to the socio-economic inequities promulgated by the policies of the apartheid regime, psychology was almost the exclusive reserve of what were perceived as an elitist group of middle-class white men. There was a crisis in public confidence regarding the applicability of psychological knowledge and practice to the majority of the South African population, and this led to a search for 'relevance'.

Against the backdrop of apartheid, several psychologists argued that the proper objective of South African psychology was to redress the consequences of human rights abuses visited upon the majority black population by apartheid policies. From the early 1990s, not long before the formal demise of apartheid, a growing number of psychologists focused on teaching and researching issues of racism, sexism and oppression. At the time there was very little being taught formally about any of these issues at universities. Offering a critical voice in opposition to the mainstream became one form of response in the search for relevance. The integration of theoretical criticism and political activism became a motif which led to the emergence of new content areas such as community psychology. Nowadays most departments of psychology teach community psychology and almost all professional training programmes in clinical and counselling psychology have a community component.

From 1994 onwards the call for relevance manifested in the form of two strands of response: first, an attempt to change the demographic profile of psychologists and second, a conscious responsiveness to post-apartheid policy imperatives and issues.

Changes in representation and focus

In an attempt to shift the racial and gender bias evident in psychological research, a number of projects aimed at the development of scholarship among black psychologists were initiated. Shortly after the launch of the Psychological Society of South Africa in 1994, the first non-racial professional organisation for psychology, a special issue of the *South African Journal of Psychology* was published focusing on black authorship. Since then there have been steady changes in the demographic profile of psychology in South Africa.

Beyond the demographics, there have been significant changes in the focus and organization of psychology. In the aftermath of the first democratic elections, psychologists made significant contributions to building a new South Africa through work on mental health policy, the provision and the accessibility of mental health services, and the Truth and Reconciliation Commission (TRC) became a focal point for South African psychology. There was the direct involvement of psychologists in the TRC process itself in the form of provision of counselling services and a few psychologists were appointed as commissioners. Psychologists also conducted research on the TRC, the process and its impact. Questions on the efficacy of the psychological support services (Hamber, 1998) healing and the TRC (De la Rey and Owens, 1998) and the impact of public testimony (Kaminer *et al.*, 2001) constituted the focus of several studies.

South African psychology today

The relevance debate has given way to contemporary debates about social responsiveness, particularly judged in terms of the degree to which psychology contributes to the social and economic challenges of South Africa as a developing country. In numerical terms psychology is one of the most popular disciplines in universities as measured by student enrolments. The responsibility of educating and training psychologists resides largely with the universities. Although institutional autonomy and academic freedom are enshrined in the South African constitution, in practice universities are not in total control of their curricula. While university senates have the ultimate decision-making power over the curriculum of any particular university, in practice curricula are shaped by the influence of statutory bodies and government policy and funding.

South Africa was one of the first countries to adopt a National Qualifications Framework (NQF). National Qualifications Frameworks are recent inventions, ostensibly to promote access and articulation for students and to enable lifelong learning. The emergence of NQFs can also be linked to globalization and human mobility. As more and more students move around the world, the need for cross-national credentialing and articulation has increased.

The NQF is a comprehensive system approved by the government for the classification, registration and articulation of national qualifications. It is intended to bring order and coherence into the complex arena of education and training, assisting students to progress in their educational and career paths, and ensuring that South African qualifications are both relevant and of high quality. The NQF is organized as a series of levels of learning achievement (arranged in the order of 1 to 10), each described by a level descriptor, which provides a broad indication of learning achievements or outcomes appropriate to a qualification at that level. National legislation prescribes that all qualifications must be categorised and registered in terms of the NQF.

The NQF is structured as a single integrated system which comprises three qualifications sub-frameworks for basic or school education, trades and occupations and higher education. Education and training in psychology falls within the sub-framework of higher education, known as the Higher Education Qualifications Framework (HEQF).

The HEQF applies to all higher education institutions, both public and private, and it determines the qualification types, characteristics and purposes of all higher education qualifications in South Africa. The HEQF covers all post-school qualifications from certificates at NQF level 5 through to doctoral degrees. A statutory body, the Council on Higher Education (CHE) is responsible for all aspects of the HEQF including quality assurance. The classification of qualifications and the purpose of each are listed in Table 10.1.

The Health Professions Council of South Africa (HPCSA) is another statutory body that shapes the education and training of psychology in South Africa. Through its Professional Board for Psychology, the HPCSA is responsible for

Table 10.1 The HEQF classification of qualifications applicable to psychology

Qualification	Purpose
Bachelor's degree	Provides a well-rounded, broad education that equips graduates with the knowledge base, theory and methodology of disciplines, and enables them to demonstrate initiative and responsibility in an academic or professional context. Principles and theory are emphasized as a basis for entry into the labour market, professional training, postgraduate studies, or professional practice.
Bachelor honours degree	Prepares students for research-based postgraduate study, and serves to consolidate and deepen the student's expertise and to develop research capacity in the methodology and techniques of the discipline. The qualification demands a high level of theoretical engagement and intellectual independence.
Master's degree	Educates and trains researchers who can contribute to the development of knowledge at an advanced level, or prepare graduates for advanced and specialized professional employment. Graduates must have the ability to deal with complex issues both systematically and creatively, make sound judgements using data and information at their disposal, and communicate their conclusions clearly to specialist and non-specialist audiences.

Qualification	Purpose
Doctoral degree	Requires a candidate to undertake research at the most advanced academic levels and to demonstrate high-level research capability, and make a significant and original academic contribution at the frontiers of a discipline or field. The work must be of a quality to satisfy peer review and merit publication. A graduate must be able to supervise and evaluate the research of others in the area of specialization concerned.

specifying the scope of professional practice and for the registration and licensing of psychologists to practice. Therefore, two statutory bodies in the form of the CHE and the HPCSA have a significant role in influencing PET in South Africa. On the one hand, the CHE is responsible for the accreditation and quality assurance of psychology programmes offered by universities, and the HPCSA, on the other hand, determines the scope of practice and licenses candidates to practise psychology in the public domain.

The curricula of universities are therefore shaped by the policies and practices of the CHE, the HPCSA and government which is a major role-player. Government shapes PET through policies, regulation and funding. All professional psychology programmes in South Africa are offered by public universities. Government via its Department of Higher Education and Training subsidises the cost of educating and training students via a formula-driven block grant which covers about 40 per cent of the cost and only those programmes accredited by the CHE are subsidised.

Implications for basic and applied psychology

The HEQF, which is the overall conceptual framework for accreditation, makes a distinction between professional qualifications and general academic qualifications. Professional qualifications are deemed to be applied in focus, comprise a service-learning or internship component and lead to a 'licence' to practise the profession, whereas academic or general qualifications are more theoretical, research-oriented and are designed to lead to academic or research careers. In practice, university psychology programmes are general in nature until the Master's level or fifth year of study, where specialisation comes into effect. At present a candidate may register as a professional psychologist with the HPCSA after graduating with a Master's degree in psychology and completing a period of internship.

At present the HEQF makes no provision for a professional doctorate and favours academic psychology, specifying that:

A Doctoral Degree requires a candidate to undertake research at the most advanced academic levels culminating in the submission, assessment and acceptance of a thesis . . . The defining characteristic . . . is that the candidate is required to demonstrate high-level research capability and make a significant and original academic contribution at the frontiers of a discipline or field. The work must be of a quality to satisfy peer review and merit publication.

This specification largely follows the traditional model of doctoral education whereby the candidate is apprenticed to a supervisor and the career objective is to follow an academic career track. Thus the degree is awarded on the basis of a research thesis alone.

Many professional associations, including the Psychological Society of South Africa, have lobbied for the inclusion of a professional doctorate and it appears that the CHE is about to accede. The CHE has received several queries about the possibility of a professional doctorate that would include structured courses and practice-based work in addition to a research component.

The proposed revision will mean that in the future there are likely to be two types of doctoral level qualifications applicable to psychology. The first, which to date has been the only type of doctorate, will be based fully on research that is conducted under supervision and then published as a thesis and/or as publications. The second, which is the new proposal, will be based 60 per cent on research and 40 per cent on coursework and/or professional and work-integrated learning. In psychology this second type of doctorate would be applicable to those who wished to obtain a doctorate in clinical, counselling, industrial and educational psychology, in other words, all categories of psychology that involve some form of therapeutic intervention with individuals, groups and/or organizations.

Implications for research: basic and applied

With respect to research, the relevance debate of the early to mid-1990s, as outlined above, led to the dominance of applied research in psychology with very few pockets of basic research. This dominance of applied research has been given further impetus by contemporary debates about the social responsiveness of university research.

The main form of public funding for the direct costs of research in universities and therefore, psychology research, flows from government via the National Research Foundation (NRF). Although the NRF allocates research grants via a competitive process, the framework for such research grants is determined by national priorities, which means that the larger proportion of public research funding is granted for strategic, applied research. Government departments such as the Department of Science and Technology set national policy and associated national priorities, after which public agencies publish strategic plans. The process takes into consideration international trends and factors such as geographical advantage and local needs. For the 2012 to 2015 period, the NRF has stated that it will deliver support 'in research fields, where South Africa has a geographical and/or knowledge advantage' (NRF, 2012, p.22). Examples of these priorities are space science, drug discovery and biodiversity. Psychology research would be considered within the area of human and social dynamics in development in competition with all the other social science disciplines. The total budget available for human and social dynamics is a small proportion of the total allocation. What is helpful, however, is that a considerable proportion of the total NRF budget is allocated for capacity development, with a strong focus on candidates who were disadvantaged under the apartheid system. This type of funding support includes scholarships and bursaries for graduate students and new and emerging researchers. The real limitation, however, is the total budget available to support scientific research in general, which is less than 1 per cent of GDP.

In a context where resources are constrained, researchers find it difficult to sustain longer-term research that can enable a desirable level of dynamism between applied and basic research and between theory development and practice. The tendency is to focus on applied research that has immediate relevance. In a developing country such as South Africa, this does have a positive impact because researchers are tackling issues that are relevant to local communities, for example, the psycho-social implications of HIV/AIDS, race attitudes and psychological resilience.

Conclusion

Notwithstanding the limitations identified in this chapter, the status of psychology in South Africa is on an upward trajectory. The registration records of the HPCSA show that across areas of specialisation there are increasing numbers of psychologists, and new registration categories such as forensic psychology and neuropsychology were declared in 2011 (Cooper and Nicholas, 2012). Psychology in South Africa is vibrant and growing significantly.

Furthermore, South Africa's hosting of the thirtieth International Congress of Psychology in July 2012 has generated significant excitement and public interest. The NRF, many public universities and private companies together provided significant funding support for the Congress and this is likely to act as a stimulus for local research. Other encouraging factors are the increasing opportunities for South African researchers to forge joint research projects with international colleagues and to become active contributors within larger research networks. Through collaboration and partnerships South African psychologists are likely to increasingly access international sources of research funding which can supplement local research grants.

References

Cooper, S. and Nicholas, N. (2012). An Overview of South African Psychology. *International Journal of Psychology*, 47(2), 89–101.

De la Rey, C. and Owens, I. (1998). Perceptions of Psycho-social Healing and the Truth and Reconciliation Commission in South Africa. *Peace and Conflict: Journal of Peace Psychology*, 4(3), 257–70.

Department of Education (2007). The Higher Education Qualifications Framework. *Government Gazette*, 958 (30353).

Duncan, N., Van Niekerk, A., De la Rey, C. and Seedat, M. (2001). *Race, Racism, Knowledge Production and Psychology in South Africa.* Huntington, NY: Nova Science Publishers.

Duncan, N., Seedat, M., De la Rey, C., Van Niekerk, A. and Gobodo-Madikizela, P. (1999). Challenging Academic Racism in South African Psychology. In K. Prah (ed.), *Knowledge in Black and White: The Impact of Apartheid on the Production and Reproduction of Knowledge*, pp. 1–27. Cape Town: CASAS.

Hamber, B. (1998). The Burdens of Truth: An Evaluation of the Psychological Support Services and Initiatives Undertaken by the South African Truth and Reconciliation Commission. *American Imago*, 55, 9–28.

Kaminer, D., Stein D., Mbanga I. and Zungu-Dirwayi, N. (2001). The Truth and Reconciliation Commission in South Africa: Relation to Psychiatric Status and Forgiveness among Survivors of Human Rights Abuses. *British Journal of Psychiatry*, 178, 373–7.

NRF (National Research Foundation). (2012). *Research Driving Sustainability: Annual Performance Plan for 2012/13–2014/15.* Pretoria: National Research Foundation of South Africa.

Commentary on 'Balancing basic and applied research with national needs in PET'

Buxin Han

Aber in Chapter 9 and de la Rey in Chapter 10 both raise the issue of how modern psychology can be applied to and satisfy the needs of a developing country, given its Western-centric nature. My commentary will initially try to find the commonalities and differences in their presentations, then discuss why it is important to study applied psychology locally and/or globally, and finally discuss such a balance in relation to psychology in China.

Aber shows us how to balance basic and applied research (BAR) with national and international needs in psychology education and training (PET). He claims that psychology is both a basic and applied science, both a natural and a social science. I agree with him that, rather than view psychology's dualities as a weakness, we can and should see these dualities as a source of creative provocation and strength. One fact that stands out is that psychology as a profession, applied, needs to develop the skills and techniques in order to serve individuals who have grown up in one particular culture but who might work globally. Psychology as a discipline, however, could be more universal: does knowledge and an approach derived from the US hold any validity for the African people and their society? Do we need culturally specific guidelines in applied psychology?

De la Rey briefly discusses the history of PET in South Africa, but places an emphasis on the policies held by universities, governmental bodies, such as the Health Professionals Council and the Council on Higher Education. South Africa's dual track approach concerning the professional qualifications, which differentiates between academic and general, is discussed, as is the role of South African psychologists in the Truth and Reconciliation Commission, headed by Archbishop Desmond Tutu. The significant developments concerning legislation on education, accrediting, and certification psychology and the involvement of the Health Professionals Council and the Council on Higher Education is interesting, but my concern is, how will they arrive at their final decision? From my own perspective, and given the important role of religion (both folk and mainstream) in South Africa, I would have been interested to learn something about religion's contribution to psychology in general and to PET in particular.

The common features in the two presentations are the passion and concern for the economically, physically, and mentally disadvantaged. They face the realities that evidence based upon applied research is rare, and that universities are not in total control of their curricula design from both international and domestic aspects. There are of course differences in the presentations, e.g., stage of development in BAR of PET, ethnic issues and different social needs reflected.

Psychology can be both culturally specific and universal, with clinical or other applied branches being more biased to the effects of culture. For example, Freud's psychoanalysis was influenced by the Jewish religious doctrine (Kabbalah) (Langman, 1997) and Vygotsky proposed social cultural development theory from his Jewish background growing up (Kotik-Friedgut and Friedgut, 2008). Such culturally specific but creative thoughts have contributed so much to dual track psychology, that Jewish psychologists have held 39 per cent of the 99 eminent psychologist positions in the twentieth century (Haggbloom *et al.*, 2002; www.jinfo.org/psychology.html).

Modern psychology has been widely accepted and promoted in China (Han and Zhang, 2007), as witnessed by the fact that nearly 300 departments, schools, and programs of psychology have been developed in China, although culturally specific elements (e.g., psychology of Chinese religion, and the culture-friend model of psychotherapy) are still rare in the PET programs (Dueck and Han, 2012, see Figure 1 in that volume). However, as the thought processes and conflicts of the Chinese people are modulated by strong cultural factors, such as *ren qing* or *guan xi*, which refers to personal relationships; *mian zi*, meaning 'face', which is very similar to the Western notion of reputation; and *xiao*, meaning filial piety (Hwang, 2010), there must be some modification of psychotherapy proposed by Western psychologists for a better understanding and outcome among Chinese people (Wang, 2012).

Regulatory bodies and policies of PET differ between countries, as indicated clearly in the two chapters, from the accreditation process to qualification criteria, from legislation to the expectation of career development, not to mention the different status of social economic development, as well as the social welfare system. While psychology as a discipline needs empirical research for conceptual and theoretical development, as a profession it has a responsibility to serve a nation by dealing with indigenous issues in the process of social economic development (Rosenzweig, 1992; de la Rey, Chapter 10 this volume). This means that an international PET program would be helpful for the developing countries, but there must be space for locally relevant thoughts. PET professionals need to think locally, but communicate globally, and psychologists in the two branches should communicate even more than before for a better approach to PET!

References

Dueck, A. and Han, B. (2012). Psychology of religion in China. *Pastoral Psychology*, 61(5), 605–22. DOI 10.1007/s11089-012-0488-2.

Haggbloom, S. J., Warnick, R., Warnick, J. E., Jones, V. K., Yarbrough, G. L. and Russell, T. M. (2002). The 100 most eminent psychologists of the 20th century. *Review of General Psychology*, 6(2), 139–52.

Han, B. and Zhang, K. (2007). Psychology in China. *The Psychologist*, 20(12), 734–6.

Hwang, K. K. (2010). *Foundations of Chinese Psychology – Confucian Social Relations*. New York: Springer.

Kotik-Friedgut, B. and Friedgut, T. H. (2008). A man of his country and his time: Jewish influences on Lev Semionovich Vygotsky's world view. *History of Psychology*, 11(1), 15–39.

Langman, P. F. (1997). White culture, Jewish culture, and the origins of psychotherapy. *Psychotherapy*, 34(2), 207–18.

Rosenzweig, M. R. (1992). *International Psychological Science: Progress, Problems, and Prospects*. Washington, DC: APA.

Wang, X. (2012). On becoming a religious therapist in Chinese culture. *Pastoral Psychology*, 61(6), 1007–1024. DOI 10.1007/s11089-012-0430-7.

Part VII
Quality control and PET

11 Quality control in psychology education and training

Views from around the world

Victor N. Karandashev

The concept of quality assurance in higher education has drawn special attention at national and regional levels in recent years. International cooperation and free trade agreements require 'borderless' higher education and international quality control of teaching and training leading to recognition of professional qualifications. Models for quality control in PET have to establish: (1) what is the quality, (2) assessment standards, (3) procedures for comparing the standards with real outcomes, and deciding to what extent they are met. All these are closely related to national systems of higher education and training, and should be considered in this context.

Typical patterns of psychology education and training around the world

Knowledge available in the twentieth century about psychology education and training (PET) in different countries was somewhat piecemeal and difficult to access. We have only recently begun to collect such information from around the world, and as the timeline below shows, most has only happened over the past two decades.

1   Until the 1990s little research was devoted to examining PET from the international perspective.
2   From 1990–1999 many publications began to shed light on national practices in teaching and training in psychology.
3   The advent of the twenty-first century witnessed a more global and systematic coverage of PET in publications and research projects (for a review, see Karandashev, 2010).

This trend has been demonstrated by the number of publications, international comparative projects and conferences concerning PET. For example, at the onset of the twenty-first century, a series of international conferences on psychology education, teaching, and training was launched; the *International Journal of Psychology*, flagship publication of the IUPsyS, published a special issue on International Practices in the Teaching of Psychology (Karandashev and McCarthy, 2006); three volumes of *Teaching Psychology around the World* collected and presented information on PET from a comprehensively global perspective (McCarthy *et al.*, 2007, 2009, 2012). As a result, more information about PET worldwide is available than ever before (see more at http:// interteachpsy.org). Complex international collaborations within particular sub-fields of psychology also took place, which contributed to internationalization of the field (Burgess *et al.*, 2004; European Network of Work and Organizational Psychologists, 2005; Helmes and Pachana, 2005; Leong and Ponterotto, 2003; Marsella and Pedersen, 2004).

Countries around the world have their own stories of how psychology became established as a discipline and of how various traditions developed concerning the organization of PET (see Karandashev, 2009). So what are the typical models and requirements in psychology programs internationally?

Generally speaking, national structures of PET are organized either as a one-level, continuous program, or as a discontinuous two-level structure comprising separate undergraduate and graduate schools. A common model across much of the world, including Europe, has been a five-year continuous undergraduate degree program, while countries such as the UK, USA, Canada, Japan, China, New Zealand and Australia have typically adhered to the discontinuous, two-level model. The Bologna reforms in education imply a transition from the continuous, one level to the discontinuous two-level model for the European Union (see Chapter 2 this volume).

In many countries outside the US and Europe, the model of PET followed often depends on historical ties in political-economic development. For example, in East African countries, the British discontinuous model seems to prevail, whereas in West African countries it is usually the French continuous model. Some Latin American countries, parts of South America, and Asia follow the European continuous one-level plan.

The European model carefully screens students for mastery of general skills, such as writing and mathematics, prior to university entry and then focuses primarily on the topic of psychology and on applied activities for the entire five years of the program. A 3+2 model seems to be the preferred transition from this model to a more discontinuous one, with the first three years encompassing general training, still primarily related to the discipline of psychology, and the last two years focusing on a particular specialty area within the discipline, such as clinical, school psychology or organizational psychology. Training in research or preparation to teach psychology at the university level is acquired later, at the graduate level. A further expansion of the discontinuous, multilevel model (Bachelor's, Master's and Doctorate degrees earned separately) seems to be the current trend. This encourages expansion of areas of expertise, re-specialization and continuous education requirements designed to keep practicing psychologists current in the field.

Despite these differences, there are also similarities among the curricula in different countries. Topics of psychology courses are classified into four groups:

- fundamental (basic or core) psychology,
- research methods and statistics,

- applied psychology,
- internships, practice placement and service learning.

Students study fundamental psychology disciplines during the first part of the program and applied topics as the second part. The list of disciplines may be different with regard to actual titles and amount of time allocated, but subject content is largely similar. Despite content similarities, however, diversification is found due to the increasing number of new fields of psychology appearing in curricula, such as the various areas of applied psychology that have become particularly popular among students.

A multilevel university structure for PET generally focuses on fundamental courses and research methodology at the undergraduate level and applied psychology and internship placement at the graduate level. In a one-level five-year structure, introductory (undergraduate) and advanced (graduate) curriculum components are organized within one and the same school or college, usually with significant and flexible interplay between the two.

Regardless of the structure, many hours of practice and internship under professional supervision, as well as a thesis, dissertation or capstone project, are generally compulsory parts of the education and training required to become a professional psychologist in most countries of the world.

The training required for the practice of professional psychology varies across countries, and has usually evolved from a combination of input from local and national regulatory bodies, legislative requirements, academic institutions, and relevant professional bodies (Helmes and Pachana, 2005). A survey of training programs in 16 countries/regions on 6 continents found significant variation in training, minimum qualification requirements, and roles of the professional psychologist (Burgess *et al.*, 2004).

PET throughout the world has traditionally striven for the highest scientific standards academically. Recently due to growing demands for psychological practitioners to enter professional work in schools and clinics, in private practice and in industry, the specialized science-practitioner curricula were introduced in many universities throughout the world. A new type of tertiary education, professional schools of psychology, which offer a professional doctorate, the doctor of psychology (Psy.D.), not a research degree, has also been introduced in many countries. At the same time, high-ranking university departments of psychology began to introduce comparable course programs, also leading to a Psy.D., many of which follow the science-practitioner model (Pawlik, 2000). As a rule, these programs contain an obligatory one-year practical internship. Similar specialized curricula have been set up at some British and German universities.

All of these factors influence the training of psychologists in countries around the world and corresponding regulations of quality assurance. National legislation and regulation, structure and methods regarding psychology education and training vary around the world, but psychology curriculum and expected learning outcomes internationally have a lot in common.

National regulations of quality control in PET around the world

Quality control becomes necessary when the number of programs on offer grows and an interest in comparing their effectiveness arises: national bodies typically provide legislation and regulation for the accreditation and evaluation of programs and are thereby the keepers of quality control. In the area of PET, the important questions are:

- Who is in charge and has the authority for quality control?
- What are the subjects and areas for quality control?
- What are the requirements for quality control and performance indicators?
- What are the procedures and functions of quality control?

International quality control in PET needs to take into account many national legal and policy environments of quality assurance and program evaluations in the individual countries involved. This information is piecemeal and not easily available in many countries. Below are the abridged and sketchy summaries of some regulations from recent publications.

Psychology program evaluations in Australia

Australian university psychology programs have to be accredited by the Australian Psychology Accreditation Council (APAC) in order for graduates to seek registration as a psychologist (Moore, 2009; Cranney and Voudouris, 2012). After a three-year undergraduate major within a Bachelor's degree program, students wishing to pursue a career in psychology must also complete an Honors year or an equivalent accredited course such as a Graduate Diploma of Psychology, both colloquially referred to as a fourth year. They then have the option of completing a coursework Masters or Professional Doctorate, a research Masters or a PhD; alternatively, they might choose to complete two years of equivalent supervised work experience pre-approved by the relevant state or territory registration board (Moore, 2009).

The Masters and Professional Doctorate programs are typically specialist programs designed around the requirements of APAC and the specialist colleges of the Australian Psychological Society (APS), such as health, counseling, and clinical etc., which evaluate and approve these programs.

While APAC and for graduate programs, the APS colleges, specify the content, standards and competencies required from graduates of each degree, universities have some autonomy in the structure and content of their programs. It is important to note that APAC does not accredit research-based higher degree programs (i.e., Masters by research, PhD). APAC assesses psychology training programs offered by institutions on application and on a five-year cycle thereafter. APAC works cooperatively with institutions by providing the rules and accreditation standards, and by advising on the design of courses for which accreditation is being sought (see www.apac.psychology.org.au/).

The postgraduate programs are Master of Psychology; Doctor of Psychology; and Doctor of Philosophy. The Doctor of Psychology, often referred to as a professional doctorate, is of three years duration, and combines the components of the Master of Psychology with a more extensive research thesis, more placements, and further specialized coursework in the third year. Recently, there has been a push for dual professional doctorates (e.g., Doctor of Psychology Health and Clinical) and for a PhD combined with a coursework Masters degree or a Professional Doctorate. The Doctor of Philosophy degree is essentially a pure research degree, modeled after the UK. Under the APAC accreditation guidelines, and the APS college approvals guidelines, professional programs in psychology are required to adhere to the scientist-practitioner model as the basis for education and practical experience (Moore, 2009).

The Federal Government's introduction of a National Registration and Accreditation Scheme (National Scheme) for ten professions, including psychology, in 2010 created one single national registration board for psychology as a profession, the Psychology Board of Australia (PBA). The PBA introduced a type of recognition for registered psychologists with specialized skills and knowledge, titled an 'Area of Practice Endorsement' (Cranney and Voudouris, 2012). Endorsement requires two additional post-graduation years of approved full-time equivalent supervised practice for Masters and combined Masters/PhD graduates, and one additional year of supervised practice for Doctor of Psychology graduates.

In 2009, the APS formed the National Education and Training Reference Group (NETRG), a group of experts who undertook a review of the existing education and training pathways in Australia and explored possible future innovations in the education and training pathways for psychologists (Littlefield *et al.*, 2009, as cited in Cranney and Voudouris, 2012). NETRG deliberately included a variety of stakeholders with a wide range of viewpoints, such as board members of APAC, academics and others from the higher education sector, psychologists from registration boards, and other practitioners, as well as receiving input from other targeted and general stakeholders. A number of different models were considered, and in the face of a host of constraints the group recommended retaining existing pathways, although some innovation in the form of an additional '5+1' training pathway was suggested. This will involve the usual APAC-accredited four-year undergraduate degree program, followed by a one-year graduate generalist professional psychology program, and then one year of PBA-approved supervised practice. APAC included this pathway in its major revision of the Accreditation Standards in 2010 by introducing a Graduate Diploma in Professional Psychology fifth-year degree (Cranney and Voudouris, 2012).

Psychology program evaluations in Africa

Collecting information on psychology programs and psychologists in Africa is a difficult task because the general understanding of psychology as a discipline is often poor. Psychology teaching is frequently avoided in many

African countries with attempts at the Africanization of psychology curricula (Thatcher, 2009).

Psychology programs regulation in Zambia: the curriculum of the University of Zambia (UNZA) follows Western theories of psychology. In addition to undergraduate degree courses, UNZA also offers a postgraduate diploma in counseling, including Masters' and Doctorate degrees. The University Act (1999) regulates higher education in Zambia and determines the minimum academic standards, but specific quality control in higher education has recently been handed over to the Zambian Higher Education Authority (Thatcher, 2009). Currently, there is no body that oversees the professional registration of psychologists within Zambia. The professionalization of psychology is still not properly established in Zambia despite psychology having been taught within a university context for more than 40 years. It has been recommended that UNZA reinstate the external examiner system in order to maintain the quality of degrees within Zambia (*Commonwealth News*, 2009, as cited in Thatcher, 2009).

Psychology programs regulation in Zimbabwe: universities and academic programs are accredited by the Ministry of Higher and Tertiary Education. The Division of Standards Development and Quality Assurance (SDQA) has been established, but nobody specifically oversees the quality of psychology teaching and degrees (Thatcher, 2009). Qualification as a psychologist essentially involves three years of practical training following a three-year Bachelor's degree (a Masters' degree is not essential to become registered as a psychologist). An MSc degree in educational psychology or a Diploma in Occupational Psychology could substitute one of the years of practical training (Gwandure, 2009, as cited in Thatcher, 2009).

Psychology program evaluations in Asia

Collecting information on psychology programs in Asia is a difficult task; publications on the topic are not easily available due to language barriers, but it is clear that the offer of higher education programs in psychology is growing rapidly in this part of the world. Psychology teaching in Asia has long-standing ties to psychology in Australia as maintained by the APS, in large part because of the number of distance education programs in psychology based in Australia that are offered throughout Asia. The recently established Asian Psychological Association has been responsible for putting forward the recommendations for standards and competencies for training and licensing of psychologists in Asia. This organization is growing and supporting psychologists and those who teach psychology in Asia (Jaafar and McCarthy, 2009).

Regulatory frameworks for psychology programs in Iran: There is a nationally defined curriculum for psychology programs in Iran that, in terms of teaching, learning and assessment, results in conformity across institutions, but little in the way of quality control (McCarthy *et al.*, 2007).

Psychology program evaluations in Europe

Although the Bologna reforms in education have drawn European PET closer together (see Chapter 2 this volume), differences in mechanisms of quality control inevitably persist (Karandashev, 2007). Information about quality control in PET is available in publications for several European countries, but not for others. We will consider only some examples.

Regulatory frameworks for programs in the UK: according to the Quality Assurance Agency (QAA) for Higher Education in the UK, universities and colleges are autonomous, self-governing institutions (see at www.qaa.ac.uk) and responsible for ensuring appropriate standards and a good quality of education. The responsibilities of QAA are to safeguard the public interest by providing quality control and to encourage continuous improvement in higher education: academic standards are set at a similar level across the UK. To monitor quality and standards, QAA conducts institutional audits based on a peer-review process where teams of academics from outside institutions conduct reviews. Subject benchmark statements provide the frameworks for higher education qualifications and serve as a set of expectations about the standards of degrees in a range of subject areas (see at www.qaa.ac.uk). The benchmarking of academic standards for psychology was undertaken by a group of subject specialists drawn from and acting on behalf of the psychological community. Psychology benchmark statements represent the standards for qualifications at a given level and articulate the attributes and capabilities that those possessing such qualifications should be able to demonstrate. A benchmark statement is not a specification of a detailed curriculum in the subject. Rather it provides variety and flexibility in the design of programs, encourages innovation within an agreed framework, and offers an important external source of reference for higher education institutions when new programs are being designed and developed in a subject area[1] (QAA, 2010).

In order to proceed to postgraduate training in professional psychology and licensure as a psychologist, a student's undergraduate psychology degree must be accredited by the British Psychological Society (BPS) as conferring eligibility for the graduate basis for registration. Graduates from non-accredited courses and institutions can achieve the graduate basis for registration by taking the Society's qualifying examination or an accredited conversion course. Regular reviews are conducted by the BPS to ensure that accredited degrees continue to meet the necessary professional standards for preparing psychologists.

Regulatory frameworks for psychology programs in Germany: The general framework of regulations applies throughout the country and is established by the Ministry of Cultural Affairs. This agency provides the regulations for examinations, which are transferrable to specific programs in the universities. Each program also has to consider the regulations that have been developed in cooperation with the German Psychological Association and ensure a framework for the contents of the curriculum. Programs and examinations follow a homogeneous structure. New regulations aimed at a restructuring of study programs to bring them in line with developments in the EU have recently been drafted and started to run. The main characteristics of these new regulations are the organization of study units into modules, the introduction of the European Credit Transfer System (ECTS) of the European Union, and steps towards greater flexibility regarding new subjects or combinations of subjects (see Karandashev, 2007 for a review).

Regulatory frameworks for psychology programs in Italy: University program assessment is conducted in each university by an evaluation panel appointed by a university's rector. Panel assessment is used both to give suggestions for improvement to university teachers and to inform program management. A national committee, appointed by the Public Education Ministry, collects data from each local evaluation committee and visits universities for further study. Data collection on student's overall satisfaction with university courses and program structure, on graduation rates, and through tracking the employment of graduates, also supports program assessment. Funding for university programs is contingent upon satisfactory assessment (Prandini and McCarthy, 2006; Karandashev, 2007).

Regulatory frameworks for psychology programs in Russia: the Russian Ministry of Education established national standards in all fields of higher education and updates these on an ongoing basis (2010). These standards describe the core content that study programs should contain, but they are flexible so that regional and university bodies can include additional topics to meet the regional, university and student needs. In terms of quality control, the Agency of Psychology Education, which includes subject specialists, such as chairs of psychology schools and departments and professors of psychology, approves and controls the standard of psychology education in universities. The standards are reconsidered every five years (Karandashev, 2007).

Regulatory frameworks for psychology programs in Norway: the Norwegian psychology curriculum is based on Standards for Norwegian Candidate of Psychology, developed by the National Council for Psychology, which comprises representatives of Norwegian universities and the Norwegian Psychological Association. These standards set out curricula and methods of evaluation that ensure the minimum requirements for psychology education and training (Karandashev, 2007).

Regulatory frameworks for psychology programs in Turkey: There are no well-established regulations either for teaching or for practice in psychology in Turkey. Graduates from four-year bachelor degree programs can use the title of psychologist without having any expertise in a specific area. Those who have an MA degree in a specific subfield can use the title of 'expert psychologist', although there is no official chamber or other legal entity regulating the practice of professional psychologists. However, two recent developments promise progress in both the teaching and practice in psychology in Turkey. First, the Council of Higher Education accepted a regulation for the accreditation of psychology undergraduate programs and empowered the Turkish Psychological Association to be the sole institution in charge. Second, the Turkish National Assembly passed legislation defining the practice of clinical psychology, which is the largest application area in Turkey. However, there are still many uncertainties related to teaching, research, and the practice of psychology in Turkey (Trapp *et al.*, 2012).

Regulatory frameworks for psychology programs in Spain: the Spanish undergraduate university degrees currently providing PET are the Licentiate's Degree in Psychology and the Bachelor's Degree in Psychology. Both provide access to the professional license and practice in psychology. The National Agency for Quality Assessment and Accreditation (ANECA) is in charge of accreditation and verifying that the curriculum meets the pertinent training goals (Garcia-Vera *et al.*, 2012).

There are various means for students to receive postgraduate PET in Spain: (1) specialized health training via the residency system in the National Health System; (2) Master's degrees organized by universities with a professional or research focus; (3) university Doctorate programs (Garcia-Vera *et al.*, 2012).

In sum, despite the differences outlined, European countries have much in common in their approach to PET, especially as they move towards consolidation of the European Higher Education Area and respond to the reforms of higher education policy according to Bologna reforms. The transformation of psychology program regulation (www.ehea.info/article-details.aspx?ArticleId=24) is discussed further later in this chapter.

Psychology program evaluations in America

Since quality control in North America and the Caribbean is covered elsewhere (see Chapter 12 by Hall and the commentary by Thompson in this volume), we present here only Latin and South America.

Regulatory frameworks for psychology programs in Mexico: here, professional organizations and societies work with government and non-government institutions for the development of psychology education and practice. The legal mandatory requirements for engaging in professional practice are (1) a degree from an officially recognized university documenting graduation from an approved psychology program, and (2) professional credential or registration documents. Psychological associations strive to enhance standards of psychological practice and teaching, and promote postgraduate specialty education in Mexico (McCarthy *et al.*, 2007).

Regulatory frameworks for psychology programs in Brazil: as in Mexico and much of Latin America, license to practice as a psychologist is granted after the successful completion of a five-year undergraduate program, for which public universities are responsible (McCarthy *et al.*, 2007, 2009). In 2004, new curricular parameters were established to guide a vast reform of psychology undergraduate programs. The first part of the undergraduate study, basic curricula, is a five-year program which provides an overview of psychology in general and leads to a degree that allows registration as a psychologist in Brazil. Students completing these five years can choose two professional areas of emphasis, which may include clinical psychology, health psychology, developmental psychology, and others (De Souza *et al.*, 2012). A four-year baccalaureate degree, similar to those in the

US, is also offered by some universities in Brazil, but this does not allow graduates to practice psychology and is rapidly disappearing.

A systematic, nationwide evaluation of undergraduate psychology programs and quality assessment is a relatively recent development in Brazilian higher education. Instituto Nacional de Estudos e Pesquisas Educacionais Anísio Teixeira (INEP), as the research and development division of the Ministry of Education, is responsible for evaluation and accreditation of all levels of education in Brazil. There are several interesting examples of innovations in a national evaluation system.

On-site visits, internal evaluation committees and official commissions assess psychology programs in such domains as didactic organization of the curriculum, faculty and staff profiles, student body, and adequacy of facilities. As a discipline, psychology has particular criteria in those domains that must be demonstrated, such as mandatory internships, required types of laboratories and other facilities, appropriate faculty/student ratios and expected proportion of faculty members with doctoral degrees or specific professional accreditation. Program evaluators assign a Preliminary Course Grade (Conceito Preliminar de Curso – CPC) to each program based on three measures. CPC is an average of students' performance on the national exam; a differential index of observed and expected performance (IDD) that compares exit scores with the entry scores of novice students; and a group of 'resource variables' that encompasses faculty training and accomplishments, infrastructure and didactics.

The National Exam of Students' Performance (Exame Nacional de Desempenho de Estudantes – ENADE), which is used for the national evaluation of students of psychology degree programs, has replaced individual university exit exams. Students take this test, popularly known as 'The Big Test', when they are nearing graduation from the university in specific programs. Its aim is to assess proficiency in the content, skills and competences covered by the psychology curriculum. ENADE is taken by both first- and final-year students. Scoring is based on minimum standards set by experts in the respective areas measured.

The Indicador de Diferença Entre os Desempenhos Observado e Esperado, referred to as IDD, provides data on the performances of graduating students compared to beginning students in the same psychology program compared to students in psychology programs across all institutions in the system. Policymakers take this as a measure of psychology program performance.

Based on an average of its undergraduate degree CPCs and graduate programs' specific scores, each university receives a general ranking known as the Índice Geral de Cursos (IGC) that provides an overall measure of the institution's educational quality at all levels. IGCs are published annually, immediately after the ENADE results (De Souza *et al.*, 2012).

Graduates of five-year psychology degree programs may progress to a two- to three-year graduate program which grants a specialist degree (a *lato sensu* degree) in a specific area. Graduate research degrees (*stricto sensu*) are also available and important for psychologists in Brazil. Two-years masters and four-years doctoral programs are evaluated by the accreditation committee which oversees psychology education on a three-year cycle. The programs are ranked on a scale of 1 to 7, based on the carefully weighted criteria established. A rank of 3 is the minimum necessary to continue granting (post)graduate degrees. Rankings of 4 or 5 are considered acceptable, of 6 or 7 – outstanding programs. Programs graded 7 are considered of competitive quality internationally.

Ranking and accrediting programs within Brazil is a complex standardized process developed in cooperation with faculty members at all of the major universities in Brazil and overseen by a committee with representation from each region. It is a model which may be valuable to study and adapt as the psychology discipline struggles with developing a viable international evaluation system over the next few years (McCarthy, 2012).

Regulatory frameworks for psychology programs in Peru: in 2005, the government of Peru started the National System of Evaluation, Accreditation, and Certification of Quality of Education (De Souza *et al.*, 2012). A workgroup of psychologists representing different universities developed a document with the new methodological foundation and competencies to be implemented to evaluate and unify psychology curricula. The new curricular system for a professional career in psychology encompasses five to six years of study for a BA in psychology and the professional title of psychologist (García *et al.*, 2006; Benites and Zapata, 2010, as cited in De Souza *et al.*, 2012).

Regulatory frameworks for psychology programs in Chile: a typical program covers four years, including two years of basic classes and two years of specialized classes in the areas of clinical psychology and mental health, community psychology, educational psychology, or others. Completion of these four years of study leads to the title of Licenciado en Psicologia. A fifth year of studies prepares students for professional practice (De Souza *et al.*, 2012). The Board of Psychologists of Chile created a committee to oversee continuing education and master's programs in clinical, educational, and social psychology in Chile. This committee is responsible for monitoring and granting accreditation to those programs. The first doctorate in psychology in Chile was offered in 1998 at the University of Chile, and the Catholic University began a doctoral program in 2000. In 2007 these and two universities, along with the University of Heidelberg (Germany) established the International Doctorate in Psychotherapy (De Souza *et al.*, 2012).

National psychology program evaluations: summary

The preceding review of national quality control regulations leads to the following conclusions:

1   Quality control in PET typically evaluates:

   (a)   program provision (amount of study in the program, its structure, contents, teaching and training methods, faculty and staff qualifications, instructional resources and facilities, etc.)
   (b)   program performance in terms of knowledge of the graduates who completed the program.

2   Professional associations and governmental bodies have their own responsibilities in quality control because higher education and training serve both public and professional purposes.
3   The interests of students and potential employers, who are the major consumers of educational services, have to be represented in quality control.
4   Internal and external quality assessments based on self-study along with an external onsite evaluation and team review are considered as an optimal model for quality control.
5   Quality control can be mandatory or voluntary. A voluntary accreditation system, such as is typical in the US, is not always applicable in education systems in other countries, for example those of Eastern Europe and South America, where a rapid increase in the private education sector has occurred. In such situations, a central (government-led, controlled, supported) body is created to ensure the private offer meets the minimum standards.

International approaches to quality control in PET
There are evident trends towards greater international cooperation in quality control for higher education and training in general and this has now begun to embrace PET as well. For example, international psychological associations, such as IUPsyS and the International Association of Applied Psychology (IAAP) increasingly influence psychology programs around the world. The development of comparative international quality standards for program evaluations is also an important aspect in the internationalization of PET.

As already mentioned, the Bologna Process in Europe is a good example of an attempt to extend international quality control beyond national borders. The Bologna Declaration (1999) encouraged European cooperation in quality assurance of higher education with a view to developing comparable criteria and methodologies (Trapp *et al.*, 2012). With regard to PET, the European Diploma in Psychology (EuropPsy) project developed a framework of minimum standards for education and training in professional psychology and is meant to form a benchmark for high quality training and professional services in psychology in EU countries (Lunt and Poortinga, 2009; Lunt, Chapter 2 this volume).

The European Federation of Psychology Associations (EFPA) has identified psychology teaching as a strategic area and plans to set up a Standing Committee for Educational Affairs. In addition, many psychology departments across the European Union have joined a Europlat network (www. europlat.org.uk) focusing on psychology education. This EC Erasmus Academic Network focuses on knowledge exchange and quality enhancement in the teaching of the psychological sciences (Trapp *et al.*, 2012). Thus, as the EU moves rapidly toward an international model, it is plausible to assume that a similar model will soon be required for the entire international community of psychologists.

Indeed, it is extremely likely that program evaluations will become more international during the twenty-first century; with collaborative program evaluation in international quality assurance being a potential and interesting approach. For example, in 2010, the graduate program at the Institute of

Psychology (PPG-PSICO) at Federal University in Rio Grande do Sul, Brazil, in cooperation with CAPES, the group within the Brazilian Ministry of Education which accredits and ranks psychology programs within that country, took an innovative step toward establishing an objective and equitable international process for comparing the quality of psychology programs between various countries (McCarthy, 2012). As part of this process, an international team from Spain, the UK and the US visited for a three-day evaluative site visit. The team learned how psychology programs within Brazil are evaluated, ranked and accredited. They shared information about how graduate psychology programs in their own home countries were evaluated, compared to each other and accredited. The team used these standards and various other applicable means of quality control in order to determine how well PPG-PSICO's program compared to other high-quality graduate programs preparing psychologists and psychology faculty members in their own countries (McCarthy, 2012). This external international program evaluation may serve as a model for programs in other countries and help to establish a pattern of external international evaluation for psychology education (McCarthy, 2012).

Another example of international evaluation was the project completed for the Centre for Quality Assurance in Higher Education in Lithuania (SKIV), which brought together two international teams chaired by Stephen Newstead (UK) and Lena Adamson (Sweden) to evaluate psychology programs, both undergraduate and graduate, at four public universities in Lithuania. The programs were evaluated against national, EU and international standards by international colleagues from many countries, including Russia, Lithuania, Estonia, Romania, Hungary, UK, Sweden, Austria (McCarthy, 2012; Newstead, personal communication, October 14, 2012).

Newstead also chaired the program evaluation in a university in Hong Kong (personal communication, October 14, 2012) which was looking at a proposed postgraduate program. This was organized by the Hong Kong Council for the Accreditation of Academic Awards and Qualifications.

Some, however, may not see the development of an international evaluation process as a positive step; convergence in accreditation systems meets resistance. The highly diversified nature of the world system of national quality assurance agencies is seen as a protective barrier against the further development of the international quality control and the loss of national sovereignty in matters held to be crucial in safeguarding national policy orientations, quality assurance, and accreditation. For example, Knight and De Wit (1997) point to the strong concerns for uniformity and imposition of Western standards in Asia Pacific countries, and to difficulties and challenges connected to policy transfer in this field relating to national and cultural sensitivities. Certainly there is a growing awareness, although no definite acceptance, that convergence and harmonization of quality assurance and accreditation arrangements are necessary in the context of increasing transnational trade in higher education (Knight, 2002).

Indeed, there are many local and contextual differences between countries, and it is unlikely that any large association from any country could develop accreditation standards that could be utilized on an international basis. A report on APA's role in international quality assurance stated that APA would not engage in quality assurance reviews of PET programs at the international level, but would strive to be a collaborating organization in developing policies to promote international mechanisms of review (McCarthy, 2012). IUPsyS, however, currently has a task force focused on PET that may move toward this end.

In general, the following questions are pertinent to the issue of international quality control of PET.

Quantity and quality: does a psychology program give enough time for teaching and training in psychology? Does the program provide enough breadth and depth of psychology knowledge and experience? As for quantity, the European Credit Transfer and Accumulation System (ECTS), for example, makes teaching and learning in higher education transparent across Europe. One ECTS credit corresponds to 25–30 hours of work. The typical credit ranges are 180–240 units for the first (Bachelor's) and 90–120 units for the second (Master's) degree. There is no credit range for the third degree, Doctoral. As another example, psychology programs in the US require 120–128 semester credit hours for a Bachelor's degree, 30–50 credit hours for a Master's degree, and 50–90 credit hours for a Doctoral degree. One may ask: what is the credit hour and how comparable are the credit units? What kind of student involvement do they take into account? Do they include in class meetings? How about online classes?

As for quality, another question arises: what is the content of these classes? Are they in psychology, related disciplines, or general education? For instance, as Cranney and Voudouris (2012) noted, on average, the amount of psychology content in a three-year undergraduate degree program in Australia is more than that in the four-year US model and less than that in the three-year British model. What degree is sufficient for independent psychology practice, research, and teaching: five-year undergraduate, Master's, or Doctoral degree? Should we count only the degree achieved or curriculum content as well? A few countries, most notably the USA, required graduate degrees for practice of psychology, but the structure of undergraduate training there also differed greatly, with more general studies courses and fewer applied courses within the discipline. It should be noted that in the US, entry to professional-level psychology does not necessarily require an undergraduate degree in psychology, thus putting into question the value of undergraduate psychology education for preparing practicing psychologists. Graduate training, in turn, focused only on the discipline of psychology or, more precisely, one of many subdisciplines within psychology such as counseling, clinical or school psychology.

Mandatory and optional requirements question in quality control: what should be the proportion of mandatory, optional, and flexible requirements in curriculum and learning outcomes? How to preserve flexibility and diversity within an international framework of quality control in PET? The development of education, training curriculum and qualification common to many countries but still regionally flexible would provide the best quality in PET. Should the quality control and registration of psychologists apply to psychologists as a generic profession, or to specializations: clinical, counseling, work/industrial/ organizational psychologists?

The review of international experiences of quality control in PET led to the following conclusions:

1   National as well as international organizations may have interests in quality control. Psychology programs have complex relations with their state system of education as well as with the international academic community and there is a need for balance between the national responsibilities and the practices of the international academic community.
2   To take into account all interested parties, quality control might be implemented by an independent agency representing the national and international groups, professional and governmental organizations, and student and consumer–employer representatives.
3   International quality control may lead to resistance, but it should transform into a process of ongoing improvement, and put quality on the agenda. International evaluation should have clear consequences, such as being linked to the funding or international degree validation.
4   Quality control should be voluntary, initiated by an institution, and bring benefits. The quality control requirements should be the optimal guidelines and benchmarks, a set of suggestions to follow, keeping the optimal proportion of national and international components.

Note

1 www.qaa.ac.uk/Publications/InformationAndGuidance/Documents/Psychology 2010.pdf

References

Burgess, G.H., Sternberger, L.G., Sanchez-Sosa, J.J., Lunt, I., Shealy, C.N. and Ritchie, P. (2004). Development of a global curriculum for professional psychology: Implications of the combined-integrated model of doctoral training. *Journal of Clinical Psychology*, *60*, 10, 1027–49.

Cranney, J. and Voudouris, N.J. (2012). Psychology education and training in Australia: Shaping the future. In McCarthy, S., Cranney, J., Dickson, K. L., Trapp, A. and Karandashev, V. (Eds.), *Teaching Psychology around the World: Vol. 3*, pp. 2–14. Newcastle upon Tyne, UK: Cambridge Scholars Publishing.

De Souza, L.K., McCarthy, S. and Gauer, G. (2012). Teaching psychology in South America. In McCarthy, S., Cranney, J., Dickson, K. L., Trapp, A. and Karandashev, V. (Eds.), *Teaching Psychology around the World: Vol. 3*, pp. 350–74. Newcastle upon Tyne, UK: Cambridge Scholars Publishing.

European Network of Work and Organizational Psychologists (2005). *European Curriculum in W&O Psychology: Reference Model and Minimal Standards*. www.ucm. es/info/Psyap/enop/rmodel.html

Garcia-Vera, M.P., Sanz, J. and Prieto, J.M. (2012). The current situation of undergraduate and postgraduate education in psychotherapy for psychologists in Spain. In McCarthy,

S., Cranney, J., Dickson, K.L., Trapp, A. and Karandashev, V. (Eds.), *Teaching Psychology around the World: Vol. 3*, pp. 311–29. Newcastle upon Tyne, UK: Cambridge Scholars Publishing.

Helmes, E. and Pachana, N.A. (2005). Professional doctoral training in psychology: International comparison and commentary. *Australian Psychologist, 40*, 1, 45–53.

Jaafar, J.L. and McCarthy, S. (2009). Teaching Psychology in Asia: Historical Roots and Modern Practices. In McCarthy, S., Karandashev, V., Stevens, M., Thatcher, A., Jaafar, J., Moore, K., Trapp, A. and Brewer, C. (2009). *Teaching Psychology around the World: Vol. 2*, pp. 186–211. Newcastle upon Tyne, UK: Cambridge Scholars Publishing.

Karandashev, V. (2007) International Perspectives on Psychology Teaching: Europe. In McCarthy, S., Newstead, S., Karandashev, V., Prandini, C., Hutz, C. and Gomes, W. (2007). *Teaching Psychology around the World*, pp. 167–214. Newcastle, UK: Cambridge Scholars Publishing.

Karandashev, V. (2009). The Internationalization of Psychology Teaching Around the World: History and Current Trends. In McCarthy, S., Karandashev, V., Stevens, M., Thatcher, A., Jafaar, J., Moore, K., Trapp, A. and Brewer, C. (Eds.), *Teaching Psychology Around the World, Vol. 2*, pp. 1–38. Newcastle, UK: Cambridge Scholars Publishing.

Karandashev, V. (2010). International Psychology Education: Retrospective and Promise for the Global Future. Paper presented at the Fourth International Conference on Psychology Education, 8–10 July, 2012, Sydney, Australia, http://icope2010.psy.unsw.edu.au/program/Karandashev.pdf

Karandashev, V. and McCarthy, S. (Eds.) (2006). *International Journal of Psychology: Special Issue: International Practices in the Teaching of Psychology*, *41*, 1.

Knight, J. (2002). *Trade in Higher Education Services: The Implications of GATS*. London: The Observatory on Borderless Higher Education.

Knight, J. and De Wit, H. (Eds.) (1997). *Internationalization of Higher Education in Asia Pacific Countries*. Amsterdam: EAIE.

Leong, F.T.L. and Ponterotto, J.G. (2003). A Proposal for Internationalizing Counseling Psychology in the United States: Rationale, Recommendations, and Challenges. *The Counseling Psychologist, 31*, 4, 381–95.

Lunt, I. and Poortinga, Y.H. (2009) Certification of Psychologists in Europe: Implications for Teaching Psychology. In McCarthy, S., Karandashev, V., Stevens, M., Thatcher, A., Jaafar, J., Moore, K., Trapp, A. and Brewer, C. (Eds.), *Teaching Psychology Around the World: Vol. 2*, pp. 293–307. Newcastle upon Tyne, UK: Cambridge Scholars Publishing.

Marsella, A. and Pedersen, P. (2004). Internationalizing the Curriculum in Counseling Psychology. *Counseling Psychology Quarterly, 17*, 413–24.

McCarthy, S. (2012) Teaching Psychology around the World: Changing Landscapes. In McCarthy, S., Cranney, J., Dickson, K.L., Trapp, A. and Karandashev, V. (Eds.), *Teaching Psychology around the World: Vol. 3*, pp. 467–80. Newcastle upon Tyne, UK: Cambridge Scholars Publishing.

McCarthy, S., Alvarez, E. and Vasquez, F. (2007) International Perspectives on Psychology Teaching: North America. In McCarthy, S., Newstead, S., Karandashev, V., Prandini, C., Hutz, C. and Gomes, W. (2007). *Teaching Psychology around the World*, pp. 275–321. Newcastle, UK: Cambridge Scholars Publishing.

McCarthy, S., Cranney, J., Dickson, K.L. Trapp, A. and Karandashev, V. (2012). *Teaching Psychology around the World: Vol. 3*. Newcastle upon Tyne, UK: Cambridge Scholars Publishing.

McCarthy, S., Karandashev, V., Stevens, M., Thatcher, A., Jaafar, J., Moore, K., Trapp, A. and Brewer, C. (2009). *Teaching Psychology around the World: Vol. 2*. Newcastle upon Tyne, UK: Cambridge Scholars Publishing.

McCarthy, S., Newstead, S., Karandashev, V., Prandini, C., Hutz, C. and Gomes, W. (2007). *Teaching Psychology around the World*. Newcastle, UK: Cambridge Scholars Publishing.

Moore, K. (2009) Teaching Psychology in Australia: Reaching out to the World. In McCarthy, S., Karandashev, V., Stevens, M., Thatcher, A., Jaafar, J., Moore, K., Trapp, A. and Brewer, C. (2009). *Teaching Psychology around the World: Vol. 2*, pp. 220–35. Newcastle upon Tyne, UK: Cambridge Scholars Publishing.

Pawlik, K. (2000). Psychological science: content, methodology, history and profession. In Pawlik, K. and Rosenzweig, M.R. (Eds.), *International Handbook of Psychology*, pp. 3–19. London: Sage.

Prandini, C. and McCarthy, S. (2006). Teaching psychology as a science in Italy. *International Journal of Psychology, 41* (1), 42–50.

QAA (2010). *Subject Benchmark Statement. Psychology*. The Quality Assurance Agency for Higher Education: UK. www.qaa.ac.uk/Publications/InformationAnd Guidance/Documents/Psychology2010.pdf

Russian Ministry of Education (2010). Федеральный государственный образовательный стандарт высшего профессионального образования по направлению подготовки психология (Federal State Educational Standard of Higher Professional Education in Psychology). Retrieved from www.edu.ru/db-mon/mo/Data/d_09/m759.html and www.edu.ru/db-mon/mo/Data/d_09/prm759-1.pdf

Thatcher, A. (2009) International Perspectives on Psychology Teaching: Africa and the Mid-East. In McCarthy, S., Karandashev, V., Stevens, M., Thatcher, A., Jaafar, J., Moore, K., Trapp, A. and Brewer, C. (2009). *Teaching Psychology around the World: Vol. 2*, pp. 87–101. Newcastle upon Tyne, UK: Cambridge Scholars Publishing.

Trapp, A., Reddy, P., Spinath, B., Marques, F. and Sumer, N. (2012) Teaching Psychology in Europe. In McCarthy, S., Cranney, J., Dickson, K.L. Trapp, A. and Karandashev, V. (Eds.). *Teaching Psychology around the World: Vol. 3*, pp. 292–310. Newcastle upon Tyne, UK: Cambridge Scholars Publishing.

12 Models for quality control in psychology education and training

A North American perspective

Judy E. Hall

This chapter examines the training model, terminal professional degree, accreditation/designation process, licensure laws, ethics and public accountability, and voluntary registers as some of the attributes to be considered in developing a model for quality control in psychology education and training. In so doing, it focuses mainly on education and training in North America for the following reasons:

- over the years individuals from other countries came to the United States and Canada for education and training as psychologists, then returned home to develop programs molded somewhat on those experiences but sensitive to local culture and concerns;
- these accreditation and regulatory systems are useful as models, as well as for considering what not to do; and
- the author is most conversant with North America and has been integrally involved in developing/implementing many of the structures.

In the United States psychology is both a scientific discipline and a science-based profession. Both characteristics influence the need for quality assurance in education and training and associated challenges. The *scientist-practitioner* training model was developed in 1949 and dominated the academic community in psychology for many years. Dissatisfaction by PhD graduates who felt inadequately prepared for health service delivery culminated in the development of a new model of training for practice. The shift to the *practitioner* training model occurred in 1974 when a new degree, the Doctor of Psychology (PsyD), was anointed as an alternative path for education and training in professional psychology. The PsyD was intended to prepare students to apply psychological principles and research as a vehicle to address individual or societal problems.

Implementation of licensure laws and regulation in the United States followed a similar timeline, starting in 1945. By 1978 all states regulated the practice or title of psychologist. In the early stages of defining the profession, it was logical that the net be widely cast. Anyone who presented as a psychologist was expected to hold the defining credential. This necessitated a broad definition of psychology from a regulatory standpoint, resulting in the generic license.

Once licensed the psychologist was cautioned to practice within their demonstrated areas of expertise as mandated by the professional ethics code developed by the American Psychological Association (APA). Although begun in 1947, APA did not approve its first code of ethics until 1953 (American Psychological Association, 1953).

The 1970s were an important developmental stage for psychology, and the themes reverberate today:

- states enact idiosyncratic rules defining education and training;
- few specialty areas announce their opposition to requiring licensure for their graduates (e.g., industrial/ organizational psychology) viewing such standards as irrelevant to competence and an intrusion on academic freedom;
- the potential for national health insurance necessitates a uniform definition and credentialing process for psychologists if the profession is to be recognized;
- the practitioner training model – the PsyD – initiated in a few institutions (and opposed by others) provides an option for those interested in entering the profession of psychology and engaging in services as an independent practitioner, regardless of whether they also conduct scientific research, publish in peer-reviewed journals or join academic faculties; and
- private, non-profit and for-profit schools compete successfully for the increasing number of students seeking a doctoral degree in psychology.

In the past forty years, organized psychology has focused on how best to (a) educate and train professional psychologists (including setting national standards for education, internship and postdoctoral training), (b) regulate professional psychologists through accreditation/designation, licensure/certification, licensure examinations, ethical standards, and credentialing, and more recently, (c) foster ways in which a country, state, province, or territory reduces barriers for those seeking geographic or virtual mobility.

The first training conference in 1949 defined the doctoral standard as the entry level for psychologists, and was codified in four APA model licensure acts, with the last model act approved in 2010 (American Psychological Association, 2010). Program accreditation began in 1947 (Altmaier, 2003). However, as graduates of accredited programs applied for licensure, regulatory boards found inconsistencies in the programs' adherence to requiring a foundation in specified scientific coursework. The tension created by the two regulatory approaches, accreditation and licensure, derived from contrasting perspectives. Millard's classification (as cited in Nelson *et al.*, 2008) is helpful in highlighting the differences, namely whether a program is evaluated against common standards of what constitutes a good program (definitional-prescriptive) or one which focuses on the mission and goals of the program (mission-objective).

Recognizing the variability in the 51 jurisdictions spotlighted by adverse legal decisions in the 1970s, the APA and the National Register of Health Service Providers in Psychology (National Register) invited organized psychology to send representatives to a meeting to define an acceptable doctoral degree in psychology. Participants in these two seminal conferences in 1976 and 1977 argued that doctoral programs must provide sufficient scientific foundation and constitute an organized program of study, with adequate faculty and institutional resources (as well as meet other criteria, regardless of specialty area and doctoral degree) (Wellner, 1978). Advancing this agenda, the Association of State and Provincial Psychology Boards (ASPPB) and the National Register independently adopted the designation criteria as policy in 1978. Over time, licensure laws came to rely on this criterion-based evaluation, focusing on input (residency, courses, faculty, and training hours) with the only outcome relating to passing the licensure examination(s).

Today, the majority of state licensure laws specify that graduates of APA/CPA accredited programs or ASPPB/National Register designated programs meet the statutory definition of minimal competence. Voluntary quality assurance mechanisms now have the force of law, as licensure laws require applicants to meet either standard. When voluntary professional standards become mandatory, the stakes are raised for training programs and for applicants seeking licensure. Some jurisdictions hold to that standard; other boards have deviated and accept graduates from other programs housed in regionally accredited institutions. Most psychologists engaged in education and training believe that regional accreditation of the institution is a necessary but insufficient criterion for approval of a doctoral program.

Voluntary mechanisms, such as professional registers, were established in the United States in 1974 (www.nationalregister.org) and in Canada in 1985 (www.crhspp.ca) for credentialing health service psychologists. More recently in 2010, the EuroPsy Register was initiated in Europe for recognizing psychologists (www.europsy-efpa.eu). All three have established credentialing standards and recognize psychologists individually but on a national basis. Voluntary professional registers assure consumers that psychologists who have been credentialed meet those standards, which may exceed the standards for licensure. Professional registers implement quality assurance by monitoring ethical conduct and the sanctioning of psychologists based upon violation of jurisdictional codes of conduct. Actions taken independently by the professional registers may be reported to professionals, the complainants, and the public.

Adding representatives of the public to boards of regulatory and professional organizations helps advance quality control through increased transparency and de-mystification of decision making. This trend was initiated in 1974 by the National Register, which appointed consumer representatives to the board of directors which set policy and to the appeal board which reviewed decisions related to charges of ethical misconduct or failure to meet credentialing standards. Then, beginning in the 1980s, licensure boards as well as other psychology organizations and disciplinary committees began to involve consumers. One could argue that including consumers is essential to effective quality control in psychology. However, the definition of the consumer varies. Students are consumers; clients are consumers; governments and agencies are consumers; registers are consumers. For the professional psychologist the label for this individual has migrated from patient, to client, to consumer (Ritchie, 2008).

A defining characteristic of the North American regulatory process is the absence of a national license. This omission leads to significant variation in laws/ rules governing the profession of psychology, with psychologists held to different licensure standards. In contrast, credible credentialing organizations are typically national in scope built upon a license to practice but independently evaluate doctoral degree, internship and postdoctoral experience using primary source documentation. Because of their national scope, credentialing organizations offer the individual both geographic and virtual mobility. In order to see what can be accomplished by the removal of those jurisdictional barriers, consider Australia, which used federal reimbursement for healthcare services to get agreement from the states and territories for creating a national license to practice. Dissension occurred when the final standards, which did not require graduation from accredited doctoral programs, were considerably more lax than expected, purportedly justified by the country needing access to more psychological practitioners.

Remaining variables in quality control include the role of the undergraduate degree; competencies: what, when and how assessed; organized training vs. supervised experience; relationship between licensure and credentialing, including mobility mechanisms; and sharing disciplinary data with the public.

The role of the undergraduate degree

In the United States approximately 25 percent of psychology baccalaureate recipients go on to graduate study in psychology (4–6 percent pursue doctoral degrees and 20–22 percent are enrolled in master's degree programs). Conversely, of those who graduate with a doctorate in psychology, 70 percent completed an undergraduate degree in psychology, where a major in psychology is offered within a liberal education curriculum with substantial coursework outside psychology (American Psychological Association, Support Center, 2012). Thus, a degree major in psychology is not a necessary precursor for admission to a graduate program in psychology in the United States, although several courses in psychology may be required. This is unlike what happens in Canada where the required *honors* degree in psychology includes senior-year coursework considered graduate-level work. As a result, these senior-year courses are often counted in the educational foundation for licensure in the United States. In the United Kingdom, applicants pursuing licensure must first gain a bachelor's degree in psychology accredited by the British Psychological Society (BPS); 20 percent of those graduates go on to professional training in psychology (Lunt, 2008).

Contrast this sequence with Mexico where education for practice begins in the final years of high school and continues for five years culminating in a degree (licentiate) that meets the requirement for a permanent license to practice (cédula) (Hernández Guzmán and Sanchez-Sosa, 2008). The doctoral degree, which focuses on research generation and scholarly activity, is needed for employment in academic settings but is earned after the license. This is the opposite of what happens in the United States and Canada, where the academic-scientific foundation and research precede professional training and licensure. A comparison of time spent in education from the entry into the educational system to independent practice as a psychologist in the United States, Canada and Mexico is presented in Hall and Hurley (2002).

Quality control in higher education

The first step in determining whether adequate quality control of education and training in professional psychology exists is to look at the context in which the degree program is offered, namely the institution and the processes in place to ensure quality. It is important to ask: who are the reliable authorities as to the quality of education or training and which programs do they accredit? Higher education may be controlled by a governmental or non-governmental agency, such as the ministry of education, a federation of institutions and private organizations, or in some instances located in institutions deemed autonomous. Finding out whether an institution has been authorized to operate by an official, external body is often quite complicated for someone outside the country. However, in the United States there is an annual printed publication which categorizes programs/institutions and the approval level, e.g., regional or specialty (American Council on Education, 2011). The two relevant bodies which *accredit the accreditors* are the United States Department of Education (2012) (USDOE; see www2.ed.gov/admins/finaid/accred/index.html) and the Council for Higher Education Accreditation (CHEA; see www.chea.org/search/default. asp). While the first exists primarily to approve institutions/programs interested in offering federal loans to students in the United States, the latter is a voluntary, standard-setting organization also involved in international programs (Council for Higher Education Accreditation, 2012). Through the Commission on Accreditation (CoA) professional psychology has a USDOE- and CHEA-approved specialized accreditation program that is self-supporting and independent of APA in terms of its decision-making.

State government may have a mechanism to determine whether an institution can offer a degree program but most do not have meaningful oversight. They may simply issue a license for the institution to operate. That means students may enter programs in which their desired goal, licensure as a professional psychologist, may not be achievable. More importantly, in some cases, the institution does not make this outcome clear to students in advance of enrollment.

Thus, the next step is determining whether the identified and recognized institution offers an acceptable program in psychology. As we have seen, the differences in psychology training models relate to the control of the curriculum, the degree that is granted upon completion of the educational program, the interplay of the degree with practice responsibilities, and whether the outcome guarantees access to the practice of the profession. In Australia and the United Kingdom, the students can easily identify programs which meet accreditation and licensure standards. For a global perspective, a method of identifying comparable institutional and programmatic resources for each country is needed. Having such a resource would also be extremely helpful for individual mobility.

In the United States and Canada, doctoral programs in professional psychology are approved by the CoA, accredited by the Canadian Psychological Association (CPA) or designated by the ASPPB/National Register Designation Project. Graduates of these programs typically meet the educational criteria for licensure. However, graduates of unapproved programs may be admitted to the licensure exam because jurisdictional boards idiosyncratically evaluate applicants and determine that the program presented is equivalent or primarily psychological. Many years ago, Mort Berger, the President of ASPPB, quipped that 'primarily psychological in nature' actually means 'not psychology' (Wellner, 1978, p. 16). Deeming an individual applicant's program equivalent, especially when the program has previously been denied as meeting accreditation or designation approval criteria, undercuts the role of accreditation and designation in the quality assurance process. Moving to the jurisdictional level, New York posts online 40 programs meeting the educational requirement for licensure as a New York psychologist. New York is the only state that guarantees licensure eligibility on educational grounds if a student completes a state-approved program. This is due to the unique hosting of the licensure review process within the State Department of Education under supervision of the New York Board of Regents, a USDOE-recognized accrediting agency.

Whereas previously doctoral programs could apply for joint accreditation by CoA and CPA, as of January 1, 2008, the CoA no longer accepts new applications for accreditation of Canadian programs. Only Canadian programs accredited by the APA prior to January 1, 2008 have the option of applying to renew their CPA/APA accreditation up to September 1, 2015. This decision came about because of differences in how the United States model applied in Canada. Recently, both CPA and APA entered into an agreement, not on reciprocal recognition of accreditation status which had been sought for many years, but on understanding the 'policies, processes, standards, criteria, guidelines and principles upon which accreditation (and/or other systems of quality assurance) of doctoral program/mes and internship program/mes in professional psychology in their respective countries are based' (American Psychological Association, Council of Representatives, 2011). This is different from the international engineering alliance where the results of member countries' accreditation processes are deemed substantially equivalent, ensuring mobility for graduates who become licensed in one member country and move to another (Washington Accord, 2012).

Separating the two countries' accreditation processes coincided with the Task Force Report of the Board of Educational Affairs (BEA)/Council on International Relations in Psychology (CIRP) on APA's role in international quality assurance. This task force recommended that APA not engage in accrediting programs outside the United States (American Psychological Association, Council of Representatives, 2009). Thus, the APA now proposes to collaborate with other organizations engaged in quality assurance of education and training.

In addition to providing a pathway to licensure, in recent years the accreditation process in the United States evaluates whether certain outcomes are met. Related indicators, high student debt and an insufficient number of qualified internships, are of primary concern. Both are due to an increasing number of students seeking graduate training in professional school programs with large class sizes. External pressure is essential as applied by the Federal Government, including a recent investigation of for-profit schools (United States Senate Committee on Health, Education, Labor and Pensions, July 30, 2012), and by organized psychology concerned about the internship crisis (Grus *et al.*, 2011). For a full-time student, the advantage of the practitioner model over the research/academic model is the fixed curriculum that guarantees graduation in a set number of years. However, if an internship position is not available in the designated year, the number of years to graduation is interrupted and the contract with the student is essentially broken. It is important to note these programs typically have the highest tuition and provide no financial support, thereby increasing hardship on students.

Many argue that the proximal outcomes of education and training are appropriate measures for assessing program quality. This trend led educational institutions and quality assurance bodies to look at competencies including identifying, assessing, and requiring them for graduation. This competencies' push in the United States began in 1986, followed by identifying foundation and functional competencies for practice in 2002, and benchmarking competencies into four stages in 2006. Building upon prior progress, the benchmarks document analyzes the competencies required to be ready for entry into practicum, internship, and then practice, with the competencies related to continuing professional development set aside for later development (Fouad *et al.*, 2009). With the change in licensing requirements in 11 states to allow the potential for licensure upon graduation (and prior to completing the postdoctoral years of experience), even more emphasis is placed on defining and assessing practica competencies. Hatcher and Lasseter created a document to identify the competencies expected. To review the report, visit (www.aptc.org/public_files/Practicum%20Competencies %20FINAL%20(Oct%20'06%20Version)pdf). The benchmarks are now tied to an evaluation system available online (www.apa.org/ed/graduate/benchmarks-evaluation-system.aspx).

Academic programs argue that because the defined competencies are demonstrated and measured by educators and trainers, there is no need for the licensing board to evaluate the individual graduate's program. Graduates' complaints are twofold: (a) additional experience beyond the doctorate is not needed because of the two years supervised experience in the doctoral degree program, and (b) the licensing exam doesn't measure ability to practice. Beginning in 2007 accredited programs were required to post outcomes on their websites, namely average program time to completion, program costs, and rates for internship placement, attrition, and licensure. However, as pointed out by Stricker (2008), it is the convergence of these measures and requirements that defines quality assurance and helps ensure that the licensee is qualified to enter practice. Debate continues on how competence is best assessed, by whom and when, and whether that is sufficient to protect the public from potentially harmful and unethical practitioners.

Terminal degree for practice

Until recently the United States was the only country with a doctoral degree as the standard for entry into the profession. Canada followed with more provinces having now adopted a doctoral standard. In the United Kingdom, a doctoral degree (DClinPsy or DEdPsy) is now the standard for licensure, even though the standard for the EuroPsy is a master's degree plus one year of experience. However, for many of the most populated Latin America countries, a professional undergraduate degree leads to practice. In terms of training, in some countries it is typical for the clinical experience to be integrated into the degree (e.g., United Kingdom, Nordic countries) or in a period that follows graduation (e.g., Mexico) or both (e.g., South Africa). The variation in these models of training adds a potential barrier to global mobility and a need for competent authorities to evaluate equivalence in education and training. Even so, within certain regions mobility may be easy, such as in Latin America, within Europe or across Scandinavia.

Internship versus supervised experience

In North America, the internship is completed prior to and as a requirement for graduation. In the United States the first internship program in professional psychology was accredited in 1956. Even at that time, the number of students seeking formal internships was higher than the number of positions available. As a result, students often used on-the-job training to satisfy the experience requirement. Initially, the APA accreditation guidelines required only 600 hours of practicum experience prior to admission to an internship (a number is no longer specified). Today, most students complete a number of different practica (face-to-face delivery of professional psychological services) distributed over several sites treating diverse populations and working under the supervision of different licensed psychologists in order to be competitive in obtaining an internship. In many programs the first year of practicum is spent in a psychology clinic run by the university or doctoral program, giving the faculty even more control over the assessment of competencies. Today, internship applicants typically document an average of 1800–2000 practicum hours in their internship application. Approved internships include an APA/CPA approved internship, an Association of Psychology Internship and Postdoctoral Centers (APPIC) listed internship, a Council of Directors of School Psychology Programs (CDSPP) internship or an internship that meets specified criteria developed by the National Register.

The National Register internship criteria were developed in 1980 based upon an analysis of the variable experience submitted between 1974 and 1979 by applicants for credentialing by the National Register. In contrast to supervised experience, an internship was defined as a training program occurring over one year full-time or two years half-time, with at least two psychologists supervising the training program and two psychology interns participating. These criteria have stood the test of time with CDSPP as well as other groups and licensure boards adopting these criteria as their own.

So while there has been a history of insufficient numbers of internship positions available, the imbalance between applicants and positions available has gotten progressively worse in recent years. Now doctoral programs are challenged to create internship opportunities for their students or potentially lose program accreditation status. Part of the reluctance in seeking internship accreditation is due to the insufficiency of federal government funding (only US$3 million awarded in 2011), unlike that for graduate medical education (US$9 billion). The modal number of psychology interns is two; therefore, the cost–benefit proposition for accreditation is not convincing. Even though APPIC encourages members to seek accreditation, about a third (200) of the APPIC internships is unaccredited, with 87 of those in private practice sites.

To stimulate applications for accreditation, CoA proposes a three-step review and approval process, with no change in application and renewal fees. Both APA and Health Resources and Services Administration (HRSA) have recently made funds available for accredited internships. The accredited internships can now compete for the US$3 million just authorized by APA. In addition, HRSA just awarded US$3.6 million to 11 accredited institutions/programs and internships (Arielle Eiser, personal communication, September 27, 2012). (HRSA is the primary federal agency for improving access to health care services for people who are uninsured, isolated, or medically vulnerable.)

The second phase of required experience for licensure, credentialing, and mobility is a year of postdoctoral supervised experience. Licensing boards and credentialing organizations have established their own criteria for this culmination of training with little commonality other than length, which is typically one year consisting of 1500–2000 hours of supervised experience. Although there have been postdoctoral training programs for many years, especially in specialized practice areas, only recently was accreditation for postdoctoral residencies initiated by CoA fostered by the United States Department of Veterans' Affairs requirement. Recently, organized postdoctoral residency training sites agreed to participate in a trial for matching applicants to training sites, similar to the process that has existed for many years for internship placement. These formal postdoctoral residency training programs and less organized experiences, such as supervised employment, meet licensure standards and credentialing requirements.

Licensing and credentialing

In North America, licensing is the function of the government, implemented by regulatory or licensing boards which determine whether an applicant meets state, provincial, or territorial requirements for entry into the generic practice of psychology. Frankly, professional licensing has very little to do with quality assurance, although most consumers think that it does, knowing that a psychologist is licensed only means that the psychologist possesses a *minimum* level of competence. This level of competence is defined as having completed a sequence of education, training, and experience followed by successful performance on an independent examination of knowledge and skills.

The final required component of the licensure process in North America is a national multiple choice examination called the Examination for Professional Practice in Psychology (EPPP) developed by ASPPB. The EPPP has been in place since the 1960s with unsuccessful attempts to add more specialized national exams. States and provinces also may require an oral exam or a jurisprudence examination to assess local knowledge of laws and other practice requirements. Variability abounds in the oral exam: the oral can be a structured examination about specific questions, the applicant's work product, jurisprudence issues or simply an interview. The role of exams *could* change if doctoral programs objectively assessed competencies before allowing students to graduate, and if licensing boards adopted a competency-based, outcome standard in addition to the current input model. As pointed out by Greenberg and Smith (2008), although test use is common internationally, countries vary, with some countries not giving structured examinations. At the present time, re-licensure exams are not required in North America so the assessment on entry-level knowledge and skills constitutes the only opportunity for the jurisdiction to independently assess competence.

Credentialing and *certification* are terms that are often used interchangeably and usually refer to individual achievement. For instance, the university certifies to the public that the graduate has met the requirements for a doctoral degree by awarding the diploma. Certification typically indicates quality, 'especially in the absence of knowledge to the contrary' (Drum and Hall, 1993, p. 151). Credentials for health care professionals are important because, 'in no other field does a consumer care so much about the quality of services and yet have so little ability to judge quality themselves . . . Credentials serve as necessary proxies for direct measurement of quality' (Stromberg, 1991, p. 1). However, only a small percentage of psychologists pursue credentials beyond licensure.

Credentialing organizations typically are pro-profession and not organized for the purpose of consumer protection; yet as voluntary organizations, they can and do play a significant role in creating a special relationship with the public. Credible credentialing organizations conduct primary source verification of credentials (education, training, and licensure) and provide an independent check on the accuracy and currency of these qualifications. Licensing authorities investigate and adjudicate professional misconduct complaints, and then report adverse decisions to professional organizations and credentialing bodies, and in the United States, to the federal disciplinary healthcare databank. With this information, credentialing bodies may take disciplinary action and report their actions to consumers, typically by posting the information online. Noting this symbiotic relationship between licensure and credentialing, in terms of protecting consumers, Hall (2000) states that 'neither licensing nor certification alone is sufficient . . . [Rather,] both are needed' (pp. 317–18). Stricker (2008) interprets the lack of interest in seeking voluntary, higher-order credentialing as a lack of concern by practitioners about quality assurance. He points to the reluctance to engage in self-regulation as likely to invite external bodies to fill the void. Ritchie (2008) suggests that by providing feedback to professionals the consumer fulfills a responsibility to demand that standards be met.

Another difference between licensure and credentialing in the United States is that holding a license in one jurisdiction does not make it easier to obtain another one. As psychologists became interested in mobility and encountered hurdles, the National Register promoted mobility by asking each state and provincial board to endorse the health service provider credential. Forty-six jurisdictions (and more in process this year) approve the National Register as a mechanism for expediting licensure. For a current list, go to www.nationalregister.org/licensure_mobility. html. Thus, geographic or virtual mobility is relatively easily achieved on an individual basis. Verification of qualifications from a credentialing organization like the National Register expedites document-gathering by the applicant and review and approval by the regulatory body. Mobility potential is sought by most psychologists, may not be acted upon immediately, but having it serves as an insurance policy that is there when needed.

Ethical and professional conduct

Psychology students, postgraduate trainees, and licensed/credentialed psychologists are responsible for adhering to scientific and professional ethics (e.g., in research, practica, or internship, in post-degree training, and attesting to whether they were the subject of ethical complaints/adjudications at the time of renewal of the license and credential). Consumer complaints to state and provincial regulatory bodies are investigated with the force of law while offering administrative due process to the psychologist. State actions are publicized and posted on the licensing board website. Disciplinary actions taken by the APA Ethics Committee are reported annually to the APA membership. Thus, at least in the United States these actions are accessible by the public. Not so elsewhere.

One could easily argue that reporting adjudicated ethical sanctions to the public balances public accountability with protection of the profession. As long as the information is accurate and timelines for posting disciplinary actions are followed, making the information publicly available is consonant with embracing a culture of accountability. The majority of regulatory boards in the United States post online the names of licensed psychologists along with information on whether the person is under any disciplinary sanction. On its website the National Register posts actions that lead to removal of the credential, with the maximum time of five years reserved for multiple offenders who pose the greatest risk to the public. This helps to diminish the perception that a conspiracy of silence exists among professionals.

Moving toward a globally accountable profession

Professional psychology can either continue its independent pursuit of quality assurance or collaborate towards common goals. Mobility does not mean that psychologists are able to freely move around the world and qualify to practice in the country of their choosing. That is unlikely, for the language and cultural barriers are too great. However, linking together professional registers into a cooperative endeavor to promote quality assurance might be worthwhile. These registers could develop and disseminate standards, share regulatory experience and methods, motivate psychologists to become credentialed, and finally join together in an effort to educate consumers about the value of psychological services. National and international leaders of psychology in countries with developed professional organizations could help build capacity in other countries and regions. The goal is to develop mechanisms which are 'sufficiently specified to be useful and accommodate variation in the definition of education, training and regulations governing professional psychology' (Bullock and Hall, 2008, p. 230).

Pieces of this strategy are already in place. In North America, the National and Canadian Registers are well established and highly respected and have significant experience in developing and disseminating standards, working within a regulatory framework, and promoting psychological services to consumers. Although in existence for many years, the initial interest in those registers led to large numbers of applicants, partly due to a grandparent clause which encouraged early commitment. The EuroPsy Register, while not yet marketed to individual psychologists at the level of the two North American registers, has tremendous potential for growth given that it invites applications from psychologists in 35 countries. However, since December 10, 2010 when the first certification was issued, only 3754 psychologists have been approved by the 19 different countries' with National Accrediting Committees (Ivana Marinovic, personal communication, September 26, 2013).

The umbrella group guiding this cooperative of registers would decide on sequential goals and strategies for linkage. Goals might include member-registries seeking a higher level of quality and uniformity in standards than licensure; and making information about the regulatory processes, accreditation systems, and other aspects of quality assurance in the geographic area available to other member registries (and in a common language); and participating in a jointly operated and global effort to educate consumers on the value of psychological services in addressing healthcare needs.

North American psychology training has influenced many countries by educating psychologists who return to their own country to establish education and training programs, just as Europeans influenced the early development of research laboratories and education in the United States and elsewhere. While dominant and useful to examine for what can be learned from its fairly extensive history and learning curve, it is not the only successful model. Other examples written by experts on their own country are available in the chapters written for *Global promise: quality assurance and accountability in professional psychology* (Hall and Altmaier, 2008). In addition to examples provided herein, those countries provide ideas on how to develop an international model of quality control. In looking at the various elements, the challenge is to build a model that reinforces a culture of accountability, while recognizing that this philosophy varies across socio-political and historical context (Hurley, 2008).

References

Altmaier, E.M. (Ed.) (2003). *Setting Standards in Graduate Education: Psychology's Commitment to Excellence in Accreditation*. Washington, DC: American Psychological Association.

American Council on Education (2011) *Accredited Institutions of Postsecondary Education*. Washington, DC: Author.

American Psychological Association, Council of Representatives. (2009). *Minutes, February*. Washington, DC: Author. Retrieved September 17, 2012, from www.apa.org/international/governance/cirp/quality-assurance-resolution.pdf

American Psychological Association, Council of Representatives. (2011). *Minutes, August*. Washington, DC: Author. Retrieved August 20, 2103, from www.apa.org/ed/accreditation/first-street-accord.aspx.

American Psychological Association, Support Center. (2012). *Statistics*. Retrieved September 17, 2012, from www.apa.org/support/education/statistics/continuing.aspx#answer.

American Psychological Association. (1953). *Ethical Standards of Psychologists*. Washington, DC: Author.

American Psychological Association. (2010). *Model Act for State Licensure of Psychologists*. Available at www.apa.org/about/policy/model-act-2010.pdf

American Psychological Association. (2011). *Competency Benchmarks Work Group*. Retrieved September 17, 2012, from www.apa.org/ed/graduate/revised-competency-benchmarks.aspx. Washington, DC: Author.

Bullock, M. and Hall, J. E. (2008). The promotion of international mobility. In J. E. Hall and E. M. Altmaier (Eds.), *Global Promise: Quality Assurance and Accountability in Professional Psychology* (pp. 216–31). New York: Oxford University Press.

Council for Higher Education Accreditation (2012). Search for accredited institutions. Retrieved September 29, 2012, from www.chea.org/search/search.asp.

Drum, D. J. and Hall, J. E. (1993). Psychology's self-regulation and the setting of professional standards. *Applied and Preventive Psychology*, *2*, 151–61.

Fouad, N. A., Grus, C. L., Hatcher, R. L., Kaslow, N. J. Hutchings, P. S., Madson, M., Collins, F. L. Jr. and Crossman, R. E. (2009). Competency benchmarks: a developmental model for understanding and measuring competence in professional psychology. *Training and Education in Professional Psychology*, *3*(4 Suppl), S5–S26. doi: 10.1037/a0015832.

Greenberg, S. and Smith, I.L. (2008). Methods to evaluate competency and enhance quality assurance internationally and across professions. In J. E. Hall and E. M. Altmaier (Eds.), *Global Promise: Quality Assurance and Accountability in Professional Psychology* (pp. 51–72). New York: Oxford University Press.

Grus, C. L., McCutcheon, S. R. and Berry, S. L. (2011). Actions by professional psychology education and training groups to mitigate the internship imbalance. *Training and Education in Professional Psychology*, *5*, 193–201.

Hall, J. E. (2000). Licensing and credentialing as quality management tools in behavioral health care. In G. Stricker, W. G. Troy and S. A. Shueman (Eds.), *Handbook of Quality Management in Behavioral Health* (pp. 317–32). New York: Kluwer Academic/Plenum.

Hall, J. E. and Altmaier, E. M. (Eds.). (2008). *Global Promise: Quality Assurance and Accountability in Professional Psychology*. New York: Oxford University Press.

Hall, J. E. and Hurley, G. (2002). Education and training of clinical psychologists: a North American perspective. In I. Wiener (Ed.), *Handbook of Psychology* (pp. 471–96). New York: Wiley.

Hatcher, R.L. and Lassiter, K.D. (2006). *The Practicum Competencies Outline: Report on Practicum Competencies*. Retrieved September 17, 2012, from www.aptc.org/public_ files/Practicum%20Competencies%20FINAL%20(Oct%20'06%20Version).pdf

Hernández Guzmán, L. and Sanchez-Sosa, J. J. (2008). Practice and professional regulation of professional psychology in Latin-America. In J. E. Hall and E. M. Altmaier (Eds.), *Global Promise: Quality Assurance and Accountability in Professional Psychology* (pp. 109–27). New York: Oxford University Press.

Hurley, G. (2008). Synthesis and concluding comments. In J. E. Hall and E. M. Altmaier (Eds.), *Global Promise: Quality Assurance and Accountability in Professional Psychology* (pp. 232–41). New York: Oxford University Press.

Lunt, I. (2008). Accountability in professional psychology in the United Kingdom. In J. E. Hall and E. M. Altmaier (Eds.), *Global Promise: Quality Assurance and Accountability in Professional Psychology* (pp. 140–7). New York: Oxford University Press.

Nelson, P. D., Belar, C. D., Grus, C. L. and Zlotlow, S. (2008). Quality assessment in higher education through accreditation. In J. E. Hall and E. M. Altmaier (Eds.), *Global Promise: Quality Assurance and Accountability in Professional Psychology* (pp. 16–37). New York: Oxford University Press.

Ritchie, P. L.-J. (2008). Codes of ethics, conduct, and standards as vehicles of accountability. In J. E. Hall and E. M. Altmaier (Eds.), *Global Promise: Quality Assurance and Accountability in Professional Psychology* (pp. 73–97). New York: Oxford University Press.

Stricker, G. (2008). Quality assurance in professional psychology education. In J. E. Hall and E. M. Altmaier (Eds.), *Global Promise: Quality Assurance and Accountability in Professional Psychology* (pp. 199–215). New York: Oxford University Press.

Stromberg, C. D. (1991). *Healthcare Credentialing: Implications for Academic Health Centers*. Paper presented at the meeting of the Academic Health Centers, Washington, DC, April. Unpublished manuscript.

United States Department of Education (2012). *Database of Accredited Postsecondary Institutions and Programs*. Retrieved September 18, 2012, from www.ope.ed.gov/ accreditation.

United States Senate Committee on Health, Education, Labor and Pensions (2012). *For Profit Higher Education: The Failure to Safeguard the Federal Investment and Ensure Student Success*, July 30. Retrieved September 28, 2012, from www.gpo.gov/fdsys/pkg/ CPRT-112SPRT74953/html/CPRT-112SPRT74953.htm

Washington Accord. Retrieved September 28, 2012, from www.washingtonaccord.org

Wellner, A.M. (Ed.). (1978). *Education and Credentialing in Psychology: Proposal for a National Commission in Education and Training in Psychology*. Washington, DC: National Register of Health Service Providers in Psychology.

Commentary on 'Quality control in psychology education and training (PET)'

A Caribbean perspective

Ava D. Thompson

The Caribbean societies share common socio-historical experiences but there are considerable differences in socio-political, cultural and economic realities that have led to variability in the development of psychology across the Caribbean region (Alvarez, 2000). Despite this diversity, there is a sense of 'Caribbean oneness' that is reflected in regional psychologists' commitment to a regional community of psychologists to advance the discipline and contribute to regional development. The first regional psychology organization was formed in the early 1970s and was followed by a conference in Haiti with participants from the English, French, Spanish and Dutch-speaking Caribbean. While the organization existed for only a short time, a foundation was laid and contemporary Caribbean psychologists have renewed efforts to establish a regional organization, but with a mandate that now includes quality control in professional practice, research and psychology education and training (PET).

For years regional psychologists have assumed critical roles in PET quality control programmes (Aire, 2012; Evans, 2012), expressed concerns about psychology's rapid, unregulated growth (Alvarez, 2000) and highlighted the need to protect consumers (Salter, 2000). Recently regional leaders convened at the 2011 Caribbean Regional Conference of Psychology with the unparalleled priority of forming a regional body to promote the growth of the discipline and to harmonize academic, national legislative and professional standards. The discussions culminated in the Nassau Declaration and the creation of The Caribbean Organisation of Psychology Steering Committee (COPSC) to establish the regional organization. COPSC has been active for one year and its PET subcommittee has begun to formally address concerns about the quality of training programmes in the region.

The issues that Caribbean psychologists have explored in their dialogue and scholarship on quality control overlap considerably with Judy Hall and Victor Karandashev's work in their respective chapters on the North American and global experiences. It is clear that psychologists not only agree on the importance of quality control for the growth of the discipline, but also recognize an inclusive, consultative approach that values diversity in context (i.e. psychology and its broader milieu) is critical to an appropriate and effective quality control framework (Chapter 12). Its need to reflect features common to many contextual realities and to balance national, regional and international requirements (Chapter 11) are equally important features in twenty-first century psychology.

While quality control frameworks around the globe have been developed to fit specific cultural contexts and are continuing to evolve, collectively they represent an invaluable resource for Caribbean psychologists. It is critical for regional psychologists to investigate the full range of intra-regional realities and possible mechanisms and conceptualize quality control as a complex, interrelated system with multiple mechanisms and stakeholders that must be harmonized to ensure sustainability (Hall, Chapter 12). The processes and length of time required to develop such systems are also instructive for the region. Caribbean psychologists must systematically build capacity, engage intra- and interdisciplinary stakeholders, anticipate challenges (including competing values and interests), and cautiously develop a strategic plan with a temporal sequencing of mechanisms that meets the current and future needs of the discipline (Amuleru-Marshall, 2011), rather than work expeditiously to meet the standards established for other contexts.

Quality control's prominent position in developing a culturally relevant Caribbean psychology is a 'take-home message' for international PET efforts. It is an integral component of the overarching goals of defining the discipline, building infrastructure, and developing appropriate psychological and research models. For example, all regional psychologists, regardless of psychology's development in their context, have a role to play in determining associated competencies to meet the needs of communities and to maximize limited resources. Essentially, quality control systems cannot develop in a vacuum, but must be congruent with the overall development of the discipline, philosophies that undergird the vision for the discipline and current paradigms, developments and models in psychology, specifically international and global psychology. Therefore psychologists from contexts with newly and well-established psychological traditions are all meaningful contributors to a globally viable system, i.e., one that represents the totality of psychology's education and training reality. Reliance on the resources and expertise from traditional centres of psychology, mere sensitivity to issues of differential cultural realities, and trivializing resistance instead of valuing a deep commitment to intellectual reciprocity and multidirectional exchange of knowledge, can ultimately undermine the development of a global psychology agenda, of which PET quality control is a critical component.

The Caribbean's mental health landscape has characteristics, including intra-regional mobility in order to provide clinical, educational and organizational psychological services, which are not typically considered in current international literature (World Health Organization, 2011). This state of affairs necessitates self-directed, innovative and collective production of knowledge (Alvarez, 2000) that reduces dependence on extra-regional expertise, and yet is grounded in a robust, globally negotiated PET quality control system. While there is a consensus that this system cannot reflect unilateral globalization, it is imperative that psychologists in all regions of the world embrace the principles of enlightened globalization (Kim and Park, 2007) to construct a solid foundation of global psychology through psychology education and training.

References

Aire, J. (2012). Local and regional issues in the training of Grenadian psychologists. Paper presented at the International Congress of Psychology 2012, Cape Town, South Africa, 22–27 July.

Alvarez, A. I. (2000). Psicología en Caribe Isleño (A history of psychology in the Insular Caribbean). *Revista Interamericana de Psicología*, (34), 235–56.

Amuleru-Marshall, O. (2011). Vision for Caribbean Psychology: Identity, practice and development. Paper presented at the Caribbean Regional Conference of Psychology 2011, Nassau, Bahamas, 15–18 November.

Evans, M. (2012). A critical review of psychology programmes offered at the International University of the Caribbean. Paper presented at the International Congress of Psychology 2012, Cape Town, South Africa, 22–27 July.

Kim, U. and Park, Y. (2007). Development of indigenous psychologies: Understanding people in a global context. In M. J. Stevens and U. P. Gielen (eds.), *Toward a global psychology: Theory, research, intervention and pedagogy*, pp. 147–72. Mahwah, NJ: Lawrence Erlbaum Associates.

Salter, V. (2000). The status of psychology in the Commonwealth Caribbean: Emphasis on Jamaica. *Revista Interamericana de Psicología*, (34), 211–21.

World Health Organization (2011). *Report of the assessment of the mental health system in the Caribbean region*. Geneva: World Health Organization.

Roles and responsibilities of international psychology organizations for PET

13 Roles and responsibilities of international psychology organizations for psychology education and training

José M. Peiró

Introduction: psychology in a global world

Globalization, technological developments, the connectivity of people and groups, socioeconomic and demographic changes, human capital mobility, transformation of ideologies and value systems, and sociopolitical dynamics represent important factors in the transformation of current societies. This transformation, in turn, has an important influence on many human activities, such as science, and more specifically, on psychology. From one side, new demands are made of psychology as a scientific discipline and profession; from the other side, psychology itself is experiencing important changes within the framework of psychology as a science and as a profession system. In this context, it is more important than ever to analyze the disciplinary and professional identity and diversity of psychology in the international scene.

Psychology as a science emerged in Europe in the last part of the nineteenth century, but was very soon grounded and developed in North America. Over subsequent decades, it grew mainly in Western developed countries, which was a relevant factor in its development. More recently, it has been growing in many other societies all over the world, so that larger diversity within what we understand as psychology is evident. The aim of this chapter is to reflect on the growing complexity of psychology and on the role of PET to promote its 'identity' and 'diversity' in the current global and local ('glo-cal') world. We also aim to analyze the main functions and roles that international organizations of psychology play in this process. These organizations may promote the quality and significance of PET around the world. By their very nature this contribution is even more important in the current situation of internationalization and in the global era.

The identity of psychology as a science and a profession: centrifugal and centripetal forces

During the last decades, the awareness of differences in psychology across regions has increased and these differences may at least partly be explained by contextual, socioeconomic, political, cultural and legal factors, as well as historical traditions. At the same time, scientific and professional mobility, international professional markets, global communication media, international scientific and professional associations, world or regional scientific events, and international cooperation, among other forces, are promoting a higher visibility, identity, image and reputation of psychology worldwide. The current situation is, therefore, a complex one and results from a dynamic tension between such centrifugal and centripetal forces. In a context where globalization is increasing, the question about the identity or identities of psychology is more relevant than ever. It is also important to analyze whether there is a dominant and widely shared paradigm or several paradigms around the world, or whether a pre-paradigmatic situation must be acknowledged with different epistemological assumptions and subsequent methods, topics and issues.

The strength of the identity of psychology as a science and a profession has differed throughout its history and across geographical regions, as has the tension between the centripetal and centrifugal forces acting upon it. In fact, several epistemological approaches have been identified (e.g.: positivistic, post-positivistic, critical, etc.); psychological subdisciplines also have experienced the tension between a unified psychology with an articulated system of sub-disciplines vs. the forces that drive some of those subdisciplines to join other disciplinary fields (e.g. neurosciences, psychiatry, education sciences, management, etc.). This tension also appeared among professional roles. While psychological roles are widely recognized, psychologists often present themselves under other professional labels and roles, such as human resources management expert, psychotherapist, mental health professional, etc. This dynamic has become even more complex in recent decades when psychology has spread across the world. During this growth process, different traditions, especially cultural and linguistic, have predominated in different regions with the result that the landscape has been enriched with the emergence of indigenous psychology movements.

The situation becomes even more complex when the nature of psychological science is considered. We refer to issues such as the natural, life or social nature of psychological science and to the universality or contextualized nature of its scientific knowledge and 'laws'. Acknowledging the critical role of culture, socioeconomic, legal, linguistic and historical factors in the study of psychology has important implications for professional practice if it intends to be 'evidence-based'. What grounds a scientist-practitioner model in professional practice is scientific evidence. However, this evidence will be understood differently depending on whether we consider psychological science as producing just universal knowledge or both universal and contextualized knowledge. If the context where evidence on a given psychological phenomenon or process is obtained plays a relevant role in such evidence, its generalizability becomes an empirical issue rather than an assumption taken for granted. So, the generalizability of knowledge gained through research may be different for different kinds of psychological phenomena, ranging from biochemical and neurological, to cultural and social ones. The generalization of evidence obtained on a psychological phenomenon in a given context may be more or less relevant to grounding professional practice in a different context and this fact must be carefully scrutinized. In fact, the debate about general laws vs. contextualized knowledge in psychological science (nomothetic vs. idiographic, emic vs. etic, etc.) emerges again here in a broader sense and with clear implications for science and practice in different regions of the world.

Thus, to identify the essential core that promotes a global identity of psychology while paying respect to regional and cultural ways of understanding, producing and implementing psychological knowledge, tools, methods and services is nowadays an important challenge. This issue requires attention and debate.

Diversity in psychology around the world is manifest in many facets: conceptualization of individual, group, and collective needs in different contexts; services offered; professional roles enacted and practices performed; methods and tools used; skills and competences for analysis, diagnosis and intervention put in place and also scientific paradigms, topics, theoretical models and research methods used. At the same time, we must consider centripetal forces that contribute to a shared view on psychology. These forces contribute to its identity, visibility and image in a way that is often recognized and demanded by users and clients in a large array of fields and in many societies and regions. We can mention among these forces the strong worldwide scientific communication systems in psychology (scientific journals, databases, etc.); the well-developed publishing industry that produces textbooks, handbooks, monographs, and other scientific and professional publications, selling them on the world market; the international organizations of psychology and the international congresses that promote exchange of ideas, experiences and research outcomes about psychology. They also facilitate interaction, contact and cooperation, and increasing mobility, among researchers, scholars, students and professionals. Other factors also play a role in this centripetal process. One is the growing international 'market' of psychology in many subdisciplines both in research and professional practice (e.g. international consultancy firms, multinational companies, non-governmental organizations [NGOs], international organizations, etc.).

Another factor is the strong development of new information and communication technologies. The growth of electronic publications, the increasing possibilities of virtual teamwork, opportunities for virtual cooperation and education, as well as virtual conferencing, may contribute to a more shared view and to a global identity for psychology. This virtual reality also facilitates the development of cross-national and cross-disciplinary networks in science and professional practice, the cooperation of professional bodies and organizations and scientific associations.

This identity is grounded in several common features such as the scientific nature of psychology (Magnusson, 2011), its emphasis on theory testing and critical analysis, and evidence-finding with methodological rigor as the basic mechanism for the advancement of knowledge. Moreover, evidence-based practice is an important inspiring principle for professional interventions that also promotes identity. Finally, but not least, the shared mission of psychology aiming to promote well-being, human and social development and the quality of life through scientific research and development and through professional interventions is also an important element that contributes to strengthening its identity as a discipline.

The identity of psychology is, in fact, acknowledged by numerous groups of people, societies and cultures around the world. So the customers, clients and actors involved in educational systems, policy makers, governments, NGOs, social agents, international bodies, etc., identify the services and contributions of psychology and acknowledge its scientific nature as one of the core elements of its identity. In this context, the processes of socialization and training of new scientists and professionals in the discipline and the dissemination of psychological knowledge among a broader interested public are important to develop both the identity and the productive diversity of psychology around the world.

The education and training of psychologists as scientists and professionals in a global world: changes and challenges

Kuhn (1996) pointed out that scientific education systems, especially in paradigmatic sciences, reflect and are inspired by the dominant scientific paradigm and that they educate and socialize new researchers and professionals on the assumptions, theories, evidence and paradigmatic exemplars of the discipline. However, the paradigmatic status of psychology as a science has been widely debated. Indeed, it has often been questioned whether our discipline has reached the stage of a paradigmatic science in the sense formulated by Kuhn and even whether this would be the most mature stage in its scientific development.

In any case, the degree of integration and similarity of the PET systems in different regions of the world is an empirical question; however, the answer is far from clear, systematic or complete. In fact, this question contains a large number of facets that require individual consideration: the core assumptions, topics, theories, methodologies, tools in use, the emphasis on producing science vs. professional models and competencies and the main features of the education process. The different combinations of cultural diversity and global views in PET are not well known, but such knowledge would be useful for a better understanding of the identity and diversity of psychology.

There are several traditions and systems for psychology education and training that have been unevenly implemented in different parts of the world, and new or adopted models are being established in the areas where psychology is developing. Innovation in PET is also taking place in universities and other educational institutions. New forms and systems of education are emerging, such as open, distance and blended education strategies. These strategies are promoting different ways of cooperation between institutions from different regions of the world (included franchising psychology education and training programs).

In this context, it is important to identify similarities and, if possible, common core features of education and training of psychology systems in the global era. This not only refers to content (theories and methods for explanation and intervention) but also to the aims and basic assumptions underlying PET (e.g.

evidence-based practice; scientist-practitioner model, critical approach, etc.), the methods used for education and its focus (knowledge, skills, attitudes, competences, etc.). The comparison of the professional models promoted and the ethics for science and profession is also of interest.

More than ever, it is necessary to recollect and share information about all the issues discussed so far because they are instantiated in the different regions of the world. We also need to identify how systems of psychology education and training promote the identity of psychology while generating several productive specifications in specific contexts that make psychology more effective and valuable in those contexts. National or regional boundaries are increasingly permeable so that a comprehensive view of the PET situation may help to better understand the 'reality' of PET and to contribute meaningfully to its future.

Yet another challenge is to identify existing forms of cooperation between educational institutions across countries and regions and their effectiveness in promoting international PET. Several options are already being implemented, such as 'franchising' of programs from one institution in a country to institutions in other countries; 'melting pot' meaning education takes place in one institution but participants come from different countries; 'mobility-based' where a period of education takes place in another country; and 'joint diplomas', which are awarded by consortia of universities in different countries oriented towards specific professional work in international settings – e.g. multinational companies, World Bank, WHO, United Nations programs; integrated approach combining some of the previous alternatives (Martinez-Tur *et al.*, in press). It is useful to identify these international programs and pay attention to the approaches and strategies they use to educate for international practice. It is therefore particularly important to find and understand those culturally appropriate diverse and global education systems that contribute to the socialization of good quality research scientists and those in professional practice, so that they fulfill the needs of the clients and society in specific contexts and cultures. In the same way, it is vital to be aware of the changes of PET needed when moving from one culture or context to another.

In some regions, guidelines for curriculum development in psychology have been established. More specifically, in Europe, the Tuning program has formulated reference points for the design and delivery of degree program profiles in psychology (see Lunt *et al.* 2011); this initiative could also be developed in other regions where the Tuning project is being operated (Latin America, Africa, Russia, USA, etc., see www.unideusto.org/tuningeu/home.html). Moreover, standards and certification processes to enhance and guarantee the quality of PET have also been established in some regions. The Association of the State and Provincial Psychology Board (ASPPB) (in USA and Canada) has since 1961 been contributing

> to enhance services and support its member jurisdictions in fulfilling their goal of advancing public protection by offering exemplary examination and credentialing programs, providing state of the art programs and services to all our stakeholders, serving as the source for the most current and accurate

information about the regulation of psychologists, and contributing to the critical consumer protection perspective in the on-going development of the profession.

(www.asppb.net)

In 2009, the European Federation of Psychology Association (EFPA) launched the EuroPsy Certificate of Psychology as a quality standard in Europe (EFPA, 2011). The International Test Commission (ITC) has also developed a number of guidelines in this specific domain (e.g. the ITC Guidelines on Adapting Tests; the ITC Guidelines on Test Use; the ITC Guidelines on Computer-Based and Internet-Delivered Testing; and the ITC Guidelines on Quality Control in Scoring, Test Analysis and Reporting of Test Scores (see www.intestcom.org/guidelines/index.php).

In sum, at the regional level, guidelines and standards on education and/or on certification and licensing exist. In a context where the mobility of professionals is increasing and their practice may occur in a different country or region than the one in which they have been educated, the internationalization of the quality assurance systems for PET is appealing. Finding consensus on a set of international guidelines and standards could be aimed for as the next step for the identification of the common core of the global PET.

Roles and responsibilities of international psychology organizations in promoting and improving PET in the international scene

As we pointed out, there is a limitation to keeping PET analysis, design, practice and evaluation within national boundaries or at the regional level. In fact, international organizations of psychology such as IAAP, IUPsyS, IACCP, etc. have been promoting, albeit by different means, the internationalization of PET. It is perhaps appropriate to mention first the International Congresses of Psychology and of Applied Psychology that, being held continuously in different places of the world, have helped facilitate knowledge and development of psychology and its education in all the continents. Moreover, attracting psychologists from all over the world has provided excellent platforms for debates, symposia, round tables, and other types of activities related to psychology education and training and its internationalization. The publication of international handbooks, monographs and journals on all areas of psychology and related disciplines has also contributed to the internationalization of PET. An analysis of the developments in PET in different countries and regions of the world has also been addressed in some of those publications.

Surveys and/or documents concerning the situation of PET in general (such as the recent survey by IUPsyS) (see Chapter 1 this volume) or in specific disciplinary fields or geographical areas are also relevant contributions to improving PET internationally. Capacity-building activities of international organizations, such as the Advanced Research and Training Seminars (ARTS) or regional conferences of psychology, which are collaborative efforts by IUPsyS, IAAP and ICCAP, also provided opportunities for the creation of networks of young scholars from different parts of the world for them to share in learning processes, methods and experiences in international education activities. The promotion of cooperation and exchange among institutions and individuals (scholars, professionals and students) from all over the world has also been effective in many instances. Finally, the development of international guidelines on some relevant issues for PET, such as those from the ICT mentioned earlier, and the Universal Declaration of Ethical Principles for Psychologists promoted by IAAP, IUPsyS and IACCP, is also an achievement that can be added to those of regional and national associations and organizations.

New opportunities and challenges for international psychology organizations to promote PET

Developments in information and communication technologies: a large number of opportunities for the international organizations to promote PET have stemmed from the development of Information and Communication Technologies (ICT). Their impact has been both extensive and intensive, and very evident in many areas relevant for PET, such as scientific communication systems, virtual interaction and cooperation among institutions and individuals around the world, and the offer of worldwide online or blended psychology education programs. In fact, the communication and advertisement of psychology courses around the world is increasing rapidly and students can follow virtual courses in universities located in other countries. The increased availability of information about psychology curricula offered on university web sites are excellent sources that can help to facilitate access to better psychology education in many regions of the world. Yet another possibility offered by ICT is the development of electronic platforms and repositories with which to communicate and exchange teaching experiences, methods, course design, etc. in PET. International psychology organizations have a worldwide membership of leading psychologists and national organizations that represent an important human and social capital worldwide. ICT provide new opportunities to facilitate effective cooperation among these actors in internationalizing and improving PET.

Increased mobility: the increasing mobility of students, teaching staff, researchers and professionals also brings opportunities for international organizations to promote the internationalization of PET. Regional and international travel, particularly related to research and study visits, has increased considerably over the last decades and seems likely to continue to do so in the near future. This situation represents an excellent opportunity for international psychology organizations to promote PET internationalization. Networking among their members, be they individuals or national organizations, may facilitate the mobility of scientists, academics, students and practitioners and this cooperation may improve the quality of research, education and practice in the different contexts. Moreover, promoting contacts among universities from different regions could contribute to the submission of joint applications for travel and cooperation related to existing international programs, such as Erasmus Mundus, Atlantis, etc. Finally, facilitating multicultural enrollment of students and the exchange of scholars in psychology programs may foster and promote international awareness and cooperation within the national contexts of PET.

Growing global and international demand: global and international demands for psychological knowledge and professional practice are also growing and represent another source of opportunities. For instance the international profile of psychology research and professional intervention is growing and diversifying in a number of fields, as witnessed by the worldwide consultancy firms in work and organizational psychology, psychologists working in international NGOs and in world organizations such as the United Nations, WHO, World Bank, the United Nations Educational, Scientific and Cultural Organization (UNESCO), and the International Labour Organization (ILO), in missions across the world. In this context international psychology organizations may be supportive of international programs in PET to facilitate the education of psychologists for these international profiles (e.g. organizing meetings of directors of international psychology programs). They can also identify new demands in the international practice of psychology and formulate guidelines for institutions delivering international PET programs.

Heightened desire for international participation: opportunities also arise from the growing interest of psychologists in international participation. In particular students and young scholars are becoming more and more active in regional and international organizations and organize their own congresses, workshops and 'schools'. All these initiatives are opportunities for well-established international organizations to reach broader audiences and actors in many regions of the world. Supporting and promoting international 'schools' and seminars for PhD students and young researchers in cooperation with universities in different disciplines of psychology could promote the emergence of research networks across countries and cross-fertilize teaching experiences through exchange of good practices among teaching staff participating in those seminars.

Growth of professional migration: the growing diaspora of psychologists coming from a region and working in another is also an important opportunity for the internationalization of PET. Such psychologists are likely to have a rich experience in cross-cultural research, professional practice, education and training in different countries or regions. This experience may be a great asset for better understanding the internationalization of psychology. International organizations could identify, analyze and disseminate these contributions as an asset in promoting cross-national cooperation.

Increase in the internationalization of universities: several policies are being put in place by governments to increase the internationalization of universities and it is a prominent goal in the strategic planning of many universities around the world. Identifying such universities and their leaders in psychology would be of interest in promoting networks with stronger ties for the improvement and innovation of PET at an international level.

Greater demands for quality assurances in PET: another opportunity is the increasing awareness and actions for the promotion of the quality of international education. Accreditation agencies, certification bodies, and the assessment exercises conducted in many countries are consolidating a 'culture' and a set of practices to promote, assess and assure quality. In many cases, these activities cover standards related to the internationalization of PET. Assessment reports and other documents (often available in the web sites of the universities or accreditation agencies) may contribute to identify good practices and to set the criteria for quality assessment. The cooperation of international psychology organizations with accreditation agencies dealing with psychology studies at a regional level could be an important resource to identify criteria and strategies to enhance quality.

Growth in level of psychological research: finally, the increasing number of countries where research on psychology is being carried out is another asset for internationalization of PET. The number of published articles with data obtained from countries other than those of North America or Western Europe is growing and represents an opportunity to extend psychology's theoretical models and empirical evidence obtained in different regions of the world. As the evidence available is increasingly international, future meta-analyses should systematically incorporate country variables in their studies and identify differences derived from cultures in psychological scientific knowledge. International organizations should promote these trends in their own journals and could stimulate 'cross-cultural research incubators' and other initiatives to facilitate international cooperation in research during their congresses. This is especially needed for applied psychology disciplines because its practices benefit largely from contextualized research.

Strategic issues for PET deserving contributions from international psychology organizations

Taking into account the main challenges concerning the identity of psychology and the demands emerging from the transformation of societies, there are some strategic issues that international psychological organizations should prioritize in cooperation with regional organizations and other important actors. More specifically, efforts should be made towards the clarification and formulation of core features, contents and standards of an international PET framework. Professional competences could be considered as one important component of the common core of education and professional practice. The progressive development and consensus on a core competence model for professional practice would represent important progress towards the formulation of criteria for quality and standards of educational systems and form common ground for the certification of professional practice.

Following this, a number of additional steps could be taken towards the identification of contents and strategies for the learning and building of these competences in different contexts (e.g. supervised practice) and its continuous professional development. The universal ethics principles should be also considered in this process as the basis for the specification of codes of ethics relevant in the different regions and countries where research and practice are implemented. Progress in these endeavors could establish the grounds for improving quality in the education systems and developing the core criteria and guidelines for the development of quality evaluation and assurance and the accreditation systems. The basis for the development of international licensure and certification systems for professionals could be drawn from these common models.

All these developments could fulfill an array of important functions, such as facilitating mobility, enhancing service quality and clients' protection in the contexts of practice. They would also contribute to a positive image of psychology as well as providing pointers for the development of new PET programs or for the improvement of existing ones.

To reach these long-term goals, we need to identify and bring together the relevant partners and develop a large number of initiatives to share information, analyze potential alternatives and develop consensus on innovative and encompassing proposals about the common core of the above-mentioned issues. At the same time, variety and diversity as well as contextual factors need to be considered. The perspective of applied psychology is an important one given the necessity of contextualized knowledge to build a competent professional practice. Moreover, the perspectives and contributions from the different disciplines of applied psychology are required for the specification and measurement of those competences in the different fields of practice and specialism.

International psychology organizations may contribute to the achievement of these goals in cooperation with other relevant partners. First, they should promote knowledge production and exchange about PET internationally. Here it is important to identify and organize existing information in the different regions of the world with the participation of relevant actors from those regions. Surveys, such as the one recently conducted by IUPsyS, are helpful in this endeavor and could be followed and complemented by qualitative analyses on relevant issues through the establishment of task forces and dedicated networks for this purpose. Symposia and round tables organized in the international congresses of psychology on these topics could also be helpful in this regard.

Finally, in order to contribute to these developments, international psychology organizations may support and stimulate cooperation among relevant actors (institutions and leading individuals) around the world to facilitate international cross-fertilization and quality of PET. They should also provide common virtual and physical platforms, for international dialogue on PET among scholars, students, researchers and professionals and to facilitate international cooperation.

References

EFPA (2011). *EuroPsy. European Certificate in Psychology. EFPA Regulations on EuroPsy and Appendices*. Brussels: EFPA.

Kuhn, Th. (1996). *The Structure of Scientific Revolutions*, 3rd edn. Chicago, IL: The University of Chicago Press.

Lunt, I., Gorbeña, S., Job, R., Lecuyer, R. and Peiró, J.M. (2011) *Tuning EuroPsy: Reference Points for the Design and Delivery of Degree Programmes in Psychology*. Bilbao: Publicaciones de la Universidad de Deusto, available at: www.unideusto.org/tuningeu/images/stories/Summary_of_outcomes_TN/Psychology_reference_points.pdf

Magnusson, D. (2011). The Human Being in Society. Psychology as a Scientific Discipline. *European Psychologist*, 17(1), 21–7.

Martínez-Tur, V., Peiró, J.M. and Rodriguez, I. (in press). Teaching and Learning Work, Organization and Personnel Psychology Internationally. The Erasmus Mundus Program. In R. Griffith (ed.), *Internationalizing the Curriculum in Organizational Psychology*, New York: Springer Science+Business.

14 Psychology education and training in Latin America

An overview

Maria Regina Maluf

Introduction

Latin America was given its name for reasons dating back to the nineteenth century. This region covers an area of around 21,000,000 km^2 with a population of approximately 500 million. It is made up of countries from South America, Central America, the Caribbean and Mexico, and is washed by the Atlantic and Pacific oceans. According to my sources, it includes 24 countries, although some other sources mention 20 or even 32 countries depending on how the different political organizations of the countries are considered.[1]

To understand the huge sociocultural diversity of the region, it is helpful to remember that the concept of 'Latin America' originates from the nineteenth century when the vast majority of countries in the region gained independence from their colonizers coming from the Iberian Peninsula, i.e., Portugal and Spain. During this time the consolidation of a culture called 'Latin' occurred largely due to the influence of the Romance languages brought to the region by the colonizers. However, one should not forget that Latin America possesses its deeper roots in the indigenous Pre-Columbian cultures, mostly Aztec, Mayan, Inca, and Moche.

The term Pre-Columbian culture refers to cultures of the Americas before significant European influence. While technically referring to the era before Christopher Columbus, in practice the term usually includes indigenous cultures because they continued to develop until they were conquered or influenced by Europeans, even if this happened decades or centuries after Columbus first landed in 1492.

Hundreds of indigenous languages are spoken in Latin American countries, in particular Quechua and Aymara, although the most commonly spoken and written languages are Portuguese and Spanish.

Since their independence in the nineteenth century, South and Central American countries have fought against very similar political and economic problems: economic stagnation, lack of good schools, health problems, great poverty, inflation and external debt, and severe inequality in living conditions between the indigenous population and the descendants of colonizers, amongst others. The twentieth century was one of revolutionary changes, dictatorships and re-democratization, and also a time when the socio-urban structure was consolidated in many of these countries. The first decade of the twenty-first century brought about significant changes in Latin America, both in its national political systems and in its foreign policy, and I agree with analysts who say that democracy in Latin America is getting stronger, albeit in different ways and unlike anything we have seen in the recent past.

In some Latin American countries (e.g. Argentina, Brazil, Chile, Colombia, Peru, Uruguay) there has been a sharp increase in the number of social movements focused on education, which is considered essential to make society more equal and more competitive. Many of these movements are led by civil organizations such as non-governmental organizations (NGOs) and private enterprises. As psychology is also considered to be of great importance for social development, it is a field, both academically and as a profession, that has shown continuous growth in Latin American countries. Therefore, psychology education and training (PET) has to be of major concern, especially for regional psychology organizations.

I will begin by considering psychology and the role of some psychology organizations in Latin America. I will then write about challenges and possibilities based on results from a survey undertaken with Latin American psychologists.

Psychology in Latin America

A quick look at the history of psychology in Latin America shows the influence of the Spanish and Portuguese colonial period that started primarily in the sixteenth century and which led to it being dominated by metaphysical, ontological, religious and ethical themes. Indeed, the region's first universities, such as the Universidad de San Marcos de Lima (1551), the Universidad de Mexico (1551) and the Universidad de Santo Tomas de Aquino de Santo Domingo (1558), were founded under the influence of these philosophical trends (Alarcón, 2002).

Although modern ideas had already gained ground in Europe, schools in the 'new world' kept the old ideas in which faith prevails over reason (Alarcón, 2002, 2004). The prevalence of these religious and philosophical ideas for more than two centuries influenced the education and training of Latin American students in a way that meant they developed an exaggerated attachment to theory and dogmatic principles and at the same time showed a lack of observation as well as a certain devaluation of the empirical sciences. A renaissance in the Iberian colonies, called the 'Ibero-American Enlightenment', began at the end of the eighteenth century (Alarcón, 2002), when the first Latin American observation-based research appeared.

In the first half of the twentieth century psychology in Latin America became more objective in its orientation due to the influence of European psychologists who had left their countries because of Nazi persecution or the Spanish civil war. Here, amongst others, Eduardo Krapf, Emilio Mira y López, Béla Székwly, Helena Antipoff, Mercedes Rodrigo, Waclaw Radecki and Walter Blumenfeld can be mentioned.

Between 1950 and 1970 the first course for professional education and training in psychology appeared in countries such as Guatemala, Colombia, Chile, Brazil,

Peru, Venezuela and Mexico. In the 1970s, several Latin American psychologists objected to what was called 'cultural colonialism or colonialism in psychology', saying that the way in which psychology was taught and practiced was far from addressing the real problems of Latin American societies.

Nowadays psychology courses are offered in all Latin American countries but there are disparities in the quality, approach, research experience and even commitment to local sociocultural realities. Nevertheless, big efforts are being made to build a psychology committed to local realities and accepting cultural influences without denying that universality is in progress. One could say that, in this context, researchers are not as interested as they were in the past in replicating research designed for other social and cultural realities. Many of them are innovating and creating new procedures and theories that are not only focused on local reality but also looking at the universality of scientific knowledge; there is also a heightened interest in applied psychology (see for instance contributions from Díaz-Guerrero, 1994, 2004; Alarcón, 2002, 2004; Ardila, 1986).

One question that arises from these developments is: to what extent is the psychology now in progress in Latin America, which is aiming to give valid answers to the social and individual needs of the population, part of 'international psychology'? Some psychologists see psychology outside the US as Rest-Of-the-World Psychology (ROW), or as Psychology from the Majority World (Adair, 2006; Adair *et al.*, 2009), which is also called 'indigenous', 'autochthonous' or 'native psychology'. In my view, psychology in Latin American countries can be called native as long as it is focused on the social, human and political reality of people from these countries, besides being based on empirical research. However, is not all psychology native? Is not all psychology subject to the same indigenization process in such a way that it always focuses on issues that are the result of a given sociocultural and economic reality? I believe that to be truly international, psychological science has to know and deal with what is going on in different cultures.

Another way of looking at this matter is that it can also be said that psychology in Latin American countries is dealing with epistemological and societal dimensions that are emerging (Santos, 1995, 2000, 2007). What I mean by this is that many researchers are looking for a psychology that opposes all forms of accumulated oppression and social exclusion, in other words, a psychology which provides a new emancipatory horizon, establishes links between epistemological and sociological truths, and accepts that knowledge can be objective but is not neutral (Maluf, 2003). From this point of view, it is evident that exchange and cooperation among Latin American psychologists is being facilitated by linguistic similarities, in addition to the similarities in social, cultural and political realities.

Psychology organizations in Latin America

In the last twenty years, many psychology organizations have been created and are playing an important role in the development of psychology in Latin America. I will mention two of these, made up of different types of national organizations and playing an important role in the psychology of the region: ULAPSI (Latin American Union of Psychology) and FIAP (Ibero American Union of Psychology Associations). I will then talk about SIP (Interamerican Society of Psychology), which is a scientific and professional organization serving psychologists internationally and in the Americas that has been both active and influential in Latin American psychology for the past 60 years.

The ULAPSI (*Unión Latinoamericana de Entidades de Psicología*) is a union of psychology organizations from about 12 countries in Latin America. It aims to be instrumental in the improvement of psychology courses and the development of psychology in this region. The ULAPSI's project was initiated by Brazil at the time of the SIP Congress held in São Paulo in 1997. ULAPSI was formally founded on November 23, 2002 in Puebla, Mexico. It presents itself as a project for the construction of a psychology committed to the social problems of Latin America. ULAPSI encourages exchanges between psychology associations from the affiliated countries, organizes regular events and has a central concern with the education of psychologists committed to building decent living conditions for the people of Latin America.

The FIAP (*Federación Iberoamericana de Asociaciones de Psicología*) was founded in July 2002 in Bogota, Colombia, by COP (*Colegio Oficial de Psicólogos de España*), ABA (*Asociación Colombiana para el Avance de las Ciencias del Comportamiento*), and other councils of psychologists. Today, eight Latin American countries are affiliated to FIAP besides Spain and Portugal. FIAP aims to promote exchange and cooperation among affiliated associations as well as contributing to the application of psychology for the well-being of all. FIAP organizes congresses and numerous activities to disseminate psychology and create cooperation among Latin American countries, Spain and Portugal.

The Interamerican Society of Psychology (SIP) (*Sociedad Interamericana de Psicología* or *Sociedade Interamericana de Psicologia*) is the oldest association present and active in Latin America. It was founded by a group of behavioral scientists on December 17 1951 in Mexico City during the Congress of the World Federation of Mental Health, and is a nonprofit, scientific and professional organization that brings together Latin American psychologists as well as psychologists from the US and Canada. The objectives of the society are to establish effective communication networks among psychologists of the American Continent and to aid in the development of psychology as a science and as a profession. The Constitution of SIP establishes that it also aims to strengthen international understanding by using 'a broader conceptualization of cultural differences and communication across national boundaries', which shows its international orientation.

Some strategies SIP uses to achieve its goals are: the official acceptance of the four most spoken languages on the American Continent (Spanish, English, Portuguese and French) in all its initiatives and activities; the sponsorship of the Interamerican Congress of Psychology every other year; the sponsorship of regional psychology congresses, which is a more recent periodical event; and the maintenance of the *Interamerican Journal of Psychology*, with three issues a year

(Salazar, 1997). The board of SIP is elected every two years and is made up of professionals from the three main regions of the Americas: North, Central and Caribbean, and South. Moreover, SIP has a network of national representatives from different countries in the Americas.

For many years SIP was the only organization to hold academic and professional meetings in Latin America, the Interamerican Congress of Psychology. The fact that Spanish and Portuguese have been used as the official languages of the event, together with English and French, facilitated the active participation of Latin American psychologists. Since 1951, these psychology congresses have taken place every two years. Three out of thirty-three took place in the US (Texas, 1955; Miami, 1964 and 1976), all of the others took place in Latin American countries.

SIP congresses played an important role in the development of psychology in Latin America and also played a role in stimulating initiatives concerning psychology education and training in the region. The First Latin American Conference on Training in Psychology took place on 17 and 18 December 1974 in Bogota, Colombia, and designed a model for the education of psychologists in the region (Alarcón, 2004; Toro and Villegas, 2001). Approximately 50 participants, representing almost all the countries of Latin America, attended the conference, which took place parallel with, but independently of, the XV Interamerican Congress of Psychology (Ardila, 1973).

During the 24th Interamerican Congress, held in Santiago, Chile 1993, one central symposium, as well as many of the invited lectures, took the theme of psychology education and training. The presenters decided that it was necessary to get systematized information about courses and programs for the training of psychologists in Latin America. The first initiative, coordinated by Modesto Alonso, who was the national representative for Argentina in SIP, resulted in the book *Psychology in the Americas* (Psicología en las Américas, edited by Modesto Alonso and Alice Eagly, 1999).

This book was the first to present systematic information about psychology in Latin America based on data collected by more than 17 psychologists from 17 countries. It has a systematized presentation of the beginnings, development and current situation of psychology in the region. SIP President at the time, Susan Pick, said about the book:

> It provides us, for the first time, with a resource which allowed us to know and to compare the development of psychology in each country, the current status of training and research and the key interests of psychologists. Upon reviewing it, we could notice that psychology had a unique history and signature in each of those countries. It made us realize that we had many things in common concerning both what we had done and what had yet to be accomplished. (Oral communication)

The next step was to sponsor a task force to study the theme 'psychology education and training in the Americas'. This task force, led by Julio Villegas, described a set of issues which they called 'Central problems for the academic formation and the psychologist's professional training', such as admission requirements, course regulations and accreditations, the conditions to obtain a graduate's academic degree and a professional title, amongst others.

As a result, a series of three books was published under the title of *Problemas centrales para la formación académica y el entrenamiento professional del psicólogo en las Américas* [Central problems for the academic formation and the psychologist's professional training in the Americas] (Toro and Villegas, 2001; Villegas, Marassi and Toro, 2003a, 2003b). The chapters were written by invited authors from different countries. Volumes 1 and 2 provided information and analysis on the central problems of training in Argentina, Bolivia, Brazil, Chile, Colombia, Costa Rica, Cuba, the USA, Guatemala, Mexico, Paraguay, Peru, Puerto Rico, the Dominican Republic, Uruguay, Venezuela, and also considerations about the Caribbean and Spain. The third volume of the book presented analyses of the ongoing situation in the different countries concerning: accreditation of training programs and the agencies that were responsible for it, the type, quality and criteria of accreditation and curricular evaluation, the regulation of the profession, and others.

Today very well structured and evaluated psychology courses can be found in many of these countries (Hernández-Guzmán and Sánchez-Sosa, 2007). In others there is still no formal system of quality assurance regarding licensure standards and accreditation for psychology courses, but it is acknowledged that there is a great need to develop formal systems to ensure quality standards for training in psychology.

To know more about what is happening in some Latin American countries today, a survey of 30 well-known psychologists and specialists in their field of psychology was conducted. The results are described below.

Challenges and possibilities in psychology education and training

The results of a brief survey on psychology education and training in the social and cultural context of South American, Central American and Caribbean countries follow. The sample comprised 30 psychologists from 12 countries in this region.[2] They constitute an intentional sample, as all of them are well known psychologists and can be seen as representatives of psychology in their country.

The psychologists were asked to give their opinion about the situation in their countries concerning the dissemination of Latin American research; the view concerning internalization of psychology in their country; the formal systems of accreditation for training programs as well as the criteria for accreditation and for curricular evaluation; the access to recent publications for teachers, students and researchers; the issue of cultural diversity in training courses; major concerns about cultural diversity and international standards. In short, we were looking for their views on the condition of psychology education and training in their countries.

The first question was: On a scale of 0 to 5, with 0 being 'not at all' and 5 being 'very well known', to what extent do you think that publications of Latin American research are known outside the region? Responses were concentrated on score 2 on the scale (16 answers out of 30); 6 psychologists chose score 1 and 7 psychologists chose score 3. Nobody attributed a score of 4 or 5 points. One of them did not answer this question. This result suggests that publications by Latin American psychologists – which are mostly in Spanish or in Portuguese – are scarcely known outside Latin America. This result is in accordance with research carried out by Adair *et al.* (2004, 2006, 2009). They showed that relatively few publications in targeted samples of North American and international journals came from psychologists from developing countries.

It is relevant to note that in addition to recognizing that Latin American research is scarcely known outside the region, some respondents added that it is also hardly known within the region. All respondents said that too few Latin American psychology journals are indexed in international databases, usually because they rarely meet the criteria for quality and lack periodicity. However, they added that there has been progress in the past ten years and that enhancing the journals' quality should be a priority for the development of psychology in Latin America.

The next question was: What is your opinion about the topic 'internationalization of psychology'? Is it considered important in your own country? Why?

The responses showed a strong tendency to consider that internationalization of psychology is important and necessary. Nevertheless, it is seen as a goal rather than a reality. The answers differed from one respondent to another, even in the same country.

They showed a tendency to say that internalization is more valued in countries where psychology is seen as more developed, like for instance in Mexico, Colombia, Brazil, Puerto Rico. For Chile and Argentina, answers were contradictory. Internationalization is seen as imposed, i.e. as a necessary consequence of Internet resources; nevertheless, many psychology organizations hang on to the approaches they already know instead of being open to new possibilities. According to half of the respondents, in some Latin American countries a major setback in attaining internationalization is caused by economic and political conditions which do not help academic advances in psychology. Some respondents argue that there are Latin American psychologists who have made important contributions to psychology. Yet their contributions are little known outside the region, because they write mostly in Spanish or Portuguese. For Peru, a significant increase in interest for internalization has been noticed over the past ten years. Respondents from Bolivia, Paraguay, El Salvador, and Guatemala tend to mention internationalization as desirable although they lack the conditions to make it work, such as easy access to publications, exchanges with researchers from abroad, knowledge of foreign language, and research funding.

Several other obstacles have been pointed out, such as the prevalence and exclusivity of English as the language of international journals while most Latin American researchers have a poor knowledge of this language; precarious and even nonexistent research activity in some countries; the precariousness or absence of publications, especially of psychology journals.

Question number three: Are there any formal systems for accreditation of psychology courses in your country? What do you think of them? The respondents considered this as a very important issue. Accreditation is recognized as a central issue, although it does not exist or is done without external controls in some Latin American countries. Bolivia, El Salvador, Guatemala, and Paraguay are among the countries which are making great efforts to achieve career recognition, to improve accreditation systems for psychology courses and to establish criteria for quality control to practice the profession.

In some countries, accreditation exists on a national level and is carried out by approved agencies external to the program. This was mentioned as being the case in Brazil, Mexico, Colombia, and Puerto Rico. It is said that in some countries accreditation has recently become a requirement. However, not all have this requirement since there are no control mechanisms. In some countries psychology courses can be accredited if they want to, but accreditation is not a requirement for all courses.

The fourth question asked about the extent to which current resources are available for professors and researchers. It was asked if they were insufficient, sufficient, good or very good. Access to up to date resources in psychology was seen as being of great importance. In some countries access is rather precarious and almost nonexistent. Respondents from countries where research is more developed said that access to resources was at least 'good'. 'Open access' is seen as indispensable to advances in research.

More than 46.7 per cent of the answers considered that access to up to date resources for teaching psychology was 'insufficient'; 16.7 per cent considered it to be just 'sufficient'. The other 36.6 per cent considered it to be 'good' or 'very good'. Some respondents mentioned that in some psychology courses, resources, especially access to data and literature, are insufficient; teachers don't do research and as a consequence their classes are obsolete.

Respondents referred to advances in gaining access to research publications in Latin American countries over the last ten years due to the dissemination of new technologies of communication, though there are still many limitations to access. From the results, it is clear that there is a wide variation among the twelve countries in the survey with regard to the availability of access to updated information.

In the fifth question we asked: How often do your students have access to scientific psychology journals? In what language do they read scientific psychology journals?

Most respondents reported that students often have access to recent publications in psychology journals, either in their native language or in a foreign language but they read very little or do not read them at all. This depends largely on the encouragement and the demands of their teachers.

In this survey 24 out of 30 respondents indicated that their students read in Spanish, 14 added they also read in English, 5 pointed out they also read in Portuguese; one mentioned French and another one German. However, preference is always for the native language, as expected. Students prefer books instead of scientific journals. Nevertheless, it should be noted that books do not mean textbooks in general, as these are rather rare in most Latin American universities.

One respondent reported a survey of 400 students which showed that 90 percent did not know of any scientific journals, and in a sample of 40 teachers with over 15 years of teaching experience, 70 percent do not read scientific journals. These results show the importance and the need to encourage good quality publications in the field of psychology in Latin America as a means to improve psychology education and training.

In the sixth question we asked how they evaluate training for research in psychology courses. There was a wide variation among respondents from the same country, and among universities in the same country. In every country there is some kind of training for research, but this does not occur at all universities or training schools. At universities considered of high quality, there is always some research training while in others it is completely nonexistent.

The orientation of the curriculum is mainly towards practical and professional activities, so that training for research occurs mainly in postgraduate programs (Master's and Doctoral programs). Currently, these programs are only offered by a few universities in Brazil, Mexico and Puerto Rico. In other countries, such as Colombia, Argentina and Peru, this type of program is just beginning. It is important to note that in many countries in Latin America postgraduate designation is applied to any course offered to those who have completed their undergraduate studies. They aim to offer specialization in any subarea of psychology with very different requirements. To finish, I will try to summarize some of the challenges and possibilities in education and training of psychologists from a Latin American perspective as a contribution to the global view and international quality assurance.

A global perspective in psychology education and training is certainly consistent with the idea of internationalization of psychological science. From this perspective, the question of the indigenization of psychology must be addressed further by expanding discussion and knowledge about all current trends in psychology. I believe that this type of reciprocal knowledge can produce advances in the development of a truly international psychology.

Psychology in American Latin countries has existed for more than a century, but its major development has occurred in the past ten years. However, an important problem still needs to be resolved, that is, how to get easy and continuous access to new research results. The lack of such access produces an exaggerated dependence on classical authors and a lack of commitment to the urgent problems in modern society. As a consequence, many students keep learning and reading translations made half a century ago, rather than accessing the latest theoretical models which respond to current problems. Moreover, the lack of funds for research hinders the dissemination of research even within their own country.

In my opinion, if we want to build a truly international psychology, we must encourge different forms of exchange and cooperation among psychologists from different parts of the world. Here international organizations have an important role to play, as they have the means to facilitate meetings, task forces, agreements and others. This can also be done by agreements among international, regional and local psychology organizations from different countries. The dissemination of writings from different parts of the world can be seen as another way to overcome obstacles to internationalization and to the establishment of basic principles for a global education and training for psychologists. International journals would help inasmuch as they agree to maintain a body of advisers including experts in different languages, who would read articles submitted in the authors' native language. If the article is approved at this stage, the authors would be invited to submit an English version. This would greatly simplify the process of article submission by writers who are not native English speakers.

Finally, a good way to improve the internationalization of psychology and of psychology education and training would be to increase training opportunities for young people in schools of excellence where psychology is more developed. In our opinion this should be achieved mainly at the postgraduate level.

Notes

1 Twenty-four countries: Argentina, Belize, Bolivia, Brazil, Chile, Colombia, Costa Rica, Cuba, El Salvador, Ecuador, Guatemala, Guyana, French Guiana, Honduras, Mexico, Nicaragua, Panama, Paraguay, Peru, Puerto Rico, Dominican Republic, Suriname, Uruguay and Venezuela; www.bvmemorial.fapesp.br/php/level.php?lang= enandcomponent=19anditem=3;Guiageográfico(www.guiageo-americas.com); *Enciclopédia contemporânea da América Latina e do Caribe* (2006), São Paulo: Boitempo; *O conceito de América Latina: uma perspectiva francesa*, Encontro Regional da ABRALIC, 23 a 25 de julho de 2007.
2 These psychologists are from Argentina, Bolivia, Brazil, Chile, Colombia, El Salvador, Guatemala, Mexico, Paraguay, Peru, Puerto Rico, and Venezuela.

References

Adair, J. G. (2004). On the indigenization and autochthonization of psychology. In B. N. Setiadi, A. Supratiknya, W. J. Lonner and Y. H. Poortinga (Eds.), *Ongoing themes in psychology and culture* (pp. 115–29). Yogyakarta, Indonesia: International Association for Cross-Cultural Psychology.

Adair, J. G. (2006). Creating indigenous psychologies: Insight from empirical social studies of the science of psychology. In U. Kim, K. S. Yang and K. K. Hwang (Eds.), *Indigenous and cultural psychology: Understanding people in context* (pp. 467–85). New York: Springer.

Adair, J. G., Kashima, Y., Maluf, M. R. and Pandey, J. (2009). Beyond indigenization: International dissemination of research by majority-world psychologists. In A. Gai and K. Mylonas (Eds.), *Quod erat demonstrandum: From Herodotus' ethnographic journeys to cross-cultural research*. Athens: Pedio Books Publishing. ebook: www.iaccp.org/drupal/Spetses

Alarcón, R. (2002). *Estudios sobre psicología latinoamericana*. [Studies on Latin American Psychology]. Lima: Editorial Universitaria.

Alarcón, R. (2004). Medio Siglo de Psicología latinoamericana: Una visión de conjunto. [Half a Century of Psychology in Latin America: An overview]. *Interamerican Journal of Psychology/Revista Interamericana de Psicología*, 38 (2), 307–16.

Alonso, M. and Eagly, A. (Eds.) (1999). *Psicología en las Américas* [Psychology in the Americas]. Buenos Aires: Sociedad Interamericana de Psicología.

Ardila, R. (1973). *La Psicología en Colombia. Contexto social e histórico.* [Psychology in Colombia. Social and historical context]. México: Trillas.

Ardila, R. (1986). *La Psicología en América Latina: pasado, presente y futuro.* [Psychology in Latin America: Past, present and future]. México: Siglo XXI.

Díaz-Guerrero, R. (1994). *Psicología del mexicano. Descubrimiento de la etnopsicología.* [Psychology of the Mexican. Discovering ethnopsychology]. México, DF: Trillas.

Díaz-Guerrero, R. (2004). 50 años de Psicología Interamericana: A view from México [50 years of Interamerican Psychology: A view from Mexico]. *Interamerican Journal of Psychology/Revista Interamericana de Psicología,* 38 (2), 333–42.

Hernández-Guzmán, L. and Sánchez-Sosa, J. J. (2007). El Aseguramiento de la Calidad de los Programas de Formación en Psicología Profesional en México [How to assure quality for training programs in professional psychology in Mexico]. *Revista Mexicana de Psicología,* 22, número monográfico especial, 271–86.

Maluf, M. R. (2003). Psicologia Escolar: reafirmando uma nova formação e atuação profissional [School psychology: Innovations in education and practice]. In O. H. Yamamoto and V. V. Gouveia (Eds.), *Construindo a Psicologia Brasileira: desafios da ciência e prática psicológica* [Building the Brazilian Psychology: Challenges for science and psychological practice], pp. 121–38. São Paulo: Casa do Psicólogo.

Salazar, J. M. (1997). La investigación transcultural en 30 años de la Revista Interamericana de Psicología [Cross-cultural research over 30 years of the Interamerican Journal of Psychology]. *Interamerican Journal of Psychology/Revista Interamericana de Psicología,* 31, 134–69.

Santos, B. S. S. (1995). *Pela Mão de Alice: O Social e o Político na Pós-Modernidade* [By Alice Hand: The social and political in post-modernity], 12th edn. São Paulo: Editora Cortez.

Santos, B. S. S. (2000). *A Crítica da Razão Indolente: Contra o Desperdício da Experiência.* [A critique of the indolent reason: Against the waste of experience], 7th edn. São Paulo: Editora Cortez.

Santos, B. S. S. (2007). *Renovar a teoria crítica e reinventar a emancipação social* [How to renew critical theory and to reinvent social emancipation]. São Paulo: Boitempo Editorial.

Toro, J. P. and Villegas, J. F. (Ed.) (2001). *Problemas centrales para la formación y el entrenamiento profesional del psicólogo en las Américas* [Central issues concerning education and training of the psychologist in the Americas], vol. I, Sociedad Interamericana de Psicología. Buenos Aires: JVE Ediciones.

Villegas, J. F., Marassi, P. and Toro, J. P. (Eds.) (2003a). *Problemas centrales para la formación y el entrenamiento profesional del psicólogo en las Américas.* [Central issues concerning education and training of the psychologist in the Americas], vol. II, Sociedad Interamericana de Psicología. Buenos Aires: JVE Ediciones.

Villegas, J. F., Marassi, P. and Toro, J. P. (Ed.) (2003b). *Problemas centrales para la formación y el entrenamiento profesional del psicólogo en las Américas* [Central issues concerning education and training of the psychologist in the Americas], Vol. III, Sociedad Interamericana de Psicología. Buenos Aires: JVE Ediciones.

Commentary on 'Roles and responsibilities of international psychology organizations for psychology education and training (PET)'

Téa Gogotishvili

The change in higher education due to globalization has become an important issue for debate. Developments in knowledge and technology have encouraged governments to reorganize higher education in order to meet the needs of a global academic industry. How globalized education systems have fulfilled the specific needs in developing countries may require further study but it has brought new demands to scientific disciplines and more specifically to psychology, which itself has experienced notable changes within the framework of sciences and professional systems.

In the context of globalization, which raises new issues on disciplinary and professional identity of psychology, Peiró underlines the differences in psychology across the world's regions and considers the identity of psychology as a science and a profession to be the result of competing centrifugal and centripetal forces. He analyses the main function of international psychology associations and the role of psychology education and training (PET) in the promotion of 'identity' and 'diversity' of psychological sciences in the current global and local world.

In my opinion, one of the core missions of and challenges for international psychology associations is to promote a global identity of psychology while paying respect to the regional and cultural ways of understanding, producing and implementing psychological knowledge, tools, methods and services.

Indeed, as Pieró suggests (Pieró, p. 236, this volume), by serving as platforms for debate, analysis, knowledge sharing, dialogue and cooperation, international organizations may also promote the improvement of PET internationally and advance progress towards common international PET frameworks and quality assurance systems worldwide. The cooperation of international psychology associations with accreditation agencies dealing with Psychology studies at a regional level could be an important resource to identify criteria and strategies to enhance quality.

Considering the global perspective of psychology education and training, it is increasingly important that international psychology organizations stimulate cross-cultural research and facilitate international cooperation in research by promoting these trends in their journals.

Other significant roles of international psychological associations are also stressed in José M. Peiró's chapter. Highlighting the importance of cooperation with regional associations and/or other relevant institutions in order to provide the clarification and formulation of core features, quality criteria and standards of an international PET framework and establishing a common ground for the certification of professional practice; including the contents for continuing professional development and universal ethics principles as the basis for the creation of a code of ethics relevant to the different regions and countries where research and practice are carried out.

Surveys like those carried out by IUPsyS help to identify and systematize the existing information on PET in different countries with the participation of the relevant national associations. This can be followed up and complemented by qualitative analyses on pertinent issues. The facilitation of international dialogue on PET among scholars, students, researchers and the promotion of international cooperation, symposia, conferences and workshops on the relevant topics would also be helpful.

In her chapter on analyzing the results of a survey composed of 30 psychologists from 12 countries in Latin America, Maluf offers the following statement:

> A global perspective in psychology education and training is certainly consistent with the idea of internationalization of psychological science. From this perspective, the question of the indigenization of psychology must be addressed further by expanding discussion and knowledge about all current trends in psychology. I believe that his type of reciprocal knowledge can produce advances in the development of a truly international psychology.
>
> (Maluf, p. 250 this volume)

These ideas are very close to my own point of view, particularly due to the existing similarities between the current needs and aspirations of PET in our home countries. Agreeing with Maluf, I believe that international psychological associations can play an important role in supporting different forms of exchange and cooperation among psychologists from different countries.

The scarcity of exchange/scholarship programs for students and academics hampers PET. Moreover, the resources of international psychology associations, especially with regard to their links with international journals and their potential to support psychologists through the promotion of international publications, could be another way to overcome obstacles to the global development of psychological science, and specifically to education and training in this field.

Regarding this issue, my vision of the way international psychology associations could help in this direction differs from Maluf's viewpoint. In particular, I think it would be almost impossible to make international journals, 'maintain a body of advisers including experts in different languages, who would read articles submitted in the authors' native language . . . [which] . . . would greatly simplify the process of article submission by writers who are not native English speakers' (Maluf, p. 251 this volume), as much as they may agree with the idea. Perhaps it would be more useful for international psychology associations to negotiate with the editorial boards of international journals with the request that they provide a body of advisors/experts who could assist non-native authors in the process of submitting articles written in English.

In conclusion, one of the best ways for the internationalization of psychological sciences, psychology education and training would be to increase the support of young people from less well-developed countries to continue their education and training in more developed and thereby better resourced countries, especially at postgraduate level.

Index

Italic page numbers indicate tables; bold indicate figures.

For Product Safety Concerns and Information please contact our EU
representative GPSR@taylorandfrancis.com
Taylor & Francis Verlag GmbH, Kaufingerstraße 24, 80331 München, Germany

www.ingramcontent.com/pod-product-compliance
Lightning Source LLC
Chambersburg PA
CBHW071354290326
41932CB00045B/1806